Work
and
Society

An Introduction To Industrial Sociology

Curt Tausky

University of Massachusetts, Amherst

F.E. PEACOCK PUBLISHERS INC.
ITASCA, ILLINOIS 60143

To Robert Dubin

Contents

Preface
1. **Looking Back: Prehistoric, Ancient, and Medieval Societies** 1
    Industrial Society and Industrial Sociology 1
    Hunting-Gathering 3
    The Agricultural Revolution 5
    City States and Empires: The Emergence of Elites 7
        Sumeria 7
        Egypt 11
        Rome 14
    The Middle Ages 17
        The Manorial System 17
        The Guild System 21
        The Putting-Out System 25
    Overview 27
2. **Looking Back: the Industrial Revolution** 29
    Industrialization in England 31
        Overview 41
    Industrialization in The United States 42
        Overview 52
3. **The Labor Force: Making a Living** 54
    Labor-Force Participation 55
    Occupations 58
        Who Gets Which Jobs? 61
        Industries 62
    Unemployment 63
    Work Outcomes: Income, Prestige, Job Satisfaction 70
        Income 73
        Prestige 85
        Job Satisfaction 92
            Productivity and Work Satisfaction 93
            The Distribution of Work Satisfaction 97
            Occupations and Work Satisfaction 98
    Overview 105

4. Changing Work Outcomes........................... 106
Occupational Mobility................................. 107
  Intragenerational Mobility and Labor Turnover.............. 107
  Intergenerational Occupational Mobility.................... 110
    Intergenerational Mobility Explanatory Variables.......... 111
    Intergenerational Mobility Data....................... 113
Unions and Collective Bargaining......................... 118
  Basic Labor Law..................................... 118
  The NLRB.. 121
  Unions... 123
  Collective Bargaining................................. 125
Overview.. 131
5. Epilogue.. 133
Retrospect... 133
Utopia Is Elusive....................................... 134
A Glance at Japan....................................... 139
  Japanese Productivity Inducements...................... 140
  Lessons from Japan................................... 141
Useful but Still Weak Reforms............................. 143
Challenge and Response.................................. 147
Bibliography.. 149
Index.. 159

Preface

In preparing this book, the most difficult decisions revolved around what to include. The theme of work, industrial sociology's focus, invites particularly thorny choices because work reaches into people's lives in so many ways. The choices made here were guided by the question: With what materials should the beginning student of work life be familiar? Long involvement with undergraduate and graduate courses on work suggested that along with conventional topics—labor force participation, pay, unions, mobility, and so forth—three other kinds of materials required attention: history, a theoretical framework, and the consequences of egocentrism.

My impression is that the majority of students is very sparingly exposed to history. Accordingly, Chapter 1 is organized around conditions of life and work up to the Industrial Revolution, and Chapter 2 addresses the Industrial Revolution itself.

Chapters 3 and 4 then present a sizable amount and variety of data on the current work scene. This kind of information, however, can be difficult for students to absorb or interpret without some aid from a conceptual framework. The framework for these chapters is quite straightforward. It assumes that individuals engage in work because that activity yields preferable outcomes compared to not working. A number of such outcomes are considered, with particular attention to income, prestige, and job satisfaction. Motion, or a dynamic element, is introduced by people's attempts to change their work rewards, notably through occupational mobility and unions. In short, people are concerned about work outcomes and express their attraction to enhanced results through individual or group action.

Egocentrism is discussed in Chapter 5. The pursuit of personal self-

interest, it seems to me, is so strongly endorsed culturally and institution-
ally that collectively damaging results have become visible. Specifically,
it is suggested that sagging productivity growth rates among American
firms can be partly attributed to members' narrowly directed self-
centeredness, which prompts adversarial, rather than more collaborative, labor-management relations. Since it is unlikely that either
exhortation or alteration of work routines can undo discordant relations,
measures with sufficient inpact to bring about cooperation are needed.
In this chapter a look at Japan's personnel practices shows a pair of
intertwined policies—also applicable elsewhere—that have stimulated
cooperation and helped to boost Japan's industrial productivity growth
rates to the world's highest.

I wish to thank Professor Richard Hall for helpful comments on the
manuscript, Mrs. Tausky-Hollocher for typing the manuscript, Mrs.
Mary-Louise Creekmore for typing the tables, and my wife for her un-
failingly sensible views on work-life matters.

Curt Tausky
University of Massachusetts at Amherst
August 1982

1. Looking Back: Prehistoric, Ancient, and Medieval Societies

INDUSTRIAL SOCIETY AND INDUSTRIAL SOCIOLOGY

In the last half of the eighteenth century, a unique set of circumstances launched the Industrial Revolution in England. The rapid reshaping of the nation's economy and society was under way; before long, even distant areas of the globe were affected.

Many factors contributed to England's emergence as an industrial society, but several stand out.[1] Enclosures had pushed people toward factory employment by not allowing farmers their traditional use of open fields, which became fenced-in property held by wealthy individuals. Canals were built, new roads laid, and existing roadbeds and surfaces greatly improved, thus bringing down the cost of transporting goods over long distances and easing the burdens of commercial travel. Metal coins were minted in greater abundance, helped by gold from the New World, while private banks issued a variety of paper money; interest rates were low, from 3 to 5 percent, so that money for new enterprises was available at attractive rates. The steam engine and numerous other ingenious machines were devised, not only replacing muscle power but proving far more productive. Agricultural innovations increased crop yields, which, along with improved transportation, made it possible to feed the growing urban populations. And the political system provided a

---

[1] A readable and useful look at these matters is T. S. Ashton's *The Industrial Revolution, 1760–1830*, rev. ed. (New York: Oxford University Press, 1969).

1

setting in which private enterprise was encouraged by Parliaments composed largely of men whose interests were furthered by "hands-off" economic policies.

The combination of circumstances shifted the localized regional market structure of England, for which small enterprises had produced a more or less fixed amount, toward large firms with costly machinery producing for national and international markets.[2] Industrial output was so vastly accelerated that a different and wealthier society emerged, an industrial society, which provided a mix of new advantages, opportunities, and problems.

Although England was the first to industrialize, it did not remain either the only nation or even the front-runner for long. With the exception of brief Prussian campaigns against Austria and France, western Europe experienced the longest period of peace in its history, from the end of the Napoleonic Wars in 1815 to the outbreak of World War I in 1914. Under the umbrella of peace, a web of financial and trade relationships developed and flourished, giving impetus to investment in manufacturing, particularly in France and Germany.

Industrialization reached the United States rather late. In 1860 there were more slaves than factory workers, and the waterwheel, not the steam engine, powered half of the country's factories until the last three decades of the nineteenth century. Yet, by the end of the century, United States production nearly equaled the combined value of English, French, and German manufactured products.[3] Thus, at the beginning of the twentieth century, the United States was well into the transition to an industrial society. Over half of the work force was in nonagricultural employment, and this proportion would continue to grow by roughly 5 percent each decade until 1970, when 95 percent of the labor force held nonfarm jobs.

This preliminary look at industrialization leads us to the central concerns of industrial sociology—the work-related features of life in industrial society. Also of interest are the events that spawned the Industrial Revolution, and conditions of life and work prior to industrialization. These are the topics discussed in this book.

Of course, more reliable and ample statistical information is available for more recent times. Indeed, it seems that one indication of an advanced industrial society is the collection of data. When it is useful to do so, we will show the information that numbers can provide. This will

---

[2]Karl Polanyi, *The Great Transformation* (Boston: Beacon Press, 1957).
[3]Herbert Gutman, *Work, Culture and Society in Industrializing America* (New York: Vintage Books, 1977), p. 33.

create no difficulty, since the data will be in a form that is easy to understand.

We begin now with a distant time and move toward the present.

HUNTING-GATHERING

Human-like creatures (termed *hominids*) appeared first on the plains of East Africa, then 1 or 2 million years ago slowly began to spread throughout the world. To date, the very earliest remains of hominids—3.75 million years old—have been unearthed in Tanzania.[4] In Kenya were found the more complete remains and campsites of hominids living 2.5 million years ago. The Kenyan hominids were four feet tall, walked erect, had a brain about one-fourth the size of a modern human's, and used simple stone tools to hack the flesh off the dead animals that they found. About 300,000 B.C. there appeared the first *Homo sapiens* (the family of modern humans). They were a foot taller than the hominids, were twice as heavy, and had a brain nearly as large as today's humans. By 40,000 B.C. evolution had produced the physical characteristics of present-day humans.[5]

For 3 million years, until the beginnings of settled agriculture (8000–7000 B.C.), food getting occupied people much of the time. Hunting, fishing, searching for berries, and digging edible roots was the way the earth's tiny population of perhaps 5 million people, scattered in small nomadic groups, attempted to avoid the constant threat of starvation. A division of labor arose, based on age and sex. Old people, lacking the stamina for hunting or foraging, worked at food and animal-skin preparation; children collected berries and nuts, and supplied the campfire with wood. As hunting developed—from small game at first to large animals tracked on increasingly lengthy expeditions—so too did the sexual division of labor, since pregnant or nursing women handicapped long hunts. Men became the hunters, and, with their hunting weapons, the protectors of their bands, leaving the women to gather food and care for the children.[6] This sexual division of labor also had an impact on physical differentiation. The skeletons of hominids and early *Homo sapiens* reveal fewer physical differences between men and women than those of more recent times. Thus, along with the development of hunting

---

[4]"Hominid Bones: Old and Firm at 3.75 Million," *Science News* 108 (1975): 292; "New Species of Man," *Science News* 115 (1979): 36.
[5]John E. Pfeiffer, *The Emergence of Society* (New York: McGraw-Hill Book Co., 1977), pp. 52–54.
[6]Melvin Kranzberg and Joseph Gies, *By the Sweat of Thy Brow* (New York: G. P. Putnam's Sons, 1975), pp. 13–14.

came an increase in the body size of males.[7] Additionally, the development of speech was accelerated by hunting, particularly big-game hunting, which demanded communication to coordinate the hunter's actions.[8]

For a very long time the wooden spear was the most advanced hunting weapon, until the bow and arrow came into use about 35,000 years ago. This innovation gave the hunter greater accuracy than was possible with a spear, and a wounding range roughly four times greater.[9] By this time, too, tools had become more "special purpose" (bone needles with eyes, stone saws, wood shovels and scoops). Tentlike structures of leather over twigs sheltered people from the weather, and the stone lamp with animal fat for fuel and moss for a wick began to come into use.[10]

Developments of this sort undoubtedly eased living conditions, but accident, disease and malnutrition made the lives of hunter-gatherers harsh and short. At least three of every four newborn babies did not survive infancy. Among those who did, the average life span was about twenty-five years, with only a few surviving to become old and decrepit in their thirties.[11] With such high infant mortality and short adult life spans, women had to bear five or six children just to maintain the population. Going about the daily round of tasks in a condition of nearly continuous pregnancy, and repeatedly exposed to the hazards of childbirth, women aged faster and died younger than men.[12]

The initial unit in the Stone Age was the band, which included about twenty-five people. Eventually, such bands formed semipermanent villages of roughly a hundred people. The great advantage of the village was that its population is big enough to send out the larger numbers of hunters that big game demanded, and more men could be mustered to defend against attack from trespassing bands. There are no indications of class distinctions within these villages. In these early human societies there were no full-time specialists whose position in the division of labor gave special privilege.[13]

The reason for this egalitarianism was the hand-to-mouth existence

[7]Amaury de Riencourt, *Sex and Power in History* (New York: Dell Publishing Co., 1974), pp. 4–6.
[8]Gerhard Lenski and Jean Lenski, *Human Societies* (New York: McGraw-Hill Book Co., 1982), p. 105.
[9]Ibid., p. 106.
[10]Ibid., p. 125.
[11]United Nations, *The Determinants and Consequences of Population Trends*, vol. 1 (New York: United Nations, 1973), p. 12. It is sobering to realize that a life span of about thirty-five years was the rule as late as the 1700s.
[12]Ibid., p. 12.
[13]V. Gordon Childe, *What Happened in History* (Baltimore, Md.: Penguin Books, 1964), p. 67.

of hunter-gatherer communities. Although there were part-time specialists—men who were particularly adept at constructing snares or at chipping flint for arrowheads, clever hunt leaders, and priests for magical-religious rituals—food was too scarce to release people for full-time activity that did not directly contribute to the food supply. What food there was, was shared. Personal belongings were scant and would only be a handicap when the campsite was moved, so accumulated belongings were not available to bestow privilege; and inheritance of position was not possible, since there was neither a full-time task to inherit nor the surplus to allow the untalented to carry out tasks affecting the whole community. Scarcity thus fostered a rough equality.

This intriguing feature of early human communities eventually gave way to more familiar forms of social organization. Human ingenuity found ways to overcome scarcity and begin to acquire surplus food, while human ingenuity also developed intricate patterns of social organization that offered privileged access to the surplus. Aside from a few small communities, the unequal distribution of the material goods of societies is today everywhere in evidence. Despite even revolutionary ideologies and events, inequality still persists after the dust has settled. This persistent characteristic of social organization first became visible in the Neolithic Era.

THE AGRICULTURAL REVOLUTION

Archeologists refer to the period from 8000 to 3000 B.C. as the Neolithic or New Stone Age. This name, unfortunately, masks the more basic change over these few thousand years, a fundamentally new way of coping with nature. Although the Neolithic was only an instant of time in the 2 million years of the Stone Age, momentous developments were compressed into this era. The descendants of nomadic people, whose survival was dependent on hunting and gathering, founded permanent settlements and fashioned new patterns of existence based on agriculture.

Agriculture developed independently in several places in the world: Mesoamerica, Southeast Asia, and the Fertile Crescent, from which it spread through Europe and Africa. The Fertile Crescent extends from the eastern shore of the Mediterranean to the Persian Gulf, arcing across present-day Lebanon, Jordan and Iraq. In prehistoric times this region flourished with game and fields of wild cereal grasses. From about 9000 to 6000 B.C., hunting and harvesting wild grasses were combined with farming, but during the period 6000 to 5000 B.C., the yield from farming became the primary food source rather than only a supplement. In addition to wheat and barley, plants such as lentils and peas were domesticated, as were sheep, pigs, and cattle.[14] There is no certain way to know, but women's knowledge of plants, gained from millennia of collecting them, points to the likelihood that the earliest sowers of seed and harvesters were women, whereas men, accustomed to the hunt, domesticated animals and herded them.[15]

With permanent settlements came more weatherproof housing. Clay slabs and bricks provided materials for housing, some of which was two-storied with a basement for food storage. In the villages of the Fertile Crescent some nine thousand years ago houses such as this were built, complete with separate rooms, hinged doors, and porthole windows.[16]

Neolithic villages contained perhaps twenty to twenty-five houses, although some became much larger, such as the town of Jericho, with an estimated population of two to three thousand inhabitants in 7000 B.C.[17] Most families were self-sufficient, making whatever they used. In the larger Neolithic towns, however, occupational specialization was advancing. Small workshops of craftsmen were making weapons, pottery, bone tools, and woven cloth. Towns as large as Jericho were centers of trade. The surrounding farmers and herdsmen brought their produce and livestock to the market town to barter for the goods available there; merchants from distant places brought obsidian (a stone highly prized for weapons) from Asia, and cowrie shells (an early form of money) from the Red Sea region to exchange for the town's products.[18] The existence of surplus food had triggered far-reaching changes, although the surplus was individually quite small: A rough estimate would be that between eighty and a hundred people occupied with farming and herding were needed to support one town dweller.[19]

The organization of early Neolithic towns and villages is clouded, but there is little evidence of distinctions in rank among the inhabitants. Warfare—which eventually gave rise to elites—was not yet prevalent, as indicated by the absence of walls around most settlements and the lack of battle weapons in men's graves. In the later Neolithic, fortified walls surround towns, and daggers and battle axes appear in the graves of all adult males.[20] It seems that the growing wealth of the towns, and their nearby herds of cattle, offered an irresistible temptation to plunder. Also

[14]For a clear and concise overview see Robert J. Braidwood and Robert H. Dyson, Jr., "Domestication," *International Encyclopedia of the Social Sciences*, vol. 4 (New York: The Macmillan Co. and The Free Press, 1968), pp. 245–54.
[15]Childe, *What Happened in History*, pp. 65–66.
[16]Pfeiffer, *The Emergence of Society*, pp. 138–39.
[17]Lenski and Lenski, *Human Societies*, p. 139.
[18]Ibid., p. 140.
[19]This estimate is based on Braidwood and Dyson, "Domestication," p. 14.
[20]Lenski and Lenski, *Human Societies*, pp. 140–41.

in the later Neolithic, bronze was coming into use in weapons, providing a further inducement to groups with metal weapons to attack those settlements defended with less sturdy arms. War had become a brutish, all-or-nothing undertaking: As a prelude to carrying off their booty, the victors usually slaughtered all survivors. In the coming period, when great empires were built, the practice grew of sparing the vanquished for use or sale as slaves, or as a source of tax revenue.

In the Middle East by the dawn of the Bronze Age, a new form of social organization was in place. Urban-based warlords with warriors armed with bronze weapons, had subdued agriculturalists whose defense still consisted of stone weapons. Warlord, officials, and priests then emerged as a privileged governing class supported by military power and religious beliefs.

CITY-STATES AND EMPIRES: THE EMERGENCE OF ELITES

Sumeria

Along the banks and tributaries of the Tigris and Euphrates rivers lie the remains of ancient cities that flourished in Sumeria (present-day Iraq). Ur in 3000 B.C. had a population of at least 24,000; Uruk had 20,000; Umma, 16,000. Each densely populated city was surrounded by a brick wall enclosing a palace, temple, granaries, workshops, and houses. With intensive cultivation and city-administered irrigation, the neighboring countryside was able to supply the city's food. Materials not locally available were imported: copper from the Persian Gulf region, tin from Iran, timber from the mountains to the northeast.[21]

Ur, Umma, and other large cities were administrative centers which controlled the surrounding farmland and organized the construction and upkeep of the water-control devices (canals, reservoirs, dams) that irrigated the land.[22] Each city with its countryside was a small kingdom, a

---

[21]Childe, *What Happened in History*, pp. 102–4, presents information on Sumerian cities.

[22]The classic study of the origin of the political state is Karl Wittfogel's *Oriental Despotism* (New Haven, Conn.: Yale University Press, 1957). Strongly impressed by the despotic regimes that arose in Mesopotamia, Egypt, India and China, Wittfogel reasoned that mass labor was required to construct and maintain their elaborate irrigation systems; and since mass labor required discipline and leadership, the centralized political state with its bureaucratic apparatus emerged as a response to the need for administrative control. Other scholars have suggested different interpretations of the origin of the state. Robert L. Carneiro, for instance, looks to warfare in "A Theory of the Origin of the State," *Science* 169 (1970): 733–38.

city-state. What made this possible? The rise of these city-states occurred in the earliest part of the Bronze Age (3000 to 1000 B.C.); by then, several technical innovations had made agriculture more productive, the transport of goods over long distances much easier, and administrative control more effective.

Agriculture had long depended on the use of hoes. This gave way to the wooden plow pulled by oxen. Because it digs deeper, a plow buries weeds, adding nutrients to the soil. By harnessing oxen, a larger land area could be cultivated, while the manure collected from the stalls of the oxen provided fertilizer. When these improvements were combined with irrigation, agricultural yields increased significantly.[23] But food produced in the countryside must somehow be transported to the urban sites. The old techniques of dragging goods on sledges or slung between poles was too slow and was not well adapted to moving large quantities. This problem was overcome by the invention of the wheel: Both two- and four-wheeled carts, pulled by oxen, donkeys, or horses, were now in use. Using wind power, small boats with sails were also available as another means of transport.[24]

One particular practice of those times, however, would horrify a modern member of the Society for the Prevention of Cruelty to Animals. The harness used for oxen was also used with horses and donkeys. The harness passed across the oxen's shoulders and throat so that the oxen pushed against the harness with their broad shoulders. Neither horses nor donkeys have broad shoulders, and when they pushed forward against the harness to move a cart, the unfortunate animals were choking themselves. Finally, in the ninth century A.D., the horse collar was invented.[25]

Organized around king and temple, a Sumerian city-state was essentially a theocracy. Each city had its own chief god, housed in a large temple. The god was provided with priestly servants, a wife, and numerous concubines.[26] The king's power in the scheme of things derived from two sources: He commanded a well-equipped and highly trained army,[27] and he was the intermediary between the city's god and the city-state's inhabitants.[28] This fusion of military might and religious belief gave awesome power to the ruler.

---

[23]With hoe cultivation, a bushel of seed yielded at best two bushels of grain. Use of the plow increased the yield to about three bushels from one of seed: Kranzberg and Gies, *By the Sweat of Thy Brow*, pp. 33–34.

[24]Childe, *What Happened in History*, pp. 89–92.

[25]Ibid., p. 91.

[26]Ralph Linton, *The Tree of Culture* (New York: Alfred A. Knopf, 1955), pp. 301–3.

[27]Ibid., pp. 306–7.

[28]Childe, *What Happened in History*, pp. 108–9.

All land belonged in principle to the city's god. To use the land, peasants paid a rent of 10 percent of everything produced.[29] This supplied food for the temple's inhabitants. To provide for their other needs, hundreds of craftsmen were employed in the workshops of the temple. To pay the artisans (pieces of silver and copper served as money), temple prostitutes sold their services to devout visitors, and priests predicted the future and conducted funerals.

As the representative of the city's deity, the king also had a claim on several hundred acres of land. The taxes from it (paid in kind) were used for the upkeep of the king's household and army. The king also, of course, was the chief recipient of booty from military campaigns. Some idea of the income required to sustain a royal household can be gained from the recent discovery of a palace in Ebla, Syria: Nearly twelve thousand people served this palace when it was at its prime in 2500 B.C.[30]

Although in theory peasants paid rent to the city's god, the actual rent collectors were, naturally, the priests. Keeping detailed records of all debts, revenues, and expenditures presented the priests with a formidable burden. Around 3000 B.C. writing emerged as a way to cope with this administrative difficulty. The Sumerian priests had developed symbols to represent spoken sounds; by combining these symbols, compound sounds could be written. This writing is called cuneiform (wedge-shaped) because a wedge-shaped stylus was used to make impressions on clay tablets. (The filled tablets were customarily baked, thus preserving them for archeologists.) Schools were set up in temples to teach cuneiform writing to priestly scribes.

Scribes were much in demand, not only as temple record keepers but also in the king's service as vital members of his growing administrative bureaucracy. In the scores of villages and towns in a city-state's domain, officials organized the irrigation work, dispensed justice, and collected taxes, while numerous other officials were responsible for administering the royal household and army. Administration had become such a complex affair that every official had a staff of scribes.[31]

The invention of writing provided a superb administrative tool for controlling a society in which everyone had a legally defined station in life. For instance, injury to an official was much more severely punished than a similar injury to an artisan, while if a slave was injured, no one was physically punished, although the owner received financial compensation for damage to his property.[32] Through the workings of the tax

---

[29]Linton, *The Tree of Culture*, p. 303.
[30]Howard LaFay, "Ebla," *National Geographic* 154 (1978): 740.
[31]Childe, *What Happened in History*, pp. 112–15.
[32]Linton, *The Tree of Culture*, pp. 305–6.

allocation systems, standards of living roughly followed class position. It is doubtful that the centralized, intricate administrative structures that maintained these arrangements could have developed without the invention of writing.

The era of independent city-states did not last long. Border skirmishes between neighboring kingdoms erupted into military campaigns of conquest. The land and treasuries of one city-state after the other fell to the king of Uruk, until, in 2500 B.C., he governed an empire extending over Sumeria. And so it went. As a dynasty weakened, the country became fragmented; the rulers of cities marched their armies against each other until one emerged victorious and reunited the empire.

The spoils of victory were great indeed. Possessing incredible riches, an army of servants, a winter and summer palace, an emperor could easily satisfy every wish except one: to stay in power. Stretching now into Iran and Syria, the vast empire and its emperor came to an end when invaded by Alexander the Great's Macedonian (Greek) infantry in the fourth century B.C.

Certainly for the great majority of people, most of whom were peasants, the rise and fall of rulers made little difference in their lives; the cleavage between commoners and the governing class persisted. Commoners labored and paid taxes. The governing class not only reaped the considerable benefits of this arrangement, but viewed physical work of any kind (except warfare) as demeaning and held in contempt those who performed it.[33]

When Alexander's troops appeared, they were armed with iron weapons, as were the opposing forces. For several hundred years iron making had been a carefully guarded secret of the Hittites in Asia Minor (now Turkey). When the Hittite empire collapsed in 1200 B.C., knowledge of iron making spread to other peoples. The scarcity of iron, and its great advantage over bronze in weaponry, initially made iron objects exported by the Hittites more valuable than gold or silver. However, once the secret of iron making was disclosed, iron weapons came into general use, and by 800 B.C. tools and plowshares were also often made of iron.[34] By this time, two discoveries had further added to the usefulness of iron: annealing (alternately heating and cooling) iron to give it greater strength, and carburizing (adding carbon to iron) to produce steel.[35] Stronger and more flexible than bronze, and able to keep an edge longer, iron had become, and still is, the supremely useful metal.

[33]Lenski and Lenski, *Human Societies*, p. 178.
[34]Childe, *What Happened in History*, p. 191.
[35]Lenski and Lenski, *Human Societies*, pp. 181–82.

Egypt

Except for members of the governing class and the craftsmen, house servants, and soldiers who served this class, agriculturally based societies provided an existence more or less at the subsistence level. In order to maintain the governing class in comfort, rents, taxes, and obligatory labor on roads, irrigation works, or (as in Egypt) pyramids were required of peasants in the appropriate seasons of the year.

To understand these arrangements more fully, consider the proprietary theory of the state, a point of view held by most people of power in agricultural societies.[36] The state, in this view, is the personal property of its owner, to be used, if he wishes, for his personal advantage, and, as property, the state can be inherited by the owner's heirs.[37]

One of the extreme cases of state proprietorship is found in ancient Egypt. In Sumeria, as we saw, a king exercised power as the representative of a god. The Egyptian kings (pharaohs) went a decisive step beyond this. Upon his coronation, the pharaoh became a god.[38]

The well-being of the land depended on the pharaoh's spiritual potency, maximized by purity of the royal blood. To ensure this, the pharaohs customarily married their own sisters. The pharaoh's palace was constructed in the form of a temple, since he was the physical embodiment of a god. It was believed that even after his death, the prosperity of the country was influenced by the pharaoh's anger or favor in the afterlife.

Egypt was unified about 2900 B.C. and fell to Alexander just before his conquest of Sumeria. Thus, for nearly three thousand years (except for sporadic interruptions by invaders) pharaohs were the absolute rulers of the country. All land was the property of the pharaoh, and the surplus produced was concentrated in the royal granaries and treasuries (filled with gold from the state's mines).

All peasants were initially serfs, bound to the royal, temple, or noble's land they cultivated. Shortly before 2000 B.C. the serfs were freed, but they could not really leave, since no other land was available. Whether serf or free, peasants were obliged to pay taxes (in kind) on all produce

---

[36]Gerhard E. Lenski, *Power and Privilege* (New York: McGraw-Hill Book Co., 1966), pp. 214–15.

[37]Involved here is the degree of control rulers might exercise in societies organized around the proprietary principle: Traditions, an aristocracy, or a state's bureaucratic apparatus may hinder the ruler's freedom of action. The best single analysis of these matters is still Max Weber's *The Theory of Social and Economic Organization*, trans. A. M. Henderson and Talcott Parsons (New York: The Free Press, 1964), pp. 324–86.

[38]Linton, *The Tree of Culture*, p. 412.

and rent to the owner of the land.

To administer taxes, a large bureaucratic apparatus was required. Priests had invented the hieroglyphic (picture-like) form of writing, which was taught to the temple-trained scribes who served as bureaucratic officials. Periodically, the government took a census. The information went to district offices that maintained records detailing land size, types of crops, and probable yields. This supplied the basis for determining the percentage of the crop to be delivered to the government as tax. Another set of officials annually issued regulations specifying when and what to plant.[39]

The use of state revenues was closely tied to position. All officials received an income—graded according to the official's rank—in the form of a daily food ration distributed from local administrative centers as loaves of bread, cuts of meat, and jugs of beer. These were prepared in the bakery, kitchens, and brewery operated by the state in each center. For exceptional service, officials were rewarded with land grants and bonuses; gold and copper rings served as money.

Selected from the hereditary nobility, royal officials serving at the pharaoh's court shared its luxurious life-style. In addition to specially trained servants, the palace was amply provided with artisans to satisfy the tastes of the governing class. In keeping with the Egyptian view of propriety, every court function involved a hierarchical ordering. In the palace kitchen, for instance, were, in descending order, the royal meat carvers, the cake bakers, the souffle makers, and the jam makers.[40]

Living in such a grand style obviously required vast wealth. Still, all this was manageable through the workings of the tax system and the government's monopoly on gold mining. What did cause strains on the economy was the curious (to the modern mind) practice of pyramid building. As soon as the pharaoh was crowned, he began to prepare for his death by building a pyramid. This was an extremely important undertaking, since the pyramid would house the pharaoh's sacred corpse. His body must be protected for the afterlife as a god; hence, the mummy was placed in an impenetrable inner room of the pyramid. Anything the pharaoh might need in the afterlife must be provided: servants (in the form of small statues), a boat, gold, prized possessions. Priests who were dedicated to the service of the pharaoh, brought offerings of food to his mausoleum for generations. The intent of these practices was to guarantee the pharaoh a satisfactory afterlife and, by so doing, assure the prosperity of the country.

---

[39]Henry Jacoby, *The Bureaucratization of the World*, trans. Evaline Kanes (Berkeley, Calif.: University of California Press, 1973), p. 10.

[40]Linton, *The Tree of Culture*, pp. 422–23.

The master builder responsible for the construction of the pyramid was a trusted noble close to the pharaoh.[41] Quarrying, transporting, and putting the stones in place was a compulsory duty that peasants performed during the season when the Nile flooded, and they could not work in the fields. Numerous craftsmen were also involved, certainly masons and carpenters (the records are very fragmentary on this), who were provided with metal tools for their work. The Great Pyramid of Cheops, built about 2600 B.C., illustrates the staggering amount of labor and other resources consumed by pyramid building. This pyramid contains 2,300,000 stone blocks, each weighing over two tons. The construction was carried out over a period of twenty years, with a labor force of thirty thousand men during the project. Everyone was housed, fed, and clothed from the pharaoh's revenues.

Working without wheel or pulley, human and animal power moved the great stones by laying greased boards underneath and sliding the stone forward. The stones were cut from rock by drilling along the grain, inserting wedges of wood, then soaking the wood with water to swell it enough to crack the rock. When this did not suffice, wooden wedges were inserted and heated with fire, then doused with cold water to crack the rock. The rough blocks were then shaped with diamond-toothed bronze saws and hauled into place. The stones fit so perfectly that no mortar was needed to hold them together.

Fortunately for the laborers, they were not, apparently, considered expendable; there are fragmentary reports by overseers' scribes on worker safety. One report on a quarry team, for instance, notes that not a man or mule was lost. Another report details the food and clothing provided to laborers: "4 lbs. bread, 2 bundles of vegetables and a roast of meat daily, and a clean linen garment twice a month."[42] Of course, since such reports went to higher officials, the information might not be wholly reliable. Still, the reports do offer a glimpse of conditions of work.

Visitors to Egypt were dazzled by its display of prosperity, but this glitter was superficial. Taxes had stifled the productive potential of the country: Too much had been taken out of the economy, while too little was left. Except when directly employed by a pharaoh, noble, or temple, the producers could afford only Neolithic equipment of copper or stone and wood. Egyptian craftsmen were superb—colored glass (used for beads and inlays) had been discovered, wood veneering was highly

---

[41]For a discussion of pyramid building, see Kranzberg and Gies, *By the Sweat of Thy Brow*, pp. 49–52, and Ahmed Fakhry, *The Pyramids* (Chicago: University of Chicago Press, 1961).

[42]Kranzberg and Gies, *By the Sweat of Thy Brow*, p. 50, and Childe, *What Happened in History*, p. 131.

developed and all the various joints known today were employed by cabinet makers, jewelers made objects of gold and electrum (a natural alloy of gold and silver) which are still copied—but the market was primarily the small governing class.

Egypt was well organized to squeeze maximum revenues from tax-payers for the comfort of its rulers. But Egypt's military forces were on occasion disastrously unreliable. Egypt fell to Alexander with slight resistance. Three hundred years later, Greek rule ended with the rise of Roman power; Egypt was now governed by Roman emperors. They used the country mainly as a source of wheat for Rome. The condition of peasants was certainly no better than before, and at times was worse. When Rome's military campaigns required more than the usual supplies of grain, the tax (in kind) on peasants was steeply increased.

Rome

After gaining control of Egypt in 31 B.C., Rome's armies marched to further conquests. Penetrating even into Britain, the empire became the largest that had ever existed in the Western world. To maintain the ar-mies required enormous revenues, obtained from Roman citizens and the conquered territories. A sales tax and a tax on inheritance were collected, as well as customs duties and a land tax. The land tax was the agricultur-alists' burden and supplied the largest share of the empire's taxes, although the majority of farms were small and provided little more than subsistence.[43]

Roman might imposed peace on the area under its domination, and with peace came trade within the empire and with distant places. Pottery, glassware, and textiles were manufactured and sold in the empire; from China and India came luxuries for the wealthy—dancing girls, parrots, silks, perfumes, and drugs.[44] The paved Roman roads, and especially control of the Mediterranean Sea, made possible the expansion of trade. Yet wealth was highly concentrated, severely limiting not only the growth of trade but also the expansion of industry. The purchasing power of the vast majority of people was quite low because the wages of laborers and craftsmen were kept down by competition from slave labor. Records in-dicate that workshops were staffed one-third to one-half by free men, while the remainder were slaves and ex-slaves.[45]

---

[43]Robert J. Antonio, "Domination and Production in Bureaucracy," *American Sociological Review* 44 (1979): 907-8.
[44]Childe, *What Happened in History*, p. 275.
[45]Ibid., p. 282.

The workshops were usually small. A "large" textile manufacturer might employ twenty-five weavers, a pottery-making shop perhaps ten to fourteen artisans.[46] Most commonly, a shop was operated by the craftsman-owner, assisted by a hired worker or slave who performed the routine preparatory tasks. Except for workshops that supplied military needs or materials such as bricks or tiles, manufacturing was a small-scale affair. The shops, though, were highly specialized. Pottery makers specialized in producing cooking pots, jars, goblets, or large urns; separate woodworking shops made couches, chests, or caskets.

Housing patterns followed craft lines. Craftsmen with a particular skill lived in one section of the city or along a certain street. Out of this spatial clustering of craftsmen developed the craft guild, a forerunner of the modern union. The guilds held religious services for their members and provided insurance by collecting money for sick members and for burial. (Later, in the Middle Ages, the guilds regulated the quality, methods, and hours of production.)

The craft guild was an important institution in Rome's attempt to stabilize the level of production when it began to decline due to internal disruptions of the empire, which prompted urban workers to leave their occupations for the countryside. In the third century, by order of the emperor, guild members were frozen in their crafts, forbidden to leave their guilds, and sons had to follow the occupations of their fathers. Voluntary membership had thus been changed into hereditary obligation.[47]

At the height of its power, Rome's architects and builders were busy with the construction of roads, aqueducts, public baths, theaters, colosseums. Although the mass of people benefited from these government-sponsored amenities, life was in other respects grim. Wages were low, as we saw, and unemployment was so high that in Rome itself a large portion of the population was dependent on the free grain supplied by the government. To keep the favor of the population, the free grain was a necessity, as were the spectacular shows provided in the colosseums and theaters. The brutality of the times is most starkly revealed in these "entertainments." For instance, the emperor Trajan celebrated his victories by providing the Roman populace with the spectacle of ten thousand captives fighting to the death in the Colosseum. In the Roman theaters, if the script called for a torture scene, a criminal was tortured to death on stage for the amusement of the audience.[48]

---

[46] Ibid., p. 280.

[47] Joseph Damus, *The Middle Ages* (Garden City, N.Y.: Image Books, 1968), p. 46.

[48] Ibid., pp. 15 and 28.

As is not unusual in human affairs, although many lived poorly, some lived very comfortably. The small middle class of merchants and the proprietors of larger workshops lived well, while the Roman hereditary aristocracy lived on a grand scale. The nobility fared well partly because, as members of the governing class in a huge empire, they filled the top administrative offices—with ample opportunities to accept bribes[49]—and because the nobility owned enormous farms, which brought large money incomes.

These large farms were operated on a commercial basis for the benefit of the landlord. Typically, an overseer was hired to manage the farm while the owner enjoyed the banquets, baths, and entertainments of urban life. Using slaves at first, and later the tenant farmers who were bound to the soil by the same decree that tied craftsmen to their guilds, the farms in an area specialized in raising grapes, olives, or livestock. A three-field system (two pieces of a farm's land were cultivated while one remained idle on a rotational basis) was used in some regions, though the more wasteful two-field system was most prevalent; in a few places the more productive wheeled plow, well suited for heavy soil, was introduced. For the most part, however, there was little change in agriculture. The Romans were ordinarily not innovative but were content to use traditional methods of doing work.[50]

Over time, the large farms held an increasing portion of the land under cultivation. Because of the civil wars of the third century, small farms were abandoned. The unused land thus created was incorporated by the large estates. Speeding this growth along were imperial decrees that directed landowners to cultivate the unused land adjoining their estates. As civil war ravaged the countryside, more and more farmers left their small plots. Those who remained were assessed heavier taxes to compensate for the government's decreasing revenues, and this stimulated further abandonment of small farms. The farmers who fled often joined the ranks of the tenant farmers on the large estates.

The large farms were initially highly dependent on urban industry. Clothes, bricks, wood, and metal objects were bought in town, and urban craftsmen were hired for repair work. Slowly, and then more rapidly, spurred by the civil wars, large farms became self-sufficient. Every large estate had weavers, tailors, potters, brick makers, smiths, and carpenters—all the crafts that were required to satisfy the estate's needs, with the exception of luxury items such as glassware.

An estate's tenant farmers were dependent on the landlord for seed

---

[49]Lenski, *Power and Privilege*, pp. 222–24; Antonio, "Domination and Production in Bureaucracy," p. 908.
[50]Kranzberg and Gies, *By the Sweat of Thy Brow*, pp. 37–38.

and equipment. In return, the farmers paid rent in kind and provided whatever labor services the estate might require. Moreover, since the imperial government was increasingly unable to operate its judicial system within the empire, the landlord became the dispenser of justice when disputes arose among his tenants. The large farm was on its way to becoming the fortified *manor* of medieval Europe. And in this flow of events, the aristocratic landlord would be transformed into the armorclad knight, absolute lord of his domain.

The empire disintegrated soon after the Huns, a Mongolian people, had pushed from their Asiatic homeland into Europe, late in the fourth century. The Huns' migration set to flight the Germanic tribes living to the north of Italy, some of whom fled south. Now weak and no longer able to withstand the large numbers and fierce combativeness of the tribesmen, Rome was sacked as the century ended, and again fifty years later. In 476, the leader of a powerful German tribe seized the throne. After this, no Roman would ever again rule the empire from Rome. With the total collapse of the Roman empire in the West, Europe entered the Middle Ages.[51]

THE MIDDLE AGES

Spanning the centuries between the ancient world and the dawn of the modern, the Middle Ages developed patterns of life based on the joint workings of the *manorial system* and the *feudal system*. The manorial system provided the economic framework for the production of food and goods in the Middle Ages; the feudal system provided its political foundation. The political system linked landowners into a hierarchical structure of lords and vassals, which gradually settled over the already existing economy of manorial production.

As we will see, the manorial system of goods production eventually gave way to the guild system. Guild production for a time existed alongside a newer form, the putting-out system. Then, displacing and finally replacing the putting-out system, the factory emerged as the dominant, modern system of production. Between the manorial system of production and the factory, over a thousand years passed.

The Manorial System

Urban life is unavoidably dependent on the transport of food from the countryside to the city and the movement of the city's products to rural

---

[51]Ruled from Byzantium (Constantinople), the eastern part of the empire managed to survive into the middle of the fifteenth century, when it fell to the Turks.

areas. Maintained roads and safety in traveling them are necessities for the survival of cities. But these necessities, which make trade possible, require effective government. With the disintegration of the Roman empire, trade withered, people deserted cities, and Europe slid into a form of economy called the manorial system.

The most distinctive feature of the manorial system is self-sufficiency. Holders of large units of land (the manor) kept men-at-arms to defend their holdings. Urban dwellers and small farmers fled to those landlords for protection; in return for security, the manor's inhabitants provided labor services, with the result that each manor produced nearly everything that it needed for survival. Every manor was, thus, a closed economy, forced by circumstances to be self-sufficient.

A manorial domain included a village, fields, pasture, woodland, and fortified manor house (castle) surrounded by a moat or wall, which also protected a building for grain storage and perhaps a chapel. Except for the landowner, his family, and some men-at-arms, the remainder of the manor's population were serfs. The status was fixed: The serf, his family, and descendants were "tied to the soil" permanently and remained with the land if it changed owners. With the absence of centralized government, the landlord was truly the lord of his land. Even a serf's marriage required the lord's consent if the wife was from another manor.[52]

The land of the manor was divided between the lord and the serfs. Half the farmland was usually the lord's, while the entire serf population used the rest. The serfs also farmed the lord's portion of the land, and the yield from it was his. Thus, from the total agricultural production of the manor, the lord directly received half.[53] In addition, the serfs had to pay (in kind) for using the lord's grain mill, wine press, and bread ovens. A portion of flour, for instance, was deducted from each sack milled. After all this, not much was left for the serfs. If things went well, if no drought, crop failure, or war came along, the serf, it has been estimated, lived on little more than 1,600 calories per day.[54]

The transition to the manorial system began in the third century. With the crumbling of Roman government in the late 400s, the self-sufficient manorial system crystallized. For the next six hundred years, Europe's economy revolved around the manor. On the political side, a seemingly minor invention had enormous consequences.

---

[52]Henri Pirenne, *A History of Europe*, trans. Bernard Miall (New York: University Books, 1955), p. 101.

[53]Zoe Oldenbourg, *The Crusades*, trans. Anne Carter (New York: Pantheon Books, 1966), p. 15.

[54]Eric R. Wolf, *Peasants* (Englewood Cliffs, N.J.: Prentice-Hall, Inc., 1966), pp. 9–10.

As late as the eighth century, warfare was conducted mostly on foot. The saddle had long been in use, giving the rider front and back support, but the full swing of an ax or sword, if it missed the target, could unseat the rider. The invention of the stirrup provided the horseman with lateral support. A sword could now be swung without fear of toppling sideways off the horse, or a lance could be thrust into an opponent while riding at full gallop. With the aid of the stirrup in the early 700s, the nature of warfare rapidly changed from foot to mounted combat.[55] No infantry could withstand the assault of armor-clad warriors on armored horses. The expense, however, was extremely high. It has been calculated that several years' income from a manor with two hundred serfs was required to equip one knight.[56]

The feudal system was under way when powerful lords gained control of the neighboring lands of less powerful lords. The latter either lost their holdings or swore loyalty, thereby keeping their land in exchange for mounted military service. Land granted by a lord was a *fief*; the fief holder was the lord's vassal. A fief could be further subdivided, so that a vassal was also a lord to lesser vassals, and so on. The limit to subdividing a fief was the amount of land required to support one fully equipped mounted knight.

The lengthy training, discipline, and wealth demanded for mounted combat forged the knights into a self-conscious class of nobles. They had contempt for those who did not bear arms, the peasants, and viewed any sort of physical work, other than combat or training for it, as degrading. (This outlook survived among European nobles well into the nineteenth century.) The right to bear arms was restricted to the nobility; their weapons made the serfs helpless to resist the nobles' demands for labor on their terms. Historical records show that over 90 percent of the rural population (which of course included almost everyone) were serfs; among the rest were a few freemen, church officials, and the tiny governing class of nobles who were 1 or 2 percent of the whole population.[57]

With little else to occupy them, the knights engaged in ceaseless feuds sparked by territorial disputes or revenge, which inevitably ended in bloody clashes, the intentional destruction of the opponent's cropland,

---

[55]Lynn White, Jr., *Medieval Technology and Social Change* (London: Oxford University Press, 1962), pp. 24–28.

[56]Stanislas Andreski, *Military Organization and Society* (Berkeley, Calif.: University of California Press, 1968), pp. 58–59.

[57]Walter P. Hall and Robert G. Albion, *A History of England and the British Empire* (New York: Ginn and Co., 1953), p. 70. As late as the eighteenth century, 80 to 90 percent of Europe's population were peasants, living from the soil and nothing else: Fernand Braudel, *Capitalism and Material Life, 1400–1800*, trans. Miriam Kochan (New York: Harper and Row, 1973), p. 18.

and the maiming of his serfs. But despite the turbulent times, a number of important innovations appeared, which greatly increased the level of production.

The heavy wheeled plow came into wide use. It so thoroughly broke earth clods that cross-plowing was eliminated. The horse shoe and padded horse collar were invented. Plodding oxen then gave way in plowing to much faster draught horses. And the greatest agricultural innovation of the Middle Ages, the three-field system of crop rotation, was adopted nearly everywhere.

Under the older two-field plan, half the usable land was planted each year while the other half remained idle. With the three-field system, the arable land was divided into thirds, keeping only one-third of the land idle in a year. On a six-hundred-acre manor, three hundred acres would be planted under the two-field system and four hundred acres under the three-field plan, an increase of one-third. The actual gain, however, was substantially more because planted land was plowed once, fallow land twice. So on a six-hundred-acre estate, plowing with the two-field plan involved nine hundred acres of annual plowing, but under the three-field plan, only eight hundred acres of annual plowing. One-third more cropland was gained with one hundred fewer acres to plow. By reclaiming land from forests and swamps, seventy-five new acres could be added to the six hundred. The serfs now annually plowed nine hundred acres under the three-field system, with 450 in crops, while they had also plowed nine hundred acres under the two-field plan with only three hundred acres in crops. With the same amount of plowing, the three-field system had a 50 percent crop production advantage over the two-field plan.[58]

The horse shoe, padded horse collar, wheeled plow, and three-field system were widespread by the eleventh century. These developments amounted to an "agricultural revolution," which supported an increase of population. About this time, too, water mills were coming into common use. Within another hundred years, the windmill was adopted where water was sluggish or unavailable. Wind and waterpower hammered iron, drove saws, crushed ore, polished armor, ground grain for bread, and even laundered clothes.[59]

The medieval interest in harnessing nature's power was intense, and the mechanisms to do so more effectively were developed in the form of complex gears and the crank (connecting reciprocating and rotary motion). Gunpowder, a new source of energy to drive mechanisms, appeared in the fourteenth century. The use of gunpowder in cannons

---

[58]White, *Medieval Technology and Social Change*, pp. 71–72.
[59]Ibid., pp. 84–89.

was militarily important, but more significant is the fact that the cannon is a one-cylinder internal combustion engine. Modern motors of this type are descended from it. A hundred years before the Industrial Revolution, attempts to drive a piston (instead of a cannonball) used powder for fuel; later, liquid fuel was substituted. Either way, the intent was to use the energy of expanding gases to drive machines.[60]

The Guild System

The self-contained manor reflects the rural, agricultural basis of the Middle Ages. Guilds arose with the revival of urban life. The manor remained the center of existence for the vast majority of people, but its self-containment gradually became less complete as money and trade began to circulate.

The origins of towns were the *bourgs* (castles) with their knights and the people necessary for their upkeep, and ecclesiastical "cities" consisting of a cathedral, one or two monasteries, and the residences of church officials. In the eleventh century a few merchants settled in these rudimentary towns; many more merchants soon followed their example. To the old order of knights, clergy, and serfs, merchants were a strange breed of man, free from the authority of a lord, and profit-minded. Their origins are unclear; probably most were the children of serfs, but they were treated as free men. As their numbers swelled, an entirely new class came into being, the *bourgeoisie*.

Attracted by the merchants' commercial activities, artisans of every kind came to the towns which grew around the walls of the *bourgs* and ecclesiastical "cities." Bakers, brewers, shoemakers, and tailors practiced their trades; others worked up the raw material imported by the merchants. These wares further stimulated export trade. In Flanders (Western Belgium) wool weavers came to the towns. The Flemish cloth trade quickly became the most flourishing industry of Europe and remained so until the end of the Middle Ages.[61] The nobility benefited from the availability of wares of many kinds and from the taxes on merchants and artisans.

Although the nobility suffered some loss of local authority, the advantages of commerce led many nobles to offer privileges and immunities to merchants to attract them. The bourgeoisie eventually developed forms of urban government wholly independent (except for taxes) of local nobles, who, however, retained their traditional privilege and jurisdiction in the predominantly agricultural society of the Middle Ages. Still,

---

[60]Ibid., pp. 99–101.
[61]Pirenne, *A History of Europe*, pp. 215–19.

the old rural order was changing; it was becoming tied to a money economy. Peasants sold their produce on local markets; the seigneur (lord of a manor) used his rent money for urban wares. Beginning in the twelfth century, serfs could gain their freedom by purchasing it from their lords. The serf, now a peasant, paid a money rent to the seigneur for use of a parcel of land, although the peasant was still obliged to work on the lord's fields a certain number of days a week. However, the traditional labor duty the peasant performed for the castle—repair of roads, bridges, moats, spinning, weaving, blacksmithing—was now done by hired hands. As before, the peasant paid a tithe to the church and fees to the seigneur for use of his grain mill, wine press, and bread ovens. On top of these, when the seigneur's son was knighted or his daughter married, the peasants made a payment; in the event the seigneur was captured, part of the ransom was paid by the peasants.[62] The local seigneur was still the master of his manor, while new wealth was developing amidst urban life.

By the fourteenth century some merchants had so financially prospered that the aristocracy felt the need to assert its status. In the main, they did so through sumptuary (consumption) decrees.[63] The intent was to show people's rank by outward appearance, rather than permit the lines between noble and commoner to become hazy. The precise color, fabric, fur trimming, and jewels that people of different rank and income level could wear were regulated. Efforts were also made to specify how many dishes could be served at meals. As might be guessed, the sumptuary regulations were a failure. The low-born, if they could afford it, imitated nobles' dress and food consumption. New wealth, like old wealth, had distinct advantages over no wealth.

Urban commercial activities, from the twelfth century through the fifteenth, were dominated by guilds. These were of two sorts: merchant and craft guilds. Their aim was the regulation of commercial activity within an area, and the exclusion of outsiders. The right to organize was given by a charter obtained from a local seigneur or ecclesiastical lord. A new member, after paying an entrance fee, was asked to take an oath of loyalty to the guild, promise to obey its laws and officers, and not divulge the secrets of his trade. Guildsmen were required to attend the funeral of a "brother" and pay the expenses. On feast days a guild's members attended devotional services in a chapel supported by the guild. Each guild enforced its rules through a guild court which could fine, expel, or seize the goods of a member.

---

[62]Barbara W. Tuchman, *A Distant Mirror* (New York: Alfred A. Knopf, 1978), pp. 172–73.
[63]Ibid., pp. 18–21.

Merchant guilds were concerned with buying and selling imported goods; craft guilds, primarily with production. Merchant guilds restricted the selling place of items—usually to the guildhall or marketplace—specified the hours during which sales could be made, and regulated who might buy, often excluding people from other communities. They possessed the right to forbid the sale of nonguildsmen's wares and had the important privilege of making a first offer on cargoes brought to certain ports.[64] Dealing in marble, herring, wool, grains, and gold, the merchant guilds were the main suppliers of desirable goods at a time when the circulation of money was increasing. Successful merchants became very wealthy and politically powerful in urban government.

Formed around specific skills, craft guilds arose, for example, among weavers, tailors, carpenters, and shoemakers. Within a craft guild there was further specialization. One carpenter made furniture, another built houses, a third did wood carving; one baker sold white bread in his shop, another only brown bread. Spreading the work around to more people was the intention and the result. Unlike merchant guilds, both employer and employee were members of the craft guild. Originally, there were two sorts of guildsmen, masters and apprentices; before long, the journeyman took his place between the two.

The master craftsman owned a shop, directed the work of apprentices and journeymen, and sold the finished products. An apprentice was a young worker whom the master was obligated to train, usually for a period of three to seven years. The master provided the apprentice with a bed, food, and sometimes a small salary. The relationship was broad, including perhaps a bit of schooling and definitely a good deal of discipline. Upon completion of his training, the apprentice became a journeyman. He was now a fully qualified artisan who held the hope of becoming a master by producing a "masterpiece" acceptable to guild officials.

Craft guilds regulated hours of work, the tools and materials that could be used, and the quality and price of products. Looking at a few examples of guild rules, we see that working at night, on Saturday afternoons, and on church feast days was everywhere prohibited. Lorimers (makers of riding equipment) specified that no cast iron should be used in making bridles and prohibited the making of saddle-bows except of specified wood; beef was not to be baked in pies and sold as venison, and rabbits were not to be baked in pies at all; cap makers should not dye white or gray wool black, since the color would be taken out by rain; baskets for fish were to be of proper size, hold only one kind of fish, and were not to be filled with better fish on top than below.[65]

---

[64]John P. Davis, *Corporations* (New York: Capricorn Books, 1961), pp. 148–56.
[65]Ibid., pp. 169–73.

For a seller to receive more than the legal price for his product was a punishable offense. If there was reason to suspect poor work, guild officers had the authority to search the houses of members for evidence. To ease the burdens of control, guild members were usually required to live in the same neighborhood. To make it easier to trace poor products to their makers, craftsmen were required to put a mark on each article produced and leave a copy of the mark with the guild. Serious and repeated offenses could result in imprisonment if fines and confiscation of goods had failed to make the point.

Craft guilds did succeed in enforcing their regulations aimed at stable employment for members and protection of buyers against overpriced, shoddy products. By the sixteenth century, however, signs of decay were visible.

Journeymen found it increasingly difficult to become master craftsmen. The fee for attaining master rank had become so exorbitant that some towns finally intervened, thereby weakening guild autonomy. Guilds became fragmented as masters set themselves apart from other members by adopting special clothing to exhibit their status. More importantly, the assembly, in which all guild members had a vote, came to be dominated by the masters, usually the wealthiest among them. This assured that guild offices went to successful masters, essentially putting control of the guilds in their hands. The concerns of the poorer masters and journeymen conflicted with the wealthy masters' interests; the earlier emphasis on control of work processes to spread the work around to all guild members gave way to cheaper and quicker production for a growing market. The medieval notion of the "just price"—that price that returned to the craftsman the cost of production plus a living wage—was on the way out in favor of profit. While the just price was a stabilizing idea, profit is open-ended, since it depends on what buyers can be induced to pay.

As craft guilds declined, some continued, though weakened, some were absorbed by merchant guilds, and some became dependent on the merchants who exported their goods. Merchant guilds and individual merchants with capital took advantage of the expanding commercial opportunities offered in the sixteenth century. With France and England in the lead, monarchies were strong enough to assure relative domestic peace and safety for the commercial traveler; sea commerce was riskier, yet often worth the risk because it was much cheaper than land freight. Now more than ever, the merchant had before him the prospect of handsome profits, but because the old guild system was ill-suited to unlimited output, another form of production was needed.

The Putting-Out System

Many products in the Middle Ages were manufactured in certain regions for export to widely dispersed markets: Nuremberg and Toledo produced arms and armor, Cordova made shoes and leather goods, Poitiers and Limoges were famous for tapestries and rugs, Venice for its mirrors and glasswares, Seville for silk cloth.[66] Although the guild system of production kept its hold on such products, merchants determined prices and profit levels. As the vital link between producers and markets, merchants were admirably situated in the export trade, but the guilds' small-shop production could not keep up with the growing demand for some commodities. The merchant-entrepreneur's solution was the putting-out system (also called cottage industry and the domestic system).

While used in supplying local markets with such goods as clothes, lace, hats, cutlery, and nails, putting-out reached its greatest importance in making wool cloth.[67] From the fifteenth century to the eighteenth, this most flourishing export was supplied by merchants through putting-out arrangements in England and Flanders. The merchant bought raw wool, usually in England, the source of the best wool. It then had to be carded (combed) to set the fibers parallel and remove undesirable ones, spun into yarn and woven, fulled by cleaning and compacting, and finally smoothed and dyed. The steps in the procedure were very old. Although peasants wore the itchy, coarse material, skipping fulling and dyeing, the complete process produced a comfortable cloth.[68] What was new in this was the manner of organizing the steps in the production process.

The merchant-entrepreneur hired workers for the final stages of manufacturing to full and dye the cloth, either in a specialist's small shop or the merchant's own establishment. The steps of carding, spinning, and weaving were done in the peasants' homes. The merchant or his agent distributed (put out) raw wool to a number of cottages, collected the yarn after a time, and then distributed it to other cottages for weaving. For each transaction the price was set by the merchant. The system was workable, though clumsy. To recruit people, the merchant went from cottage to cottage until enough workers were found. Between the

---

[66]Kranzberg and Gies, *By the Sweat of Thy Brow*, p. 71.

[67]Harry Braverman, *Labor and Monopoly Capital* (New York: Monthly Review Press, 1974), p. 61.

[68]Kranzberg and Gies, *By the Sweat of Thy Brow*, pp. 68–69. They point out that the severe skin afflictions prevalent among medieval peasants were very likely the result of wearing coarse wool cloth.

merchant's establishment and his spinners' and weavers' homes, a distance of fifteen or twenty miles was not unusual.[69]

The workers continued to earn part of their living from farming, but especially during winter, they turned to spinning and weaving for extra income. The work, as we saw, was done in the home, often a cottage with one room serving as workshop, kitchen, and bedroom. Windows were few and narrow, with movable wooden shutters against storms and sometimes oiled paper to let in light. A fireplace gave heat, but barely so if one were a few feet from it.[70]

While his children carded the fleece, the peasant or his wife sat at the spinning wheel; also, among weavers, both men and women operated the hand looms. And if the children were old enought, they too spun or wove. Considering the dawn-to-dusk hours worked by so many family members, the economic returns were quite skimpy. This system is sometimes described favorably because family members worked together in familiar surroundings, using their own tools and not bound to specific work hours and rules set by an outsider. But as with admiration for other bygone times, a close look often dispels the illusion. Cottage industry was dreary and grim for the peasant families.

In years of poor harvest the peasant had to borrow money. The most likely source was the merchant, and he was usually willing. Security was demanded for the loan; spinning wheel and loom provided it. From the seventeenth century into the eighteenth, more often than not, the peasant permanently lost his tools.[71] Unable to get out of debt, he rented tools from the merchant. Gradually the domestic workers had become employees.

Here and there a merchant collected ten or twelve workers and production equipment in his own workshop, while at the same time continuing to use workers in their own homes. This mix of old and new arrangements existed a long time in woolen goods manufacturing, despite the distinct advantages of centralized production. Compared to carting material between widely scattered cottages, not only were transport costs drastically reduced by bringing employees into a factory, but once there, it was easier to supervise them to assure consistent product quality; waste

---

[69]Paul Mantoux, *The Industrial Revolution in the Eighteenth Century* (New York: Harper and Row, 1961), p. 63.

[70]Braudel, *Capitalism and Material Life, 1400–1800*, pp. 214–17. Cold rooms were common everywhere until the 1700s, when changes in fireplace and chimney design finally brought relief. An observer remarks on cold so intense in the palace at Versailles that liquids shattered their bottles: Saint-Simon, *The Age of Magnificence: Memoirs of the Court of Louis XIV*, ed. and trans. Sanche de Gramont (New York: Capricorn Books, 1964), p. 44.

[71]Mantoux, *The Industrial Revolution in the Eighteenth Century*, pp. 64–65.

and loss of material were more controllable; and the division of labor was in the owner's hands.

In the first half of the eighteenth century England's largest export was wool cloth, produced to some extent in factories. However, industrialization was speeded by developments in another branch of the textile industry—cotton cloth. It, too, had been produced by putting-out arrangements, but only in relatively small quantities for local markets. By the close of the eighteenth century, cotton cloth had displaced wool as the primary export. For reasons involving the nature of the materials, the production of cotton cloth was more readily mechanized than woolens, and a number of mechanical inventions were adopted which reshaped the methods and location of work. The transformation of the way in which goods were produced was by later generations termed the Industrial Revolution. The results of this revolution eventually affected all the nations of the world.

OVERVIEW

Within a few millennia after hunter-gatherer nomads settled in villages and planted crops, cities arose. About 5,000 years ago in Sumeria and Egypt, kings, nobles, priests, professional armies, and tax-paying peasants were firmly in place. The division of society into rulers and ruled occurred swiftly when agriculture provided the surplus food needed to support urban, administrative centers. From then until well into the 1800s, the privileged classes, often hereditary, would feel dishonored by performing work other than administration or combat.

No matter who held power, whether Greeks or Romans, the lives of peasants were little changed. They lived close to the level of subsistence. Labor and taxes were their lot.

Rome governed a huge empire for several hundred years, but Rome's power decayed and finally crumbled in the late 400s A.D. With the disappearance of central administration, cities, and roads, trade withered, and the manorial system of production settled over the Western world. The castle of the Middle Ages was by necessity self-sufficient. Serfs worked the land and performed the tasks necessary for sustaining themselves and their lord.

In the eleventh century trade revived. Merchants settled around the castles and in ecclesiastical cities. Merchant and craft guilds formed to protect their members from outside competition and regulate business practices among guild members. By the sixteenth century, guilds had weakened, as did the concept of "just price" when confronted by the lure of open-ended profit. Merchants saw the opportunities available in an expanding market.

The putting-out system was created by merchant-entrepreneurs to supply the growing demand for goods. Putting-out produced a variety of goods for local markets, but wool cloth was the system's major international trade commodity. English wool was the best, and could handily be distributed to the nation's many peasant families who were eager to earn a little extra income from spinning or weaving. The putting-out method of making wool cloth and a few other items survived in England long after the factory system had demonstrated its ability to produce goods faster and cheaper. The ability was decisively shown in the manufacturing of cotton cloth in English factories.

2. Looking Back: The Industrial Revolution

No political revolution has so thoroughly altered so many people's lives as has the Industrial Revolution. Even those areas of the globe—China, India, Africa, South America—that were not swept by the wave of nineteenth-century industrialization nevertheless felt its effects through the overwhelming military power of industrialized countries determined to acquire colonies. With varying degrees of success, many of these formerly colonial regions are now attempting to industrialize. Why?

Even a partial answer must touch on two related issues: national power and standards of living. To begin, we notice that as industrialization proceeds, the labor force shifts from agriculture to manufacturing, then gradually to the service industries.[1]

During the nineteenth century in Western Europe and the United States, agricultural productivity had greatly improved and large portions of the labor force were absorbed into manufacturing. With manufacturing came a slow but persistent rise in the level of wages and an outpouring of goods from increasingly productive machinery. Goods once made in the home became items of mass consumption. Over time, then, people in the industrialized countries ate more and better food than before and gained access to a great variety of factory-made products. Compared with still largely agricultural societies, the inhabitants of industrialized countries certainly enjoy more physically comfortable lives.

---

[1]The service industries include government, education, health care, communications, transportation, wholesale and retail trade, insurance, entertainment, utilities and so on—manufacturing and construction are secondary industry. Primary industry refers to agriculture, fishing, mining, and lumbering.

People in industrialized countries more often survive middle age into old age and are much less likely to die as infants. The infant mortality rate (annual number of deaths per 1,000 live births) at present is 15 in North America and 14 in Western Europe, but soars to 84 in Latin America, 147 in Africa, and 105 in Asia; the world rate is 99.[2] Nearly every indicator of physical well-being closely corresponds to the extent of industrialization.

Among the Western industrialized countries, an average of 40 percent of the labor force is employed in manufacturing industries; in the developing countries of Africa and Asia, the figures range between 7 and 20 percent. Looked at another way, about two out of three working adults in the various countries of Asia and Africa are in agriculture; in the Western industrialized countries the average is one in ten.[3] These differences are vast. They represent the gulf between rich and poor countries, the difference between living into old age or dying young, having access to goods or going without. One response, then, to the question, Why industrialize? points to improvements in material life.

Military power provides the second response to our question. The technical know-how and machines developed with industrialization can also provide a nation with the technical skills and equipment to manufacture weaponry. In the world as it exists, not as one might wish it, there is scant assurance of national sovereignty for nations unable to assert their independence. Of course, one of the "great powers" may offer protection to a weaker nation, but there are inevitably strings attached to client-nation status; the price of protection is likely to include some loss of control over those aspects of domestic or foreign policy that can be shaped to benefit the powerful protector. To the extent that a country can muster the know-how and resources to make modern weapons, its dependence on others is decreased. The only path this effort can take is industrialization. There is no realistic alternative.

In our world's scheme of things, standard of living and national power rise together.[4] That is the fundamental answer to Why industrialize?

---

[2]*1978 World Population Data Sheet* (Washington, D.C.: Population Reference Bureau, 1979).

[3]International Bank for Reconstruction and Development, *World Tables, 1976* (Baltimore, Md.: Johns Hopkins University Press, 1976), p. 516.

[4]An interesting variation on this pattern occurs in the Soviet Union. Although its industrial base can provide the means to improve consumption and national power, the planners have chosen to defer consumption. The Soviet Union's Gross National Product (GNP) equals between one-half and two-thirds the GNP of the United States. Yet the Soviet Union equals or exceeds the U.S. in military expenditures while its citizens enjoy roughly one-quarter of the U.S. level of consumption: Robert W. Campbell, *The Soviet-Type Economies* (Boston: Houghton Mifflin Co., 1974), p. 105; R. W. Davies, "Economic Planning in the USSR," in Morris Bornstein, ed., *Comparative Economic Systems* (Homewood, Ill.: Richard D. Irwin, 1979), p. 225.

We turn back now to the eighteenth century and British industrialization. With smoke belching from factory chimneys and machinery rumbling, England entered the modern age.

INDUSTRIALIZATION IN ENGLAND

Industrialization involves a shift in production from households to factories, a division of labor emphasizing task specialization, the replacement of muscle and wind and waterpower with other sources of energy, and the application of this energy to drive machines.[5] Although it may seem an unlikely candidate for such a historic role, humble cotton cloth led the way toward industrialization.

The stumbling block in textile production was a persistent shortage of yarn, which held back the output of weavers. Traditionally, four spinners were needed to supply one weaver with yarn. This ratio was upset when John Kay introduced the flying shuttle in 1733. So greatly did this device increase the speed of weaving that either more spinners had to be employed or a way found to spin faster. In the 1760s James Hargreaves invented the spinning jenny. It permitted a worker to spin six or seven—eventually eighty—threads all at once.[6] The jenny was small and cheap, and required no great strength to operate. It fit into the domestic system of production but had a serious drawback. Yarn from the jenny was soft and thus suitable only for weft (horizontal strands); the warp (vertical strands) still had to be spun on the slow hand wheel. This limitation was overcome by Richard Arkwright, wigmaker. In 1769 he was granted a patent for a "frame" which produced a yarn strong enough to be used as warp, and cheaper than the linen which had usually served as warp. For the first time, a durable and cheap all-cotton cloth was made in England. Calico (cloth made entirely of cotton) had previously been imported from India, but shipping costs boosted its price. Demand for inexpensive English calicoes was immense.

The power needed to drive Arkwright's frame was more than human muscle could deliver, so from the beginning the process was carried out in a factory. Using waterpower, Arkwright set up a factory in 1771. He soon employed six hundred workers, mostly children. Now the old method of carding cotton by hand proved too slow to supply the spinners' needs. To get around this problem, Arkwright devised a way to card mechanically with cylinders. This also required waterpower, so the processes of carding and spinning were ordinarily carried out at the same

[5]Ivar Berg, *Industrial Sociology* (Englewood Cliffs, N.J.: Prentice-Hall, 1979), p. 9.
[6]A good description of these developments is presented by T. S. Ashton, on whom this discussion draws: *The Industrial Revolution, 1760–1830*, rev. ed. (New York: Oxford University Press, 1969), pp. 42–65.

location. Other entrepreneurs quickly established more factories, using the new methods of production.

Muslin, a fine cotton cloth, had been imported as a luxury from the Near East. Samuel Crompton, a weaver by trade, built the mule, a water-driven machine that was suited to produce both warp and weft for soft yet strong muslin. No longer a luxury, muslins, too, became affordable and extremely popular. After 1790, steam engines were used to drive the mules and other machinery.

The clergyman-poet Edmund Cartwright devised a power loom in 1784 that could be driven by horses, waterwheels, or steam engines. After two decades of improvement, Cartwright's power loom proved superior to the frame and mule. Estimates suggest that 2,400 power looms were operated in 1813; by 1833 steam was driving 100,000 of them.[7] Hand-loom weavers attempted to, but could not, compete with the factory and steam power. Especially in the woolen and worsted (wool cloth with a smooth, hard surface) branches of the textile industry, hand looms continued to operate into the mid-1800s. Whether woven by hand or mechanically, woolen cloth was more costly than calicoes or muslins and therefore far less in demand at home and abroad.

The printing of calicoes had been done by craftsmen; using wooden blocks they printed the pattern on the cloth by hand. This changed in 1783 with the use of large, revolving, power-operated cylinders. About the same time, bleaching and dyeing methods, too, were revolutionized. These processes drew on the discoveries of Scottish and French scientists and were closely tied to the rise of industrial chemistry in England.

By the end of the 1700s, the large factory using steam-powered machinery and integrating all the steps in production was a reality. The machines built for factories had to be more sturdy, because of vibrations, and more durable, because of cost, than was possible with equipment made of wood. Iron was required. Stimulated initially by demand for military equipment, the iron industry developed rapidly in the eighteenth century. Charcoal, a wood product, had been required in smelting iron. But England's forests were depleted by the seventeenth century, raising the price of charcoal. Coal, however, was more plentiful. It was found that when coal was heated, its gases could be removed, leaving a substance called coke, which burns with an intense heat and little smoke. In 1783 Henry Cort successfully applied coke to iron making. He heated pig iron (impure iron from the blast furnace) with coke till it became pasty, stirred it until the impurities had burnt away, then passed it between rollers to press out the remaining dross.

---

[7]Ibid., p. 53.

Cort's process liberated iron making from dependence on forests and freed England from the need to import iron. Large, integrated iron-making establishments arose, which controlled all the processes from coal mining to shaping iron objects. Now available in vastly increased supplies, iron came to replace wood in machinery, buildings, and ships.

Cort's inventions, like many others of his time, would have had only a limited effect without a new source of power. Inspired by Theodore Newcomen's "atmospheric engine," James Watt invented the steam engine. Devised in 1712, the atmospheric engine had been used only for pumping water. A counterweight lifted a piston, then steam under very low pressure flowed into the piston cylinder. When the steam condensed it formed a vacuum and atmospheric pressure pushed the piston down. While repairing a Newcomen engine in 1765, Watt saw a way to improve its efficiency. To keep the steam in the piston cylinder hot enough to prevent premature condensation, a cylinder jacket was used, and a separate condensing chamber, with cocks and valves to connect the two chambers. Steam pressure pushing against the piston now did the work. In 1782 he developed a double-acting engine which applied the force of expanding steam to both sides of the piston. And if this were not enough, Watt designed the gears to transmit the engine's action to machinery. Finally, in 1788 he introduced the "governor," which automatically maintained an engine's constant pace.

These and numerous other innovations stimulated industry, which in turn inspired further inventions. The acceleration of patents reflected the tempo of innovation. Almost never, before 1760, were more than a dozen patents granted in any single year. Thirty-one were granted in 1761; this more than doubled by 1783. The peak was reached in 1825 with 250 patents.[8] Accompanying this unprecedented outpouring of technical innovations were changes in transportation.

On land, the movement of people and goods had been difficult at best. With mud in winter and clouds of dust in summer, roads resembled obstacle courses. The main reason for poor roads was that the communities through which roads passed were responsible for their upkeep. This changed after 1750 with the formation of turnpike companies which charged tolls for travel on their roads. Over solid foundations, road surfaces were pressed to form a hard finish. As roads became usable, wagons replaced pack horses and coaches sped passengers to their destinations at the heady pace of twelve miles per hour.

The period from 1760 to 1830 was the canal age. Waterways were dug

_____

[8]Ibid., p. 63.

for barge traffic, knitting England together as never before. Coal, iron, stone, and other bulky commodities were transported more efficiently and much less expensively than earlier, and agricultural products from remote regions reached urban markets, blunting the age-old problem of scarcity in one area and abundance in another. Canal building was nearly a mania in this period. Supervised by scores of civil engineers, armies of diggers were set to work. To raise the gigantic amounts of money required for these projects, the entrepreneurs who organized canal construction sold transferrable shares. As it turned out, the investments were sound.

The utility of canals can be seen in the load that a horse can move: a horse can carry about one-eighth of a ton, pull a one-ton wagon, or draw a barge of fifty tons. Canals thus provided a reliable and relatively cheap means to transport goods.

But the peak innovation in methods of transport was the steam locomotive. Inspired by this awesome invention, great cathedral-like terminals were erected to house the engines. As early as 1803, a high-pressure steam engine had been built and run through London's streets. No rails were used because it was believed that a smooth wheel could not get traction on a smooth rail. A dozen years later, rails and smooth wheels were demonstrated to be practical in a coal mine. This led to a much more ambitious project—a thirty-one-mile railroad connecting Liverpool and Manchester.[9] The physical obstacles were formidable: a steep climb at the Liverpool end, bridges to cross, a treacherous marsh. In 1829 the Liverpool and Manchester Railway was completed and the *Rocket* successfully traveled its tracks.

Now that steam-powered transport had been convincingly demonstrated, stronger engines and more railways soon appeared. By 1850, 6,000 miles of track had been laid; only twenty years later this mileage was more than doubled. Although the railroads were built primarily for movement of freight, passenger traffic provided half the railroad companies' earnings by the mid-1800s. No other means of travel could match the comfort and speed of trains. Offering three and sometimes four classes of seats, people from all walks of life took advantage of this new opportunity for travel. The Great Exhibition of 1851 attracted over 6 million visitors to London; many among this huge crowd arrived by train.

In addition to people and freight, trains also carried newspapers and mail. Though it would have been astonishing only twenty years earlier, by the time of the Great Exhibition most areas of the country could

---

[9]Michael Robbins, *The Railway Age in Britain* (Baltimore, Md.: Penguin Books, 1965), pp. 24–25.

receive London's morning newspapers before evening. Within a decade
of the *Rocket's* success, the postal service adopted a device for receiving
and distributing mailbags from moving trains. If even greater speed than
that offered by trains was required for communicating a brief message, a
mid-nineteenth-century individual could go to the nearest train station
and make use of Samuel Morse's ingenious invention, the telegraph. And
before the century ended, another American invention was
enthusiastically imported: Alexander Graham Bell's telephone provided
instantaneous communication with unexcelled convenience. A young
Englishman, Michael Faraday, had constructed a crude generator for
producing direct electric current in 1831. A compact generator to
produce alternating current was soon built, making possible such devices
as the telegraph and telephone.

The technical triumphs of the Industrial Revolution brought the
harnessing of new sources of energy to drive machines and the defeat of
physical distance by inventions which moved people, goods, and
messages at undreamed-of speeds. Although no one can say with
certainty, it is quite likely that industrialization, with its many
opportunities for applying technology to business enterprise, also
brought more mobility up the social class ladder than at any time before
or since.

One of the peculiarities of this age was that all manner of people were
drawn into money-making activities. Those who have no other resources
to draw upon must work. In England, however, since only the eldest son
could inherit his father's title of nobility and estate, noblemen's younger
sons, too, were obliged to find work. And they did, in medicine, law,
politics, teaching, and business. But it was not only that English society
was so oddly organized that even the elite's sons sought to make a living;
by the mid-1800s a cultural emphasis on work as a virtuous use of time
had crystallized. The origins of this concept can be traced to the late
Middle Ages, particularly Martin Luther's view that work is a form of
serving God.[10] (Remnants of this can be seen in the German word *Beruf*,
which combines the concepts of profession and religious calling.)
Various Protestant groups, most markedly the Calvinists, elaborated the
theme that work is demanded by God; to waste time is sinful.

The "Protestant Ethic," as it is now called, came from these medieval
origins but not without obstacles along the way. The virtue of work was
always less apparent to those who could avoid it. If fate generously
provided aristocratic parents, or merely wealthy parents who managed to

---

[10]For the clas.ic treatment of culture and work, see Adraino Tilgher, *Homo Faber: Work
Through the Ages*, trans. Dorothy Fisher (Chicago: Henry Regnery Co., Gateway Edition,
1958).

raise their offspring into the ranks of the nobility, work was hardly an attractive use of time that could more pleasantly be spent in less burdensome ways. The "Protestant Ethic," however, was certainly important among common people, particularly those of the growing middle classes for whom hard work and thrift could make a difference.[11]

In the 1700s, the religious impulse to work—perhaps tinged with the spirit of acquisitiveness—was exercised mainly by the urban middle classes. The gentleman with land and a title, on the other hand, expertly idled away his days in the manner of this vivid description:

> ...he spent his time as such men have probably spent it from the beginning of things: hunting, shooting, fishing, quarrelling, dicing, and drabbing...; retailing his day's adventures before the fire of an evening, or towsing Liselotte in the barn; riding out on a non-hunting morning to look at his fields, or to call on a neighbor..., and killing the day with a dinner lasting three or four hours.[12]

But what was accepted in the boisterous 1700s was condemned in the mid-1800s. In Queen Victoria's Britain, every stratum of society was encouraged to use time properly:

> ...*all* respectable early Victorian citizens were expected to fill six days a week with work...; the merely amusing or relaxing, the utterly uneducational, was deprecated as morally feeble.... [For men of all stations] leisure should be devoted to self-improvement, not self-indulgence.[13]

Although the early religious message that work served God was still heard from many pulpits, it was now the worldly desire for respectability that urged work. Religious inspiration and secular culture had blended around the theme that steady effort at one's work was a good thing. Of course all Victorians did not eagerly embrace work; still, acceptance by polite society required at least the appearance of well-spent time.

Several other developments were definitely more grim. The pace of industrialization was so rapid that cities could not decently house the workers crowding into them. Manchester, Leeds, Birmingham, and Sheffield, for instance, had about 30,000 inhabitants in 1760; within a hundred years each had grown tenfold to over 300,000.[14] Cellars and

---

[11]Max Weber, *The Protestant Ethic and the Spirit of Capitalism*, trans. Talcott Parsons (New York: Charles Scribner's Sons, 1958), p. 37.

[12]W. H. Lewis, *The Splendid Century: Life in the France of Louis XIV* (Garden City, N.Y.: Anchor Books, 1957), p. 157.

[13]Geoffrey Best, *Mid-Victorian Britain, 1851-1875* (New York: Schocken Books, 1972), p. 211.

[14]Walter P. Hall and Robert G. Albion, *A History of England and the British Empire* (New York: Ginn and Co., 1953), p. 494.

garrets were crammed with families enjoying little, if any, privacy for dressing, sleeping, or just relaxing. With the exception of grand houses, the outside privy serving one house, or more likely, several houses, was the rule. Excrement dropped into a pit or pail, renewed sporadically. The mechanical water closet was officially discouraged because sewage systems were inadequate. Not until the late 1890s did sewage systems catch up with the need for them. Since cooking and heating, in addition to factories, depended on coal, soot settled over everything exposed to the air. Cities were undoubtedly stimulating, but they were also extremely smelly, grimy, and unsanitary.

Movement to cities was prompted by the pull of higher wages and the push of deteriorating rural conditions. Factory wages were higher than what a tenant farmer or agricultural laborer could earn. Even if they had been making extra money through putting-out, rural people's earnings fell, since domestic methods of production could not compete with factories. The price of factory-made items was always lower, thus continually forcing down domestic workers' earnings. Moreover, the enclosure of former open fields had removed "commons" land from its traditional use by tenant farmers and agricultural laborers for grazing cows or pigs and gathering firewood. In the early 1800s an act of Parliament had eliminated most of the legal obstacles to enclosures, and landlords took this opportunity to proceed with them. All in all, leaving the countryside was sufficiently appealing to induce large numbers of families to move to cities.

Once there, everyone searched for work. And here we confront child labor, one of the most dismal aspects of British industrialization. Judged by current standards, child labor is shocking. Yet, even prior to the Industrial Revolution, children were sent into mines, performed endless farm chores, and worked long and hard under the domestic system. Life was harsh for most people; the notion that children should be spared from doing their share to help the family survive was a luxury that only a few could afford. As a result of the Industrial Revolution, we can afford this belief.

Technical improvements in spinning and weaving made it possible for children to do factory work. Children as young as seven toiled in factories for twelve and sometimes sixteen hours a day, six days a week, with forty minutes or so for the day's meal.[15] The owner usually left it to an overseer to administer the factory and foremen to supervise the work. If a foreman had a brutal nature, he was free to exercise it, and the young workers suffered the most. The foreman was primarily interested in

---

[15]An illuminating and judicious overview of child labor is E. P. Thompson's, *The Making of the English Working Class* (New York: Pantheon Books, 1964), pp. 331–49.

maintaining production, since his wages were linked to output. Especially toward the end of a day, when the children were utterly exhausted, the foreman might strike young workers with a stick to keep them awake for their work and to prevent accidents with machinery.

Legislation began to chip away at child labor in the 1840s, but reform was sluggish. Employers had an obvious interest in hiring children at low wages, and many parents, prompted by a combination of necessity and greed, were eager to put their children to work at the earliest possible age. In what remained of cottage industry, the very worst conditions went untouched for a long time. In hosiery, lace, ribbons, plaited straw, five- or even four-year-old children labored full-time.[16] By 1870 Parliament had extended the ten-hour day to all workers in officially inspected work places, although this still neglected domestic industry. In that same year Parliament accepted and soon enforced the principle that every child under the age of ten must be a full-time student.[17] With that act the cruel expoitation of young children finally ended.

The conscience of Britain had been stung by child labor; yet, it is doubtful that conscience alone would have been sufficient to end the practice. During the nineteenth century, as a result of greatly increased industrial output, the wages of men and women gradually rose, especially in the last twenty-five years of the century.[18] This decreased the hardship of losing a child's income and weakened parents' insistence that children work. The Parliament was dominated by men who had little need to send their young children to work and, after a series of investigations reported the shameful conditions of child labor, were willing to eliminate it.

Conditions of work were harsh, of course, for most people. Not only long hours but injury or death confronted many workers. In most years of the nineteenth century, a thousand English miners were killed and nearly eight hundred railroad workers died from accidents; in manufacturing, moving parts of machinery, chemicals, and gases contributed their share to injury and disease.[19] And also pressing was the discipline imposed by the division of labor in factory and workshop. The tremendous increase in industrial productivity was typically accompanied by an extreme elaboration of task specialization. Agricultural labor and domestic work can also be grindingly repetitive

---

[16]Best, *Mid-Victorian Britain, 1851-1875*, pp. 114-15.
[17]Ibid., p. 117.
[18]Ibid., p. 123. For a detailed look at wage trends and unemployment, see Neil J. Smelser, *Social Change in the Industrial Revolution* (Chicago: University of Chicago Press, 1959), pp. 213-24; also Paul N. Rosenstein-Roden, "The Modernization of Industry," in Myron Weiner, ed., *Modernization* (New York: Basic Books, 1966), pp. 270-71.
[19]Best, *Mid-Victorian Britain, 1851-1875*, pp. 119-20.

and dull; yet, there is at least the possibility of pauses, slowing down or speeding up one's work at self-determined intervals. It would be misleading to romanticize either farm work or domestic industry, but they did permit a small measure of independence that vanished in the many factories and workshops which minutely subdivided tasks in order to gain the swiftest possible pace for each operation.

The most famous description of finely divided tasks is Adam Smith's revealing illustration of pin making, published in 1776, just as the Industrial Revolution was gaining momentum. He noted:

> ...a workman not educated to this business...could scarce, perhaps, with his utmost industry, make one pin in a day, and certainly could not make twenty. But in the way in which this business is now carried on, not only the whole work is a peculiar trade, but it is divided into a number of branches, of which the greater part are likewise peculiar trades. One man draws out the wire, another straights it, a third cuts it, a fourth points it, a fifth grinds it at the top for receiving the head; and to make the head required two or three distinct operations; to put it on is a peculiar business, to whiten the pins is another; it is even a trade by itself to put them into the paper; and the important business of making a pin is, in this manner, divided into about eighteen distinct operations, which in some manufactories, are all performed by distinct hands, though in others the same man will sometimes perform two or three of them.

Smith went on to explain why the division of labor was useful:

> I have seen a small manufactory of this kind where ten men only were employed, and where some of them consequently performed two or three distinct operations. But...they could, when they exerted themselves, make among them about twelve pounds of pins in a day.... Those ten persons, therefore, could make among them upwards of forty-eight thousand pins in a day.... But if they had all wrought separately and independently, they could certainly not each of them have made twenty.... In every other art and manufacture, the effects of the division of labor are similar to what they are in this very trifling one.... The division of labor, however, so far as it can be introduced, occasions, in every art, a proportionable increase of the productive powers of labor.[20]

From this point of view, the greater the subdivision of work, the better the productivity. Many employers attempted to follow this path to maximum output. The disadvantages, however, fell upon the workers who repeated identical motions hundreds of times a day. For a large proportion of workers, though certainly not all, such routine was then, and still is, highly monotonous. (It has only been in the last few decades,

---

[20]Adam Smith, *The Wealth of Nations* (New York: Random House, Modern Library Edition, 1937), pp. 4–5.

however, that notions such as *job enlargement* and *job enrichment* have
been seriously considered as ways to design tasks, resulting in scattered
though well-publicized applications.[21])

As in any massive social transformation, the Industrial Revolution
generated both benefits and ills. Perceiving in the Industrial Revolution
an inherent trend toward increasing misfortune and upheaval, Karl Marx
(1818–1883) predicted rising unemployment and declining wages, and the
eventual division of the population into two armed camps, the owners of
the means of production and the workers who sold their labor; through
the revolutionary overthrow of capitalism, the exploitation of labor
would end and a better society, politically and economically egalitarian,
would ultimately emerge.[22] Although the actual course of events eluded
these dramatic predictions, other equally far-reaching changes unfolded.

As a result of the occupations stimulated by the Industrial Revolution,
the middle layers of society thickened beyond any preceding era. A
reconstruction of census data for 1851 and 1881 shows expansion over
these years in the professions, particularly teachers, writers, scientists,
lawyers; in commerce, among clerks, accountants, bankers, and
wholesale and retail dealers; and foreshadowing later developments,
more workers occupied with public administration.[23]

Growth of the middle classes in turn generated a spectacular rise in the
employment of servants. Their number just about doubled between 1851
and 1881 and represented the single largest female occupation. When
both men and women are included, nearly 16 percent of the entire work
force in 1881 were domestic servants.[24] Every family that laid claim to
exclusion from the working class hired at least a cleaning woman, while
the display of higher status required at a minimum three servants to
clean, cook, and serve guests. The wages of servants were low, but crept
upward as industrial productivity rose and wages generally notched up.

Social reform and wages were helped along by labor organizations.
The Combination Act of 1799 had prohibited any association of workers
for the purpose of striking or in any other way combining to influence
conditions of work. Nevertheless, trade unions formed and were quietly
active among wool combers, hatters, shoemakers, shipwrights, and

---

[21]For a review of job redesign theory, efforts, and outcomes, see Curt Tausky and E.
Lauck Parke, "Job Enrichment, Need Theory and Reinforcement Theory," in Robert
Dubin, ed., *Handbook of Work, Organization, and Society* (Chicago: Rand McNally College Publishing Co., 1976), pp. 531–65; Louis E. Davis and Albert B. Cherns, eds., *The
Quality of Working Life* (New York: The Free Press, 1975), vol. 2.

[22]An exceptionally clear statement of Marx's thought is presented in Joseph
Schumpeter's *Capitalism, Socialism, and Democracy* (New York: Harper and Brothers
Pubs., 1950), Parts I and II.

[23]Best, *Mid-Victorian Britain, 1851–1875*, pp. 84–85.

[24]Ibid., pp. 102–5.

tailors.[25] Wages and hours demands, though illegal, were presented to employers; with some, they met with success while other employers brought legal action against the petitioners. The Combination Act was repealed in 1824, largely on the grounds that *laissez faire* was the wisest policy: If workers and employers were left alone to reach their own bargains, unionists would soon realize that combination brought no advantage. But advantage there often enough was. Close on the heels of repeal, a great surge of union-joining occurred among miners, building-trades workers, wool combers, and cotton spinners.[26] On occasion, using the now-legal tactic of the strike, organized workers nudged employers to make wages and hours concessions.

It remained for a later age to initiate new programs for shifting money to those in need. The groundwork for this was laid by the national wealth that industrialization generated, and the extension of the vote to working men in 1867. England had several such schemes in place by the early years of the twentieth century: The Workmen's Compensation Act of 1906 made employers liable for industrial injuries and occupational diseases; the elderly received assistance through a national pension system, which came into being in 1908; and the fear of unemployment was lessened in 1911 by unemployment insurance. Although these and other programs are now firmly entrenched, each was met with heated controversy.

Though industrial societies have nowhere given enough attention to erasing the misery of poverty, inadequate housing, and medical care, legislated attempts to whittle down such conditions are a characteristic of industrial societies.[27] Just a little over two hundred years ago, before the Industrial Revolution, to consider seriously the reduction of life's hardships among whole populations would have seemed crazy. Marx's mid-nineteenth-century vision of a better life was inspired precisely by the Industrial Revolution's display of immense productive potential. For the first time in history, sufficiency rather than scarcity had become a possibility.

Overview

England was the homeland of the Industrial Revolution. There, by 1800, the centralized factory was creating the pattern for making goods

---

[25]Thompson, *The Making of the English Working Class*, p. 503.
[26]Ibid., p. 511.
[27]Current social programs in "rich" countries are usefully compared by Harold Wilensky, *The Welfare State and Equality* (Berkeley, Calif.: University of California Press, 1975).

in greater quantities and more cheaply than ever before. Putting-out could not compete against factories' steam-powered machines and elaborate division of labor.

Transportation also benefited from steam power. The steam-driven locomotive transported people and goods swiftly and economically. The development of railroads, canals, and paved roads reduced the isolation of England's rural areas, facilitated commerce between regions, and made feeding large urban populations possible.

Enclosures and dwindling income from putting-out, and the hope for employment in factories, attracted people to cities. When possible, the whole family worked; often, however, the women and children were hired. Cities grew very rapidly, with newcomers crowded into cellars and garrets. Sanitation consisted of the outdoor privy for all but the grandest houses.

In the early 1800s, wages were low and conditions of life harsh. Gradually, however, incomes rose and conditions improved. Before the century ended, the middle layers of society had thickened, child labor had been nearly eliminated, unions had become legal, and working men were allowed to vote. By the early 1900s, employers were liable for compensation for industrial accidents, a national pension system was in place, and unemployment insurance had come into being. In the span of a hundred years, England was transformed from an agricultural to an industrial society.

INDUSTRIALIZATION IN THE UNITED STATES

Only the most optimistic observer of the colonial population could have believed that it would be the base for a nation whose industry would lead the world. In addition to "conventional" immigrants—adventurers, artisans, laborers, farmers—the population was expanded by large numbers of indentured servants, "transported" criminals, and slaves.

Traveling through the towns of Germany, England, and Ireland, hucksters passed out leaflets advertising the abundant wealth of America. They peddled voyages, the payment being seven years of domestic service. The recruiters were paid by the head by merchants who specialized in importing indentured servants. Undersupplied with food and overfilled with passengers, the immigrants' ships often had mortality rates approaching 50 percent. Criminals were another source of labor in the worker-short economy. English courts could sentence murderers or other criminals to an overseas colony. This relieved England of many disreputable characters and served as punishment, on the presumption that life outside England was definitely unpleasant. America became home for thousands of criminals evicted from England. Transporting evildoers was a profitable business for shipowners, but hardly as lucrative as the slave trade.

English, Dutch, and Portuguese ship captains obtained slaves by kidnapping or by selling rum to African tribal chiefs in exchange for slaves. Shipboard conditions were nightmarish. Clever arguments in defense of the slave trade were constructed, not surprisingly, since reputable colonial merchants such as the Cabots and Faneuils were in the business and seaport towns, notably Boston, Salem, New York, and Newport, earned large profits. In the 1700s the colonies received about 30,000 slaves a year; by 1800 over half a million slaves had been brought to, or born in, America, accounting for roughly one-quarter of the entire labor force. As late as 1860, the proportion was about one-fifth.[28] Most were sold to plantation owners in the South, since gang labor was impractical on the smaller holdings in the North.

Industry and commerce developed slowly in the colonies. Still, furniture, wheels, farm equipment, cloth and leather, mostly made in homes, were sold in local markets; furs, fish, and timber, however, were exported, along with Southern tobacco and rice, and later the cotton that fed British industrialization. (Eli Whitney's cotton gin, invented in 1793, cleaned cotton ten times faster than a person could.) Shipbuilding and the processing of naval stores—pitch, tar, resin, hemp—became significant early industries. Luckily, iron ore was plentiful and furnaces spread through the colonies so quickly that by 1775 America was producing one-seventh of the world's iron supply.[29]

As in England, American manufacturing was spurred by textiles. An Englishman, posing as a farmer to evade emigration restrictions on mechanics, had memorized the design of Arkwright's yarn-spinning frame, and a factory with seventy-two frames was opened in 1790 at Pawtucket, Rhode Island, using waterpower to drive the machines. More factories then began to dot the landscape, such as John Lowell's large plant in Massachusetts. He recruited mainly farmers' daughters eager to leave the isolated dullness of rural life and earn some money; to house them, dormitories were built. Company towns with houses, banks, and stores soon appeared. Lowell and Lawrence, Massachusetts, were among the most thriving company towns organized around cotton mills. The operatives' pay was largely returned through the stores to the companies.[30]

The rubber industry developed after Charles Goodyear discovered

---

[28]U.S. Department of Commerce, Bureau of the Census, *Historical Statistics of the United States, Colonial Times to 1970*, Bicentennial Edition (Washington, D.C.: U.S. Government Printing Office), Part 2, p. 139.

[29]Ben B. Seligman, *The Potentates* (New York: Dial Press, 1971), p. 23.

[30]Ibid., pp. 86–87.

vulcanizing by accidentally dropping rubber, sulfur, and lead on a hot stove. A large market for rubber boots launched this industry. By 1850, firearms, clocks, locks, power-driven machine tools (boring and grinding lathes and a turret lathe with six to eight cutting tools mounted on it for successive operations), sewing machines, and farm equipment were produced in large numbers by the "American system," as it came to be called, meaning standardization and interchangeability of parts. By producing numbers of identical parts on precision lathes, the parts can be interchanged, providing an obvious advantage for machine repair.

But the strongest push toward industrialization came with the Civil War (1861–1865). Until then, cottage industry was dominant; now the factory became the undisputed model for manufacturing, sped by the demand for enormous supplies of military equipment. Many factories, however, were dependent on waterpower: in the 1860s half of the nation's factories still used waterwheels. Within the next few decades waterpower gave way to steam power, a surge of immigration enlarged the work force, and by 1895 the value of products manufactured in the United States equaled the combined output of England, France, and Germany.[31] The momentum of industrialization can be seen in the labor force of 1860–1890. In 1860 the majority of workers were in agriculture; by 1890, manufacturing accounted for over 60 percent.[32]

To make sense of this development we need to notice underlying changes in transportation, agriculture, and the scale of industry. The movement of goods was a difficulty for which a partial solution was found in canals. As in England, canal building, once started, became nearly a mania. From small beginnings in New York just before the end of the eighteenth century, over three thousand miles of canals were in use by the 1840s, financed by a mix of private, state, and local government money.[33] The canals were so impressive that the crude railroads just coming into use were sneered at as fit only to serve as feeder lines for the canals.

The rickety trains that appeared in most of the states in 1840 became a roaring success by 1850, and in so doing stimulated the construction, iron, and coal industries. The extent of activities related to railroads was so vast that 15 percent of all capital investment from 1849 to 1858 has been attributed to railroads.[34] The later expansion of industry and commerce would have been far less remarkable without the railroads to move goods and people.

---

[31]Herbert Gutman, *Work, Culture and Society in Industrializing America* (New York: Vintage Books, 1977), p. 33.
[32]Bureau of the Census, *Historical Statistics*, Part 2, p. 127.
[33]Seligman, *The Potentates*, pp. 76–79.
[34]Ibid., pp. 80 and 103.

Throughout the nineteenth century agricultural productivity rose. In 1800, for instance, 100 bushels of corn consumed 340 hours of labor; this fell to about 150 hours over the century.[35] Among the mechanical devices that aided agriculture, Cyrus McCormick's reaper and John Deere's steel plow were major advances. McCormick's reaper and Deere's plow were especially useful in the Midwest with its large wheat and corn fields and heavy soil. Before the end of the century, the reaper had evolved into the combine, cutting, bundling, and tying grain as it rolled along. Synthetic fertilizer and pesticides, and early in the twentieth century, new varieties of corn and wheat helped boost crop yields. Contributing to the creation and spread of these science-based innovations was the land-grant college with its agricultural research and extension services. As a result of better seeds, fertilizers, and pesticides, yields became more abundant, while through mechanization the amount of labor needed to plant and harvest crops drastically decreased.

The scale of farming also changed, though slowly until fairly recently. Interest in large-scale farming had long been present; it was most successful in the South where first the slave, then the tenant farmer, were available as cheap labor. In the Midwest, farm owners had to compete for labor with the frontier's promise of cheap land and the attractions of urban industry. Still, the larger-than-family farm survived with the help of machinery and harvest crews recruited in urban areas. But farming as big business, the corporate farm, did not come into its own until the 1950s.

The corporate farm is capital-intensive, substituting machinery for labor whenever possible. Capital investment in this sort of large farm, with up to 10,000 acres, may be as high as $165,000 per worker. This is far beyond the reach of smaller farms with their average investment of $21,000 per worker.[36] In the late 1950s the Internal Revenue Code was altered in a manner that made shares in corporate farms an appealing investment. Agricultural corporations' profits were allowed to "pass through," meaning that a corporation pays no federal tax; only the shareholders do. And the income to the shareholders is regarded as a capital gain, which is taxed at more favorable rates than most other forms of income. Thus, someone who knows little or nothing about agriculture might nonetheless find farming a good investment. There are over 21,000 incorporated farms.[37] Some of these are actually incorporated family farms or ranches, but many (the data make no

[35]Melvin Kranzberg and Joseph Gies, *By the Sweat of Thy Brow* (New York: G. P. Putnam's Sons, 1975), p. 140.

[36]Ibid., p. 142.

[37]Philip M. Raup, "Corporate Farming in the United States," in Edwin J. Perkins, ed., *Men and Organizations* (New York: G. P. Putnam's Sons, 1977), p. 90.

distinction) are much larger than family members could finance.

Corporate farms are organized mainly around poultry and eggs, fruit orchards, beef cattle, sugar cane, and vegetables for canning or processing.[38] Corporate farm expansion reached a peak in the late 1960s and then subsided. With the current cost of land and labor, corporate farming is likely to be restricted to those products that particularly benefit from large infusions of capital. There are about 1.5 million farms in the United States. Of these, 20 percent produce 75 percent of farm products sold.[39] Not all the larger spreads are corporate farms, but it is clear that the greatest share of the market for agricultural products is supplied by a relatively few large farms.

We saw how a change in tax rules had a significant effect on agriculture. Now let us notice another federal policy with much greater economic impact. With the onset of the Civil War, commercial and industrial activities accelerated. Although market demands stimulated the rapid climb to world industrial leadership, the legal framework smoothed the road to it. In the U.S. Constitution the right to charter corporate bodies is left to the states. Each state, therefore, could structure its own laws of incorporation. Not surprisingly, many state legislatures, eager to attract business, made incorporation simple. The great benefit of incorporation is the principle of *limited liability*. With limited liability the stockholders in a corporation risk only their investment and can not be held personally liable for the corporation's debts.

As a vehicle for generating investment in business ventures, limited liability performed impressively. (One student of such matters observed that as one traveled east from America to England, Western Europe, then Eastern Europe, the ease of incorporation declined and with it the growth of business activity.[40]) In 1889, New Jersey instituted a variation on laws of incorporation, permitting "holding companies." A holding company owns sufficient stock in other corporations to control their affairs. A number of corporations can thus be jointly controlled to form a powerful industrial or commercial empire. Delaware and Nevada, copying New Jersey, facilitated the formation of holding companies. Such companies contributed to the shift toward larger firms and concentration of control.

By a variety of means, business in many sectors of the economy became big business. In 1851 there were fifty telegraph companies; in

---

[38]Ibid., p. 93.
[39]Kranzberg and Gies, *By the Sweat of Thy Brow*, p. 146.
[40]James S. Coleman, *Power and the Structure of Society* (New York: W. W. Norton and Co., 1974), p. 31.

1866 Western Union operated fifty thousand miles of line and had bought up all but a few remaining telegraph companies.[41] Andrew Carnegie, beginning in 1863 with a modest iron works, expanded into steel production just as the railroads began to replace iron with steel rails; in the 1890s Carnegie's steel factories controlled two-thirds of steel production in the United States.

John D. Rockefeller invested five thousand dollars in an oil refinery. The market for kerosene lighting was strong, so he invested in a second refinery, forming in 1870 the Standard Oil Company of Ohio. Following a course of swallowing rival refineries through any available means, including the most unsavory, Standard Oil in the 1870s controlled about 90 percent of the refining business. The tactics of men like Carnegie in steel, Rockefeller in oil, J. P. Morgan on Wall Street, and Cornelius Vanderbilt and Russell Sage in railroads bestowed on the years following the Civil War the label, Age of the Robber Barons.

In tobacco, the American Tobacco Company had by 1890 stretched its control over 90 percent of the cigarette business. And meat packing, too, was consolidated, though not as tightly. The giant firms of this industry—formed in the 1880s by Philip Armour, Gustavus Swift, Nelson Morris, Michael Cudahy—from their base in Chicago were shipping large amounts of meat to the East in refrigerated trains and supplying an increasing number of items rescued by chemists from the bones and hair of cattle and hogs: fertilizers, glue, buttons, combs, felt, glycerine, oleomargarine. Organized initially around electricity-generating equipment for public utilities, but soon moving into household illumination, the Westinghouse Company came into existence in 1886, followed in 1892 by General Electric, which soon out-maneuvered and outdistanced it.

The shape of retailing also changed from the small independent store to the consolidated chain. In 1879 Frank Woolworth opened his first successful store in Lancaster, Pennsylvania, soon followed by another and another. The key was customer selection of items from open shelves. With his numerous stores Woolworth could buy in quantity and press his suppliers for favorable prices. This, combined with cheap labor—check-out clerks earned two to three dollars a week—allowed the stores to sell goods at attractive prices. By 1910, a chain of over seventy Woolworth stores had been created. To tap the huge rural market, Aaron Montgomery Ward, in 1871, acted on the notion that a mail-order house could supply goods to consumers; it could and did. About fifteen years later, Richard Sears teamed up with A. C. Roebuck to start a mail-

---

[41]This description of firms' growth draws on Seligman, *The Potentates*, chapters 2–3.

order business. To that they added a retail outlet, then another, eventually hundreds. Perhaps as much as five of every hundred dollars spent on merchandise touched a Sears outlet.

Into the last third of the nineteenth century, business in America was predominantly small business. Then came the great wave of corporate expansion and the large-scale enterprises of the modern economy appeared. Until 1920, corporate integration well summarizes the trend: horizontal integration merged firms with similar product lines, and vertical integration (back into sources of supply and forward to wholesale and retail networks) extended the scope of firms' activities. After 1920, growth through diversification rather than integration became the rule.[42] Diversification (buying firms or starting divisions with dissimilar products but similar production processes or distribution channels) was the growth strategy followed by General Electric, General Motors, and DuPont, for instance. Among the five hundred largest manufacturing firms, nearly 90 percent are highly diversified.[43] Yet another growth strategy appeared in the 1950s, the conglomerate enterprise, which searched for acquisitions in any industry that offered profitable opportunities.

Increases in the scale of operations were accompanied by greater complexity. The corporations that resulted from horizontal and vertical integration could not be administered by individual captains of industry, no matter how energetic. The situation demanded coordination among a firm's units. Thus, the numbers of managers and office clerks, stenographers, typists, bookkeepers and accountants swiftly grew. Most of the clerical employees, including typists—the typewriter was invented in the late 1870s—were initially men, although this changed with such rapidity that by 1910 over 80 percent of the clerks, stenographers, and typists were women.[44] With the diversification movement of the 1920s, the need for office personnel was greater than ever. Under pressure for

---

[42]Jon Didrichsen, "The Development of Diversified and Conglomerate Firms in the United States, 1920-1970," in Perkins, ed., *Men and Organizations*, pp. 38-50; also Alfred D. Chandler, Jr., "The Structure of American Industry in the Twentieth Century: A Historical Overview," in ibid., pp. 26-37.

[43]Didrichsen, "The Development of Diversified and Conglomerate Firms," p. 39. The long-term trend toward bigness in manufacturing had these striking results: as of 1977, in terms of value added (the market price of goods minus the cost of wages and materials), the fifty largest companies accounted for 18 percent of the total value added by all 311,000 manufacturing firms in the U.S.; the one hundred largest accounted for 25 percent, and the two hundred largest for 34 percent. Moreover, 44 percent of all employees in manufacturing work for the two hundred largest firms: U.S. Department of Commerce, Bureau of the Census, *Statistical Abstract of the United States*, 1981 (Washington, D.C.: U.S. Government Printing Office, 1981) p. 793.

[44]Rosabeth M. Kanter, *Men and Women of the Corporation* (New York: Basic Books, 1977), p. 27.

providing direction, coordination, and oversight, the multilayered bureaucracy arose in the attempt to get a firm grip on operations.

Circumstances had overwhelmed the simple plan of organization, which called for the owner or his deputy, assisted by a few key men, to oversee the superintendents and check on the foremen directly. It is worth noting that throughout much of the nineteenth century, factory operations were often in the hands of foremen who were essentially labor contractors, determining wages, rest periods, hiring, and firing. If the foreman got the work out, he could manage the workers as he wished, without interference from higher-ups.[45] Moreover, workers often used tools they had purchased, operated machinery at a self-chosen pace, trained new workers if this fit into their work, and coordinated tasks among themselves unless the foreman intervened. In short, the shop floor was to a considerable degree independent of higher management but subject to the whims and often heavy-handed actions of the foreman.

The ideas of Frederick Taylor, the father of "scientific management," comfortably fit the awakened concern for tighter control. Taylor insisted that planning and doing must be separated. It was management's task to plan precisely the division of labor, select tools, determine machine speeds, working pace, rest periods, and even the motions with which work should be done. After careful studies, management can allocate tasks (preferably small and easily learned) and prescribe quantity, quality, and time standards for each operation. Writing in the mid-1890s, Taylor and others similarly inclined found a receptive audience.[46] Although Henry Ford's manufacturing of cars with moving assembly lines was inspired by the powered overhead trolleys used to move carcasses in the Chicago meat-packing industry, he brought the concept of top-down management to its peak.

---

[45]Dan Clawson, *Bureaucracy and the Labor Process* (New York: Monthly Review Press, 1980), chapters 3–5.

[46]For a handy collection of Taylor's ideas, see Frederick W. Taylor, *Scientific Management* (New York: Harper and Row, 1947). Interestingly, Lenin became an enthusiastic advocate. In 1918 Lenin wrote:

> . . . we must raise the question of applying much of what is scientific and progressive in the Taylor system. . . . The task that Soviet government must set the people in all its scope is—learn to work. The Taylor system, the last word of capitalism in this respect, like all capitalist progress, is a combination of the refined brutality of bourgeois exploitation and a number of the greatest scientific achievements in the field of analyzing mechanical motions during work, the elimination of superfluous and awkward motions, the elaboration of correct methods of work. . . . We must organize in Russia the study and teaching of the Taylor system and systematically try it out and adapt it to our own ends."

James E. Connor, ed., *Lenin on Politics and Revolution, Selected Writings* (New York: Pegasus Books, 1968), p. 260.

When the Model T first appeared in 1908, it cost $850. Refining the assembly process and shifting to a moving assembly line reduced assembly time by 1913 to twelve and a half hours per car and brought down the price. Pushing the technique further, assembly time in 1914 fell to ninety-three minutes. The speed of work and its repetitious nature, however, created problems in retaining workers. Ford's solution was the unheard-of five-dollar day, and people lined up at the factory gates for jobs. By 1924 the price of a Model T was $290 and half the cars on America's roads were Fords.[47] The basic notions of elaborate division of labor, repetition, output and time standards, as urged by Taylor and so dramatically practiced by Ford, became widely accepted as sound managerial techniques, for manufacturing as well as paper processing in large offices.

A day's wage of five dollars was a lot of money back in 1914. Other employers, shocked by Ford's apparent folly, were fearful of the ideas it might give their workers. But such concerns were premature; no widespread, rapid upswing in wages resulted. Still, wages were generally rising, though slowly, not only in Ford's time but especially over the last decades of the nineteenth century as the economy expanded. To put this into perspective, let us glance at some income data. Between 1780 and 1840 farm laborers' daily wages moved from about forty cents to fifty cents; skilled workers earned roughly $1.75 a day, up from $1.35, while laborers gained twenty-five cents, for daily earnings of around a dollar.[48] The years 1840 to 1860 were less favorable. A rise in the cost of living wiped out wage increases and resulted in a lower living standard among workers.[49] Between 1860 and 1880 wages rose. But the cost of living again played tricks, with the result that—except for skilled workers —wages at the beginning of these two decades could barely purchase more than at their end.[50] The decades between 1880 and 1900 brought significant improvement, despite the arrival of 10 million immigrants, many of whom were men seeking work as laborers and factory hands.[51] Prices came down by 15 percent, and the average annual wage rose a hundred dollars.

For a five-person family of the 1890s to enjoy some degree of comfort—newspapers, outings, beer, tobacco—required a yearly income of about 500 dollars; 50 percent or so of workers' families were living at

---

[47]Kranzberg and Gies, *By the Sweat of Thy Brow*, pp. 118–22; Seligman, *The Potentates*, pp. 247–53.

[48]Bureau of the Census, *Historical Statistics of the United States*, Part 2, p. 163.

[49]Norman Ware, *The Industrial Worker, 1840–1860* (Chicago: Quadrangle Books, 1964), pp. 26–70.

[50]Bureau of the Census, *Historical Statistics*, Part 2, p. 165.

[51]Irwin Yellowitz, *The Position of the Worker in American Society, 1865–1896* (Englewood Cliffs, N.J.: Prentice-Hall, 1969), pp. 10–11.

that level of income.[52] But even among those, a good deal of endurance was necessary.

Workmen's wives, though ordinarily not in the labor force—except before marriage, and then probably as domestic servants—faced endless chores without the aid of washing machines, gas stoves, or iceboxes. Washing was done by hand, clothes had to be mended, bread baked, and the coal stove which provided heat and cooking required frequent attention. Leisure was a scarcity that only wealthy women with servants enjoyed. Shopping for groceries was a daily task requiring ingenuity, since half of the family's income went for groceries (compared to about one-quarter currently).[53] For workers' wives, the saying that a woman's work is never done was all too true.

Long hours were also, of course, usual for men. In 1890 the average weekly hours in manufacturing was sixty, while a small unionized segment put in fifty-four. Sunday was the only day off, and paid vacations were a rarity.[54] If an injury befell the workman, that was his problem. He could sue, but lawyers cost money and employer negligence was difficult to prove. In the late 1920s a few states passed workmen's compensation laws, but in most states the courts were not inclined to interfere with the right of an employer to write labor contracts which placed the risk of injury on the employee. Unions at that time could bring only limited pressures to bear on work-place safety.

At the turn of the century, less than 1 percent of the 24 million people in the labor force belonged to trade unions. About half of the union members were in transportation and construction, with the rest scattered in the mining, manufacturing, liquor, and tobacco industries.[55] Samuel Gompers had organized the American Federation of Labor (AFL) in 1886, but it was mainly an umbrella organization for craft unions. The potentially large unions in mass-production industries—later affiliated in the Congress of Industrial Organizations (CIO)—were generally stifled until federal legislation in the mid-1930s compelled employers to bargain. Before the passage of this and other workers' protection laws, the courts were ordinarily unsympathetic to challenges to freedom of contract or property rights.

By the beginning of the twentieth century, the vast American economy had created great wealth for a few, modestly comfortable living

---

[52]David Montgomery, "American Labor, 1865–1902," *Monthly Labor Review* 99 (1976): 13.

[53]U.S. Department of Labor, *A Century of Change in Boston Family Consumption Patterns* (Washington, D.C.: Bureau of Labor Statistics, Regional Report No. 79-5, 1979), pp. 22–23. The data reported in this publication draw on surveys of food expenditures in the entire country.

[54]Eli Ginzberg and Hyman Berman, *The American Worker in the Twentieth Century* (New York: The Free Press of Glencoe, 1964), pp. 35 and 344.

[55]Ibid., pp. 37–38.

conditions for many, and quiet desperation among those afflicted by unemployment, ill health, or old age. From 1900 to 1929 wage rates improved, then tumbled as the Great Depression deepened: A quarter of the labor force could not find work and many others were put on short hours. The greatest impact of the reform laws passed in the mid-1930s would be felt most strongly later, when unions expanded their membership and the safeguards we now take for granted—such as Social Security, unemployment insurance, and minimum wage standards—were fully implemented.

As late as the third decade of the twentieth century, legislative remedies for economic ills were shunned. The economy was generally left to the contestants under the dominant principle of economic competition (in contrast to the principle of economic allocation, which animates the socialist approach to industrial development in the U.S.S.R., China, and Cuba).[56] Massive long-term unemployment in the 1930s prompted governmental action, with the result that legislated choices became the economy's visible switchtender and were increasingly employed. Competition remained, but the rules of the game were altered to make the power of the contestants somewhat more even and provide at least minimal protections for the losers; moreover, judicious use of fiscal and monetary policies, it was (and is) assumed, could level out the economy's ups and downs.

Although the anticipated results may often fall short, we now demand such interventions. Peter Berger, a perceptive social analyst, has remarked that this outlook is essentially that of the engineer: "In principle there is the assumption that all human problems can be converted into technical problems, and if the techniques to solve certain problems do not as yet exist, then they will have to be invented."[57] Rooted in the ability to overcome technological problems, this view of life, in which economic (and social) troubles can be solved by the correct legislative solution, is perhaps the most far-reaching legacy of industrialization.

Overview

Industrialization in the United States was stimulated by the Civil War. The demand for goods was too large for cottage industry to satisfy;

---

[56]Competition and allocation as alternative engines of development are insightfully examined by Peter Berger, *Pyramids of Sacrifice* (Garden City, N.Y.: Anchor Books, 1976), p. 33ff.
[57]Ibid., p. 20.

factories were better suited to supply the enormous markets of the 1860s. The pace of industrialization was very rapid. By the mid-1890s, the value of products made in the U.S. equaled the combined output of England, France, and Germany. As in England, canals, and especially railroads, aided the growth of industry and commerce.

Agricultural productivity had steadily improved in the nineteenth century. With a decreasing proportion of people needed on farms to supply food for urban areas, and huge numbers of immigrants, workers were available for industrial growth. Investment in business ventures was facilitated by the ease of incorporation. The American Constitution left to the states the right to charter corporate bodies. States competed for businesses by legislating easily met requirements for incorporation.

The outlines of our modern economy were already visible in the last decades of the nineteenth century. Large enterprises had developed by buying up competitors (horizontal integration) and acquiring sources of supply and outlets (vertical integration). In the 1920s, another growth strategy became popular, diversification. This prompted the rise of firms with multiple divisions, each organized around a product line. Then, in the 1950s, the conglomerate enterprise searched the economic landscape for acquisitions in any profitable industry.

As firms grew, they also became more complex. Coordination and control required an increasing number of managers, bookkeepers, clerks, and typists. On the shop floor, the semiautonomous foreman lost his power to hire and fire, and workers' tasks became more regulated through detailed plans formulated by officials. Frederick Taylor's ideas on "scientific management" found a highly receptive audience in the 1890s. His conception of separating doing from thinking had an enduring influence on the theory and practice of management. Even Lenin became an enthusiastic advocate of "the Taylor system" in the U.S.S.R.

Until the mid-1930s, unions had slight legal support, and their membership was accordingly stunted. The Great Depression, however, prodded Congress to pass a number of measures, including the right to organize and the stipulation that employers must recognize the right. Social Security, unemployment insurance, and minimum wage standards were also legislated into existence in the 1930s. Government's role as bystander to economic ills had changed to that of interventionist.

3. The Labor Force: Making a Living

The preceding chapters discussed past events that influenced the present. In this chapter, the focus shifts to the present time. We begin by looking at how the labor force is counted.

There are now over 110 million people in the U.S. labor force. This number represents a particular way of counting. Some other rules for counting—such as including housewives—would produce a different image of the size of the labor force.

As defined by the Department of Labor, the labor force includes people sixteen years of age and older who had a particular relationship to work during a specified week: (1) employed or self-employed persons who received pay for full- or part-time work, or who worked at least fifteen hours as unpaid workers in a family business; (2) people who had jobs from which they were absent due to illness, vacation, or strikes; (3) unemployed persons who looked for work within the past four weeks by answering advertisements, checking with friends, writing letters of application; and (4) people waiting to be called back to a job when business picks up, or waiting to start a new job within thirty days.[1]

These, then, are the people who are counted in the labor force. As mentioned, if some other rules of classification were used, perhaps including housewives or "discouraged" persons who have given up looking for work, the entire labor force would appear larger, and one component of it, the unemployed, would certainly be greater.[2] Be this as

[1]U.S. Department of Labor, Bureau of Labor Statistics, *Employment and Earnings* 30 (January 1983): 194. As of 1983, members of the armed forces are included in the labor force.

[2]Classified as not in the labor force are persons doing their own housework, in school, retired, institutionalized, or mentally or physically disabled, seasonal workers in the "off" season, the voluntarily idle, and discouraged people who no longer look for work because they believe that no job is available. In 1982, the last group would add about 1.5 million persons or roughly 1 percent to the unemployment rate.

it may, "official" labor-force data generated by monthly surveys, and once every ten years by the census, provide much useful information, as long as it is kept in mind that the numbers represent people with specific involvements in the world of work through employment or availability for employment.[3]

The *labor force participation rate* tells us what percentage of the total population, or of a particular age group, sex, or race, is in the labor force. Let us see what this statistic shows.

LABOR-FORCE PARTICIPATION

Labor-force membership reflects both stability and change over time. Men are expected to work for pay, and their labor-force participation has been quite stable, as is evident from the third column of Table 3-1. About 80 percent of men sixteen years of age and older join the labor force; this was the case earlier and still is. But notice that the rate for women increased and then doubled between 1940 and 1980. The total labor-force participation rate has therefore risen (column 2), due to the increased presence of working women.

TABLE 3-1

Labor Force Participation Rates, 1880–1982
(in percent)

	Total Noninstitutional Population, 16 years or older (in thousands)	Total Participation Rate	Men	Women
1880	36,762	47	79	15
1900	47,950	50	80	19
1920	82,739	50	78	21
1940	100,147	53	79	25
1960	124,517	56	79	35
1970	139,130	59	78	42
1980	169,886	64	79	52
1982	174,020	64	77	53

Sources: Bureau of the Census, *Historical Statistics of the United States, Colonial Times to 1970,* Bicentennial Edition (Washington, D.C.: U.S. Government Printing Office, 1975), Part 2, pp. 127–28; Department of Labor, Bureau of Labor Statistics, *Employment and Earnings,* 29 (May 1982): 7–8.

---

[3]Concern for accurate counting and consistent definitions emerged in 1940, probably as a result of the depression and the war that threatened to entangle the United States. Information collected before that time must therefore be treated with caution. This is no major problem here, since I rely on earlier data mainly to indicate large shifts; for this purpose the data are adequate.

As the nation swung into expansion of its defense industries in the early 1940s, the participation of women was needed. This helped to stimulate a redefinition of women's roles. The impact of this change is so enormous that a nonworking wife, if asked what she does, might very well answer with a twinge of embarrassment, "I am only a housewife." Additionally, a working wife's pay is often a significant contribution to family income.[4] Here culture and economics intertwine.

Single and divorced women, and of course women whose husbands received low wages, were in earlier times the most likely to work, since they had little choice. But over the last several decades, women whose husbands earn solid incomes have also joined the labor force. If the husbands' earnings are in the top quarter of income, their wives are less inclined to enter the labor force than are others' wives. However, the difference between the labor-force participation rates of wives with husbands in the top quarter of income and those with husbands in the lowest quarter is only around 10 percent.[5]

Children do make a difference, but much less now than just twenty years ago. This is clearly visible in Table 3-2. By 1980, nearly half of the mothers with one or more children under six years old were in the labor force, compared to 19 percent in 1960; and over 60 percent of the mothers with children six to eighteen years old were working or looking for work in 1980, compared to under 40 percent in 1960.

TABLE 3-2

Married Women's Labor Force Participation and Children, 1960–1980
(in percent)

Presence and Age of Children	Wives' Labor Force Participation Rates	
	1960	1980
Children under 6 yrs.	19	45
Children 6 to 18 yrs.	39	62
No children under 18 yrs.	35	46
All wives	31	50

Source: Statistical Abstract of the United States, 1981, p. 388.

[4]On average, wives working full-time contributed about 38 percent of their families' income (70 percent of working wives presently hold full-time jobs). Adding part-time earnings, the overall average contribution to family income by working wives is about 25 percent. U.S. Department of Labor, Bureau of Labor Statistics, *Perspectives on Working Women* (June 1980), p. 1.
[5]Paul Ryscavage, "More Wives in the Labor Force Have Husbands with Above-Average Incomes," *Monthly Labor Review*, 102 (1979): 41.

We thus see increasing numbers of women entering the labor force from every type of family situation and economic condition. An earlier comment bears repeating: culture and economics in varying combinations for different women nudge them into the labor force. We have paused to look at this in some detail because it is among the most fundamental social changes of the twentieth century and is bound to affect family relationships. After all, a woman who works need not tolerate an unhappy marriage, while a disgruntled husband may with a less guilty conscience file for divorce. Whether less constrained relationships are liberating or disruptive will necessarily hinge on one's point of view.

Clearly, the "traditional" family with a working husband whose wife keeps house has dwindled; about half of all married couples now both work. The two-earner family, however, may produce not only more income but serious marital strains as well. Several studies have found that couples in which the wives have high earnings or strong career commitments also have higher divorce rates.[6] The difficulty perhaps lies in the distribution of household tasks, creating frictions over who should do what.[7] As it turns out, working wives still do most of the household chores, with their husbands ordinarily not helping much.[8] In this sense, working wives have dual careers, work and home, which together require a good deal of energy and time.

That dilemma pales by comparison to the situation of unmarried, divorced, separated, or widowed women with children to raise and feed. Not surprisingly, many are in the labor force—especially the divorced (78 percent), separated (59 percent), and unmarried mothers (56 percent)—but as breadwinners heading a family they fare poorly: on average, their income is only about one-third that of intact husband-wife families with children.[9] To make ends meet on that level of income is surely difficult at best. Having to "go it alone" is among the most forceful pressures that urge women into the work force.

We have looked at labor-force participation, so we turn now to what labor force members do—their occupations.

---

[6]Kristina A. Moore and Isabel V. Sawhill, "Implications of Women's Employment for Home and Family Life," in Ann H. Stromberg and Shirley Harkess, eds., *Women Working* (Palo Alto, Calif.: Mayfield Publishing Co., 1978), p. 205.

[7]Lotte Bailyn, "Accommodation of Work to Family," in Robert and Rhona Rapoport, eds., *Working Couples* (New York: Harper and Row, 1978), especially p. 163.

[8]Juanita M. Kreps and R. John Lieper, "Home Work, Market Work, and the Allocation of Time," in Juanita M. Kreps, ed., *Women and the American Economy* (Englewood Cliffs, N.J.: Prentice-Hall, 1976), p. 74.

[9]Beverly L. Johnson, "Marital and Family Characteristics of Workers, 1970–78," *Monthly Labor Review*, 102 (1979): 51.

OCCUPATIONS

When we meet someone for the first time, the conversation before long usually turns to the sort of work each person does. Discovering another's occupation is a socially acceptable shortcut to gaining information that permits people to estimate whether a relationship might be established: Occupations signal approximate income level, education, prestige, and tastes. There is an enormous variety of occupations, but these become grouped into layers of ranked categories, which allow mental images to be constructed around the individuals in these categories. As we will see in a moment, one system of categories (corresponding, apparently, to popular conceptions) became the basis for official data collection.

Every so often the Department of Labor revises its *Dictionary of Occupational Titles*, the most inclusive list of job descriptions available anywhere. The most recent dictionary lists 20,000 distinct occupations. No individual or federal agency could track occupational matters without somehow grouping so many occupations into manageable categories. This feat was accomplished by Dr. Alba Edwards of the Census Bureau, who constructed a classification system of six broad categories based on socioeconomic commonalities within a category and differences between categories. Edwards pulled together Census Bureau returns from 1870 to 1940, making information available on long-term trends. The occupational categories he used were:[10]

1. Professionals
2. Proprietors, managers, and officials
3. Clerks and kindred workers
4. Skilled workers and foremen
5. Semiskilled workers
6. Unskilled workers

With a few adjustments, Edwards' classification scheme is still widely used.

We can see how people are distributed among occupations in Table 3-3. Several features are notable, though not surprising. Since 1900 the white-collar jobs have tremendously expanded, from 17 percent to over 50 percent. Thus, one out of every two job holders now has some sort of white-collar (or "pink-collar") job. An important aspect of this growth is that it fostered upward occupational mobility into the professional,

---

[10]Seymour Wolfbein, *Work in American Society* (Glenview, Ill.: Scott, Foresman and Co., 1971), pp. 43–44.

TABLE 3-3

Occupational Distribution of the Labor Force, 1900-1982
(in percent)

	1900	1950	1960	1970	1980	1982
WHITE COLLAR	*17*	*37*	*43*	*48*	*52*	*54*
Professional & technical	4	9	11	14	16	17
Managers & officials	6	9	11	11	11	11
Clerical workers	3	12	15	17	19	19
Sales workers	4	7	6	6	6	7
BLUE COLLAR	*36*	*41*	*37*	*35*	*32*	*30*
Foremen & skilled workers	10	14	13	13	13	13
Semiskilled workers	13	20	18	18	14	13
Laborers	13	7	6	4	5	4
SERVICE	*9*	*11*	*12*	*12*	*13*	*13*
Private household workers	5	3	3	2	1	1
Other service workers	4	8	9	10	12	12
FARM	*38*	*11*	*8*	*4*	*3*	*3*
Farmers & farm managers	20	7	4	2	2	2
Farm laborers & foremen	18	4	4	2	1	1

Sources: Data for 1900 and 1950, Bureau of the Census, *Historical Statistics of the U.S., Colonial Times to 1970*, Bicentennial Edition (Washington, D.C.: U.S. Government Printing Office, 1975), Part 2, p. 139; 1960, 1970, *Statistical Abstract of the U.S., 1973*, p. 230; 1980, 1982, U.S. Department of Labor, Bureau of Labor Statistics, *Employment and Earnings* (June 1980): 35, and 29 (May 1982): 24.

technical, and managerial ranks. Blue-collar employment has remained relatively stable as a proportion of all jobs, but notice that laborers are much less in demand than formerly; the uneducated, unskilled individual seeking a job will obviously have a difficult search. And, of course, farm work, now involving 3 percent of the work force, is not a likely source of employment, nor is domestic service, which under the more genteel label of private household workers has dwindled to near disappearance. Still, the category of "other service workers" has absorbed numbers of people who lack the appropriate education, technical skills, or social graces to find other employment.

The "service workers" category covers a diversity of occupations and includes many jobs on the lowest rungs of an occupational cluster. For instance, in food services, counter workers, waitresses, waiters, and dishwashers are included, as are cooks, but bakers are counted as skilled workers, and food-service supervisors are classified as managers. In health services, practical nurses and attendants are counted as service workers while registered nurses appear in the professional, technical category. Also among service workers we find guards, doorkeepers, watchmen, porters, janitors, bootblacks, as well as barbers and beauticians, midwives, firefighters, police, and detectives. Many of these occupations are low-skill, minimum-wage jobs, so people who can not compete for better work may find themselves in the least desirable of the service jobs.

The process by which people are sorted and sort themselves into occupations is complex, although we know that education plays a major role in this process. In turn, the duration of individuals' education is influenced by parents' education and especially one's father's occupation.[11] Looking at occupations in combination with education, it is clear that the more highly rewarded occupations go to people with lengthier education. This relationship is sketched below by listing occupational categories and the median education of people in those categories in 1981:[12]

Professional, technical	16.9
Managers, proprietors	14.0
Sales workers	13.2
Clerical workers	13.0
Foremen, skilled workers	12.7
Semiskilled workers	12.3
Laborers	12.2
Private household workers	11.0
Other service workers	12.5
Farmers and farm workers	12.2

Since the median locates the midpoint (50th percentile) of a distribution, we can see that the chances for selection into jobs with training and promotion opportunities are brighter for people with lengthier education. It is also possible, of course, that individuals have more education than a job actually requires to perform it. People may be underutilized, as is probably the case among many sales and clerical workers. The median education for these groups indicates some college attendance. But whether underutilized or not,[13] getting a job is certainly more difficult if one's education is below the average for the occupation one wishes to enter.

---

[11]David L. Featherman and Robert M. Hauser, *Opportunity and Change* (New York: Academic Press, 1978), pp. 338–39.

[12]Estimated from data in Anne M. Young, "Educational Attainment of Workers, March 1981," *Monthly Labor Review*, 105 (1982): 54, and Anne M. Young, *Educational Attainment of Workers, March 1979*, Special Labor Force Report 240 (Washington, D.C.: U.S. Department of Labor, Bureau of Labor Statistics, 1981), Table A-19.

[13]The issue of underutilization is examined in Ivar Berg, Marcia Freedman, and Michael Freeman, *Managers and Work Reform* (New York: The Free Press, 1978), chapters 6–7.

The number of years of schooling has persistently moved upward among the American labor force: Each decade since 1940 has added just about a year to the median education, which is now almost thirteen years.[14] This has encouraged employers to opt for employees with more schooling because they are available. However, the connection is very unclear between longer education and employee performance.[15] This suggests that educational requirements, especially in the middle layers of the occupational structure, reflect rather arbitrary notions more than verified criteria.

Who Gets Which Jobs?

We continue now to look at occupations by asking, Who is in which jobs? Important influences are sex and race, as shown in Table 3-4. For

TABLE 3-4

Occupations, Sex, and Race, 1982
(in percent)

	Men		Women	
	White	Black	White	Black
WHITE COLLAR	*46*	*33*	*69*	*51*
Professional & technical	17	14	18	15
Managers & officials	16	8	8	4
Clerical workers	6	8	35	29
Sales workers	7	3	8	3
BLUE COLLAR	*42*	*48*	*12*	*18*
Foremen & skilled workers	21	17	2	2
Semiskilled workers	15	20	9	15
Laborers	6	11	1	1
SERVICE	*8*	*16*	*18*	*30*
Private household workers	—	—	2	5
Other service workers	8	16	16	25
FARM	*4*	*3*	*1*	*1*
Farmers & farm managers	3	1	—	—
Farm laborers & foremen	1	2	1	1

Note: Black refers to "black and other nonwhites"; about 90 percent of this category is composed of black workers.
Source: U.S. Department of Labor, Bureau of Labor Statistics, *Employment and Earnings,* 29 (May 1982): 24.

---

[14]U.S. Department of Commerce, Bureau of the Census, *Statistical Abstract of the United States, 1981* (Washington, D.C.: U.S. Government Printing Office, 1981): p. 142.
[15]Berg, Freedman, and Freeman caution in *Managers and Work Reform,* "Indeed, a crude test we conducted in the late 1960s...provided no evidence whatever that marginal increments of education are predictive of proportionate improvements in the performance of employees" (p. 77). See also John W. Meyer, "The Effects of Education as an Institution," *American Journal of Sociology,* 83 (1977): 55–77.

white-collar workers, the most striking contrasts occur among managers
and officials—16 percent of white males are in that occupational
category compared to 8 percent of black men. Among blue-collar
workers, half the white males are foremen or skilled workers, whereas
everyone else is more likely to be semiskilled. In the service occupations
we see that one out of every three black working women is in a service
job.

Looking back, say to 1960, only 4 percent of black men were in the
professional and managerial occupations, 10 percent were employed as
foremen or skilled workers, and 24 percent worked as laborers. In that
same year 35 percent of black working women were private household
workers. Significant, though slow, occupational upgrading of black
workers has taken place. White working women have enjoyed less
substantial occupational gains. Earlier, a larger proportion were
employed as semiskilled workers and service workers, but the movement
out of these occupations has been mainly toward clerical work and only
modestly into the managerial ranks, with little change, actually, in the
professional, technical jobs (a gain of only 4 percent since 1960).[16]

Two developments, one might reasonably suppose, have helped to
reduce occupational disparities between the sexes and races: equal
employment–affirmative action regulations, and more equal educational
credentials. Government enforcement of equal employment
opportunities has had mixed reviews, not only for creating paperwork
for employers, but also in terms of results. The weight of the evidence,
however, comes down on the side of favorable results; enforcement of
equal opportunity has contributed to a measurable degree of
occupational upgrading, particularly among younger blacks and women
with college degrees.[17] As Table 3-5 indicates, the trend is toward more
college graduates among minorities, thereby contributing to
occupational upgrading. This will also, of course, make the competition
for "better" jobs increasingly keen among college graduates.

Industries

An aspect of occupations not yet touched on is the industries in which
people work. Table 3-4 showed people's occupations but not the types of

---

[16]For more detail on women and black workers, see Howard Davis, "Employment Gains
of Women by Industry, 1968-78," *Monthly Labor Review,* 103 (1980): 3-9; Diane N.
Westcott, "Blacks in the 1970's: Did They Scale the Job Ladder?" *Monthly Labor Review,*
105 (1982): 29-38; *Statistical Abstract of the United States, 1982-83,* pp. 386-90.

[17]The reader who wishes to pursue this topic would benefit from the volume by Leonard
J. Hausman et al., eds., *Equal Rights and Industrial Relations* (Madison, Wisc.: Industrial
Relations Research Association, 1977), especially chapter 9.

TABLE 3–5

College Graduates by Race and Sex, 1940–1982
(in percent)

| | | | College Graduates | | |
| | | | Persons Age 25 and Over | | |
	1940	1960	1970	1980	1982
White:					
Men }	5	10	15	22	24
Women }		6	9	14	16
Black:					
Men }	1	3	5	8	10
Women }		3	4	8	10

Sources: Statistical Abstract of the U.S., 1979 (p. 136), and 1981 (p. 142); U.S. Department of Labor, Bureau of Labor Statistics, News, August 10, 1982, Tables 1 and 2.

industry in which their jobs are carried out. One might, for instance, be a manager or clerk in an insurance company or a manufacturing firm. The insurance company would be classified as service-producing and the manufacturing firm as goods-producing. Table 3-6 shows this sort of classification.

It was mentioned earlier that in industrial societies the service-producing sector expands and eventually employs the largest share of the labor force. Without dwelling on the obvious, Table 3-6 shows at a glance that the service-producing industries are indeed the growth industries. The service industries creating the largest number of jobs since 1950 have been government, especially in education at the state and local levels, and business, personal, and professional services. About one out of every five workers is currently in manufacturing, and just about the same proportion of the work force is in trade, buying and selling the manufactured goods. With over 70 percent of the work force now in the service industries, all indications point to a continuation of the story in Table 3-6—employment prospects will be strongest in the service industries.[18]

Employment's other face is unemployment. To this we now turn.

UNEMPLOYMENT

Unemployment may be *frictional* or *structural*. Frictional unemployment refers to the short-term lack of work while changing to

---

[18]Between 1925 and 1975 the service-producing industries generated nearly three of every four new jobs in the economy. U.S. Department of Labor, Bureau of Labor Statistics, *U.S. Workers and Their Jobs: The Changing Picture* (Washington, D.C.: U.S. Government Printing Office, 1976), pp. 8–9.

TABLE 3-6

Employment in Goods-Producing and Service-Producing Industries, 1890–1982
(in percent)

	1890	1950	1970	1982
SERVICE-PRODUCING INDUSTRIES	**26**	**51**	**65**	**71**
Finance, insurance, real estate	1	4	5	6
Business, personal, professional services	8	10	19	20
Trade: wholesale and retail	9	18	20	22
Transportation, utilities, communications	6	8	6	6
Government: federal, state, and local	2	11	15	17
GOODS-PRODUCING INDUSTRIES	**74**	**49**	**35**	**29**
Manufacturing	20	29	25	21
Construction	6	4	5	4
Agriculture, forestry, mining, fishing	48	16	5	4
Total employed labor force (in millions)	23.3	58.9	78.6	98.9

Note: Business, personal, and professional services include, for example, consulting and legal services, health services, private education, repair, cleaning and gardening services, entertainment, hotels and motels, barbershops and beautyshops, private household services. The military services are here excluded from federal government employment. In 1982 the armed forces employed about 2 million uniformed persons.

Sources: 1890 and 1970 distributions are calculated from labor force data in Delbert C. Miller and William H. Form, *Industrial Sociology* (New York: Harper and Row, 1980), pp. 66, 68–69. 1950 data are drawn from *Statistical Abstract of the U.S.*, 1974, p. 228; 1982, U.S. Department of Labor, Bureau of Labor Statistics, *Employment and Earnings*, 29 (May 1982): 25 and 56.

another job or seeking a new job. Economists tell us that an unemployment rate of about 3 percent is normal and unavoidable, even in good times, because that rate reflects frictional unemployment. Structural unemployment is more ominous. It refers to the long-term or permanent unemployment brought about by technological change or decline in an industry, leaving some people unable to find work because their skills are not needed. Older workers are especially vulnerable, since they may find it difficult to learn new skills or move to another community. Steel, automobiles, furniture, textiles, and railroads are industries that have structural unemployment.[19]

Over time, unemployment rates have risen and receded: If a rate over 6 percent is considered high (a rate arbitrarily set at double the "normal" rate of frictional unemployment), then high unemployment has afflicted the United States five times from 1890 to the present. As can be seen in Table 3-7, the longest and deepest unemployment occurred in the Great Depression of 1930-1940. It can also be observed that from 1975 on,

TABLE 3-7

Unemployment Rates for Selected Years, 1890-1982

1890	4.0%	1965	4.5%
1895	13.7	1970	4.9
1900	5.0	1971	5.9
1910	5.9	1972	5.6
1920	5.2	1973	4.9
1929	3.2	1974	5.6
1930	8.7	1975	8.5
1933	24.9	1976	7.7
1940	14.6	1977	7.0
1943	1.9	1978	6.0
1945	1.9	1979	5.9
1950	5.3	1980	7.1
1955	4.4	1981	7.6
1960	6.5	1982	9.7

Note: The unemployment rate is defined as the number of unemployed persons divided by the number in the labor force.

Sources: 1890 to 1929, Bureau of the Census, Historical Statistics of the U.S., Colonial Times to 1970, Bicentennial Edition (Washington, D.C.: U.S. Government Printing Office, 1975), Part 2, p. 135; 1930 to 1978, Philip L. Rones and Carol Leon, Employment and Unemployment During 1978, Special Labor Force Report no. 218 (Washington, D.C.: Department of Labor, Bureau of Labor Statistics, 1979), p. A-4; U.S. Department of Labor, Bureau of Labor Statistics, Employment and Earnings, 29 (May 1982): 7.

---

[19]Delbert C. Miller and William H. Form, Industrial Sociology (New York: Harper and Row, 1980), p. 86.

TABLE 3–8

Unemployment Rates and Selected Characteristics, 1982

	Percent Unemployed			Percent Unemployed
RACE, SEX, AND AGE			**OCCUPATION**	
White, total	8.1		Total white collar	4.4
Men: 20 years and over	7.6		Professional & technical	2.7
16 to 19 years	21.6		Managers & officials	3.2
Women: 20 years and over	6.7		Clerical workers	6.5
16 to 19 years	18.8		Sales workers	5.3
Black, total	17.8		Total blue collar	13.9
Men: 20 years and over	16.8		Foremen & skilled workers	9.9
16 to 19 years	48.5		Semiskilled workers	15.3
Women: 20 years and over	14.1		Laborers	19.3
16 to 19 years	44.0		Service workers	10.4
			Farm workers	6.0
EDUCATION				
Less than high school	12.4		**TYPE OF WORKER**	
High school completed	8.5		Full-time workers	9.2
College: 1 to 3 years	6.2		Part-time workers	10.9
4 or more years	3.0			
			INDUSTRY	
FAMILY STATUS			Goods-producing	11.4
Married men, spouse present	6.0		Service-producing	6.9
Married women, spouse present	7.8			
Women who head families	11.5			

Sources: U.S. Department of Labor, Bureau of Labor Statistics, Employment and Earnings, 29 (May 1982): 13, 17–18, 22, 25, 32. All data are for April 1982, except education, which shows March 1982 data reported in Department of Labor, Bureau of Labor Statistics, News, August 10, 1982, Table 1.

rates of unemployment have remained disturbingly high.[20]

Unemployment does not affect everyone equally. Table 3-8 shows the situation in 1982, but the relationships are more enduring. The young, the less educated, and the less skilled are the most likely victims of unemployment. The very highest rates (over 40 percent) occur among minority youths; yet, the rate of unemployment among older black men and women is also high, about twice that of adult whites. (Although Hispanics are not separately shown in Table 3-8, their unemployment rates average midway between white and black rates.) It can also be observed that women heading families are unemployed at a rate close to twice that of married men, and part-time workers are more likely to be out of work than full-time workers.

When the economy slumps, generating higher unemployment, there is no arguing the fact that minority workers are especially vulnerable.[21] As

TABLE 3-9

Unemployment Rates in Eight Countries,
Adjusted to U.S. Concepts, 1960–1982

	1960	1970	1974	1976	1978	1981	1982
United States	6.5	4.9	5.6	7.7	6.0	7.4	9.7
Canada	7.0	5.7	5.4	7.1	8.5	7.3	10.9
Australia	1.6	1.4	2.7	4.8	6.3	5.7	7.0
Japan	1.7	1.2	1.4	2.0	2.2	2.2	2.4
France	1.9	2.6	3.0	4.6	5.1	7.8	8.0
West Germany	.8	.8	1.7	3.6	3.4	4.1	6.1
Sweden	1.5	1.5	2.0	1.6	2.3	2.3	3.1
England	2.2	3.1	2.9	5.5	6.3	10.7	12.7

Sources: Joyanna Moy and Constance Sorrentino, "Unemployment, Labor Force Trends, and Layoff Practices in 10 Countries," Monthly Labor Review, 104 (December 1981): 4–5; U.S. Department of Labor, Bureau of Labor Statistics, Handbook of Labor Statistics 1975—Reference Edition (Washington, D.C.: U.S. Government Printing Office, 1975), p. 437; Main Economic Indicators (Paris: Organization for Economic Cooperation and Development, March 1983), p. 16.

---

[20]For a variety of reasons—high interest rates and energy prices, large federal deficits and tax policies that adversely affect savings rates, increasing female labor force participation, legal and illegal immigration, attractive imports, weakened exports and domestic sales due to our manufacturing costs, export of advanced technology under licensing agreements, and restrictive government regulation of doing business abroad—recent high unemployment rates may not soon dip below 6 percent. A number of the listed reasons for unemployment are ethically insoluble; no purpose is served, however, by ignoring them.

[21]A study of 1,250 married men, over the ten-year period from 1967 to 1976, showed that the risks of unemployment for all races are quite high; within these ten years, one-third of the men had experienced some unemployment. But the incidence of unemployment was highest among blacks who were blue-collar workers and poorly educated: Martha S. Hill and Mary Corcoran, "Unemployment Among Family Men: A 10-Year Longitudinal Study," Monthly Labor Review, 102 (1979): 19–23.

a statistical rule of thumb that has held true since 1950, black workers average twice the unemployment rate of white workers.

Focusing again on the overall unemployment rate, we can place the U.S. experience in the larger context of international comparisons. A look at Table 3-9 will show that the U.S. has sometimes fared better than a few industrialized countries, but generally not as well as others. Canada's rates frequently rank highest among these eight countries while Germany's, Japan's, and Sweden's are the lowest. After 1974, all of these countries experienced rising unemployment. Although the German, Swedish, and Japanese rates for 1982 seem relatively low, they are the highest in those countries in thirty years. As one or a few nations head into slow economic growth, they import less, which in turn reduces the exports (and employment) of countries that sell manufactured goods. In short, the ripples of economic troubles touch economically interdependent nations, with unemployment consequently increased.

Putting it this way, however, understates the reach of the unemployment problem. In the 1960s and early 1970s, the European countries listed in Table 3-9 were hosts to huge numbers of "guest workers" attracted from Spain, Yugoslavia, Algeria, Greece, Turkey, and Italy. For instance, an astonishing 20 percent or so of Sweden's and Germany's labor forces were composed of guest workers. As economic growth in the host countries began to slow down in 1975, guest workers were advised to go home, and many did.[22] The consequence was an international passing along of unemployment.

The nations to which the guest workers returned have higher unemployment and lower wages than the European countries that hosted them. But here we see a curious situation: The poorer countries with their weaker economies also have the most sharply rising consumer prices. Inflation also troubles the more industrialized countries, but not as severely. Table 3-10 shows the rates of inflation in eight industrialized nations, and the inflation rates of the less industrialized countries from which the majority of guest workers originated. The trends are clearly visible.

To read Table 3-10, it is only necessary to notice that all index numbers are adjusted to the base year 1967, which equals 100 on the indexes of inflation. For example, in the U.S. in 1950, only seventy-two cents could

---

[22]By no means, however, did that signal a universal return to home. A recent estimate suggests that worldwide some 20 million people are working outside their own countries. In the very poorest regions, many of those whose skills permit them to leave do so. Thus Pakistan loses over half of its medical school graduates each year, and India loses about a third of its graduate doctors and engineers to Europe and the U.S.: "Brain Drain," *World of Work Report*, 5 (March 1980): 24.

TABLE 3-10

Inflation Rates in Selected Countries, 1950–1982

	Consumer Price Indexes (1967 = 100)						Average Annual Percent Change in Consumer Prices:		Rate in 1982
	1950	1960	1970	1975	1980	1982	1950–1970	1970–1980	
United States	72	89	116	161	247	270	3	8	4
Canada	69	86	112	160	244	278	2	8	9
Australia	48	86	110	179	296	329	4	10	11
Japan	46	68	119	205	282	291	5	9	3
France	45	79	117	179	294	337	5	10	10
West Germany	69	83	107	144	176	186	2	5	5
Sweden	48	75	112	164	271	303	2	9	10
England	53	79	117	217	424	467	4	14	6
Italy	55	74	109	187	403	479	4	14	16
Spain	38	63	113	171	448	537	6	15	14
Yugoslavia	n.a.	n.a.	126	245	609	846	n.a.	19	33
Greece	n.a.	n.a.	106	167	378	495	4	15	19
Turkey	27	68	120	239	1378	1971	8	34	33

Note: Price indexes are cumulative (like compound interest); even a relatively small annual increase compounded over several decades generates a sizable result.

Sources: U.S. Department of Labor, Bureau of Labor Statistics, Handbook of Labor Statistics 1975—Reference Edition (Washington, D.C.: U.S. Government Printing Office, 1975), p. 442; Main Economic Indicators (Paris: Organization for Economic Cooperation and Development, May 1980), pp. 162–65, and February 1983, pp. 174–77; World Tables (Washington, D.C.: The World Bank, 1980), et passim; Statistical Abstract of the United States, 1981, pp. 880–81.

purchase what in 1967 cost one dollar; in 1982, $2.70 was needed. Looking at the indexes shows that among these industrialized countries the period 1950–1970 was one of moderately rising prices, with an accelerated rise after 1970. In the less developed countries, price rises were recently explosive. It is no wonder that the guest workers had misgivings about going home. Unlike the current slowing of inflation in the U.S., England, and Japan, prices in the less developed countries contined their steep climb through 1982, as can be seen in the last column of Table 3-10.

No one has a crystal ball that reveals the future, but having looked now at rising prices and unemployment, it is difficult to avoid the prediction of a continuation of these twin problems in the 1980s. The combination of inflation and unemployment is unwelcome anywhere, but the magnitude of these interacting problems is heightened in the less developed countries, and their ability to cope with them will be severely strained.

With the discussion of unemployment and inflation as a backdrop, we focus on the comparatively less somber topic of American workers' job outcomes.

WORK OUTCOMES: INCOME, PRESTIGE, JOB SATISFACTION

The term *work outcomes* directs attention to the consequences that flow from having a job. Social scientists have detected a variety of possible work outcomes:[23]

— Time-filling; without work the hours of the day would present chunks of time which produced boredom.
— Respectability; nonworking sources of income (such as welfare) are culturally disapproved, while working gains others' approval.
— Purposiveness; a feeling of personal usefulness through contributing to society's stock of goods or services.
— Maintaining "headship"; since the male is still culturally defined as the appropriate primary breadwinner in an intact family, work provides a major basis for remaining "head" of the household.
— Subjective gratification; the content of work may provide psychological pleasure.
— Prestige; more highly regarded occupations bestow socially higher status and, therefore, enhanced self-regard.

---

[23]For the basis of this list, see Curt Tausky, "Meanings of Work Among Blue Collar Men," *Pacific Sociological Review*, 12 (1969): 49–55.

— Income; money received (plus fringe benefits) directly affects standard of living and has an impact on regard by others, self-regard, future of children (ability to pay for their education), and security (savings for a rainy day).

— Work satisfaction; the combined impact of work rules, supervision, work relations, work content, promotion chances, job security, job status, pay, and fringe benefits.

— Identity; a job's skill requirements, prestige, and income contribute to forming and validating one's self-definition as a particular kind of person, shading from the "highly successful," to the "solid citizen" who works and pays taxes, to the "loser" whose sporadic jobs are poorly rewarded.

There are several interesting features in this list of outcomes. Notice that the work outcomes are in some instances tightly linked. For example, identity formation–validation involves most of the listed outcomes, and work satisfaction is related to, among other factors, subjective gratification, prestige, and income. The brief descriptions accompanying the outcomes may suggest additional links. The outcomes may also be seen in a different light, as motivational factors—we might then think of them as rewards. To the extent that rewards such as respectability, prestige, income are highly valued, then the work setting is the location for attaining them and conformity to work rules and requirements is the means. Thus, values and motivation combine and prompt behavior toward alignment with a work organization's role demands. Viewed this way, people exchange their compliance for valued rewards. For instance, college graduation—a reward akin to income—may be highly valued. If so, the individual will be motivated to comply with university requirements in order to receive the reward (graduation). This is the basic notion underlying outcomes (rewards) as motivational factors. Finally, the outcomes may be seen simply as work attachments—a set of factors that provides the glue between work and people: They desire outcomes that only work offers.

These several ways of understanding work outcomes are important: Each in a somewhat different way points to a linking of people and their work. Such connections are reasonably firm for many people, since both values and necessity urge work.[24]

---

[24]A combination of cultural values that encourage work, and social organization that rewards it, is found in all modern societies regardless of their location on the political-economic spectrum. Clearly, if both attitude (through socialization) and behavior (by rewarding work and making nonwork aversive) can be influenced, then a rather powerful combination of elements is operating to elicit work. The Soviet Union and particularly Cuba and China attempt to teach proper attitudes, that is, ideology, to induce work, while also materially rewarding appropriate work behavior.

The remainder of this section examines three major work outcomes—income, prestige, and satisfaction. Before doing so, however, we will observe two things about the settings that generate the distribution of these outcomes.

First, the vast majority of people earn a living by working for others, in contrast to self-employment. In farming this is less true; about half of the work force in this sector is self-employed, although only a small proportion of people are engaged in farming. In the nonagricultural sectors, only eight of every hundred workers is self-employed. Thus the United States must be described as an employee society.[25] Second, in our society several million small organizations employ nearly half the work force, while a relatively tiny number of large and very large organizations employ the rest. This is shown in Table 3-11. It shows the distribution of workers among organizations of various employee size classes and the percentage of organizations in each employee size class.[26] This table indicates that over 50 percent of organizations have only four or fewer employees, accounting for under 7 percent of employment. At the other extreme—employee size class 1,000 and over—we find that .1 percent of organizations employs close to 15 percent of the work force. Those organizations with a hundred or more employees represent slightly over 2 percent of all organizations, yet hire almost one of every two workers; the remaining 98 percent of smaller organizations employ the rest.

Overall, then, most people are employees, and the chances are about equal that they work in an organization with less than one hundred employees or more than a hundred. Thus, though a relatively few larger organizations employ nearly half of our labor force, millions of smaller organizations employ the other half.

---

[25]That this situation has not greatly changed over the century is indicated by these rates of nonagricultural self-employment:

1900	9%
1920	9
1940	8
1960	1C
1982	8

Self-employment in 1900–1920 is estimated from Bureau of the Census, *Historical Statistics of the U.S., Colonial Times to 1957* (Washington, D.C.: U.S. Government Printing Office, 1960), p. 74; 1940, Bureau of the Census, *U.S. Census of Population, U.S. Summary, 1960*, Final Report, PC(1)-1C, p. 215; 1960, *Statistical Abstract of the U.S., 1975*, p. 350; 1982, Department of Labor, Bureau of Labor Statistics, *Employment and Earnings*, 29 (May 1982): 36.

[26]These data are based on Census Bureau and Internal Revenue Service records. When Social Security coverage is used as the data source, nearly identical results are produced: Curt Tausky, *Work Organizations: Major Theoretical Perspectives* (Itasca, Ill.: F. E. Peacock Publishers, 1978), p. 4.

TABLE 3-11

Employment by Size of Employing Organizations, 1980
(in percent)

Employee Size Class	Employees	Employing Organizations
1–4	6.7	54.3
5–9	8.5	19.8
10–19	10.8	12.4
20–49	15.9	8.3
50–99	12.4	2.9
100–249	14.4	1.6
250–499	9.4	.4
500–999	7.6	.2
1,000 or more	14.3	.1
	Total number of employees: 74,835,525	Total number of organizations: 4,543,167

Note: Organizations here represent reporting units; employers with units in several locations report the units separately. The data are compiled from the administrative records of the Census Bureau and the Internal Revenue Service.
Source: Bureau of the Census, County Business Patterns 1980: United States (Washington, D.C.: U.S. Government Printing Office, 1982), Figure 2, p. xiii.

Income

Who gets what and why do they get it? is a question that intrigues us, but this has not always been so. When slaves, serfs, and peasants did the world's work over the centuries, and made do with what the customs of the times provided, intellectual interest in their "pay" slumbered. Concern quickened, however, with the dawn of the Industrial Revolution's factory system and its growing numbers of wage earners whose level of pay was now not decreed by custom.

The issue of national wealth had already aroused intellectuals' attention. The prevailing doctrine in the seventeenth century was called *mercantilism*.[27] Its basic principle was that a nation's wealth is created in the way a merchant's prosperity is produced. To prosper, a nation must sell (export) goods that bring in more money that those it buys (imports). Import tariffs to discourage consumption of other countries' goods, cheap labor at home, and colonies abroad would then aid in the pursuit of national wealth. (Mercantilist doctrine has survived in a weaker form,

---

[27]Useful overviews of economic thought are: George Soule, *Ideas of the Great Economists* (New York: Mentor Books, 1952); K. W. Rothschild, *The Theory of Wages* (New York: Augustus Kelley, Publishers, 1967); Paul Montagna, *Occupations and Society* (New York: John Wiley & Sons, 1977), pp. 65–83.

which encourages the government's concern with a favorable balance of trade and balance of payments.) In the early 1700s a challenge to the mercantilists came from the physiocrats. The physiocrats held that a nation's wealth is derived from the land and water—thus the farmer, miner, and fisherman are the only true producers of wealth, while all other activities are derivatives. The only tax that should be levied, therefore, is a land tax; any other taxes, such as import duties, should be abolished. The proper role of government is not the fostering of a trade surplus, rather, the government should keep its hands off economic activities. It should practice *laissez-faire* (don't interfere). Government intervention, the physiocrats warned, would impoverish the real producers of wealth by raising the price of manufactured goods.

Was a country's wealth based on trade or land? Neither, wrote Adam Smith in *The Wealth of Nations*. With the publication of Smith's book in 1776, a new and modern view of national wealth was born: The source of national wealth is production by the proper combination of labor and resources; the path to increased production is machinery and division of labor. The more that is produced in relation to population, the better off will be the average person. National wealth and individuals' economic betterment are thus mutually dependent on raising industrial output. In a static economy, Smith went on to note, wages will not increase; the necessary condition for increased wages is a growing economy in which employers compete for workers.

Now directly interested in the wages issue, other theorists expressed a much gloomier outlook than Adam Smith's. David Ricardo's *The Principles of Political Economy and Taxation*, published in 1817, received wide and favorable attention. In it he argued that wages would always remain close to the subsistence level. Ricardo elaborated the theme that the demand for and supply of labor inevitably caused wages to fluctuate around that amount which maintained a worker and his family at the subsistence level. Higher pay would increase the supply of labor because more children would survive into adulthood; they would swell the labor supply and wages would sink below the level of subsistence. Fewer children would then survive, creating a labor shortage. Employers must then compete for workers by raising wages above the level of subsistence, and the cycle would be repeated. The "iron law of wages," as this theory came to be called, was very influential. Before long the iron law of wages, though in altered form, received support from another persuasive writer.

Karl Marx, talented economist, historian, philosopher, and revolutionary, believed that Ricardo was correct in thinking that wages could not long rise beyond the workers' subsistence needs, but for different reasons from Ricardo's. In *Capital* (1867), Marx reasoned that the operation of a capitalist system suppressed wages. An employer hires labor at a particular cost, but sells the manufactured products at a price greater than the total costs of production, thus gaining a profit. (Marx called profit "surplus value," and viewed it as exploitation of labor.) If the employer introduces machinery, which raises the workers' output, wages remain as before while surplus value increases. Since other employers are also attempting to increase surplus value and remain competitive, nearly all employers will invest a portion of their surplus value in more and more machinery. But since workers do not receive in wages the full money value of their labor, capitalism tends to produce more goods than the market can absorb. This creates recurring periods of excess goods, reduced wages, and rising unemployment, with each recession leaving behind a larger pool of unemployed who compete for jobs. Thus not only in the long run, but in the short run as well, workers competing for jobs drive wages toward the subsistence level.

Marx, as a revolutionary, predicted the overthrow of capitalism because Marx, as an economist, predicted that the supply of labor would inevitably outstrip the demand for labor, which could only result in the deepening misery of falling wages and growing unemployment. Compared to its predecessor, this version of the iron law of wages was even more pessimistic.

With the exception of Adam Smith, who noted that real wages would increase with mechanization, the dour vision of subsistence-level income pervaded the writings of early wage theorists. Current wage theories are less pessimistic, though not necessarily more useful. Let us briefly examine four of these—the first is important in economics, the second in sociology, and the last two have found an audience in both disciplines.

The *marginal productivity theory* of wages tells us that the wage for a particular kind of work will approach the value of the total output that would be lost if one more worker is not hired. If his or her "marginal productivity" (the increased value of the output because of that worker) would exceed the offered wage, then the worker will be hired, and that worker's wage will determine the wages of other workers (previously hired) performing similar jobs. Put another way, an employer will hire a worker if by doing so the employer can gain a profit; and wages reflect the relative contributions of workers to production.

The marginal productivity theory assumes "perfect competition" among many firms so that product prices are determined by market demand, a mobile labor force which responds to alternative employers' pay offers, full employment among workers with various skills, and no bargaining coalitions (unions) among workers. Obviously, all of these conditions are rarely met. Moreover, the core assumption of the theory is questionable: Do employers really know the contributions of particular kinds of workers to production? It seems that this theory leaves much to be desired.

The major sociological attempt to explain income differences informs us that the world of work contains jobs which differ in (1) the degree of difficulty of finding qualified workers (scarcity of trained personnel), and (2) the consequences to an employer if a position is not filled (functional importance of a task). The theory then states that the highest income and prestige go to those positions that have the greatest functional importance and scarcity of competent personnel. Thus, the distribution of rewards (income and prestige) reflects workers' relative contributions to output and their availability.[28] The difficulty, of course, is determining "functional importance." This concept—which is not much different from "contribution" in marginal productivity theory—has troubled the theory since its inception.[29] Nonetheless, one can not say that the theory is necessarily wrong, but it is not research-based and thus remains a perspective that sparks debate.

There has recently been great interest in *dual labor market theory*.[30] As the label implies, the labor force is viewed as employed in two sectors: a monopolistically concentrated *primary sector*, whose jobs are relatively well paid and offer pay progression and stability of employment, and a *secondary sector* with the opposite features. Professionals, managers, sales workers, and skilled workers are in the primary sector, while clerical, semiskilled workers, laborers, and service workers are in the secondary sector. (Age, sex, race, and prior work history are proposed as important characteristics which filter workers into one or the other sector.) The theory provides some clues to wage differentiation, but, like its forerunners, also contains problems.

Sectors are much less clearly bounded than the theory suggests. Skilled workers, say in the automobile and steel industries, do not enjoy stable employment. Poor economic conditions often have an impact on employees in the primary sector as well as the secondary. Also, just where to locate a segment of workers is problematic. For instance,

---

[28]Kingsley Davis and Wilbert Moore, "Some Principles of Stratification," *American Sociological Review*, 10 (1945): 242–49.

[29]A useful look at "functional importance" is Robert Dubin's "Power, Function, and Organization," *Pacific Sociological Review* 6 (1945): 242–49. For an assessment of the general theory, see Melvin Tumin, "Some Principles of Stratification: A Critical Analysis," *American Sociological Review*, 18 (1953): 387–94.

[30]Peter B. Doeringer and Michael J. Piore, *Internal Labor Markets and Manpower Analysis* (Lexington, Mass.: D. C. Heath and Co., 1971); Randy Hodson and Robert L. Kaufman, "Economic Dualism: A Critical Review," *American Sociological Review*, 47 (1982): 727–39.

semiskilled workers may be employed in prosperous industries in the primary sector or poor ones in the secondary. Development of the sector approach, nevertheless, may be useful.[31]

Finally, we consider one more perspective, conflict theory. It assumes:

> There is no minimum absolute standard of living that will make people content. Individual wants are not satiated as incomes rise, and individuals do not become more willing to transfer some of their resources to the poor as they grow richer. If their incomes rise less rapidly than someone else's, or less rapidly than they expect, they may even feel poorer as their incomes rise.[32]

This suggests that employees compete for income with each other, and with their employers. Conflict theory proposes a clear-cut principle of competition in income allocation: Who gets what depends on the relative power (resources) of employers to give as little as possible, and employees to obtain as much as possible. The result is that workers (or levels of employees) will receive that amount of income and benefits an employer believes must be offered to attract and retain persons with the required skills. Thus, the elements of power (skills, unions, the right to strike, alternative available jobs, on the one hand, and on the other, alternative locations with cheaper labor, economic climate, alternative available employees) intersect and shape income allocation. As a leading advocate of conflict theory put it, "each individual is basically pursuing his own interests and...there are many situations, notably ones where power is involved, in which those interests are inherently antagonistic....Social structures are to be explained in terms of the behavior following from various lineups of resources...."[33]

Conflict theory's emphasis on power, self-interest, and insatiable wants is perhaps distasteful. The perspective, however, does have these advantages: It probably reflects reality rather closely, and it directs the

---

[31]An extension of dual labor market theory has developed around the concept of *sheltering mechanisms*. These involve restrictions on entering an occupation by licensing, union membership, or educational qualifications. Such shelters are then linked by the theory to industry characteristics (degree of concentration, for instance) to form fourteen occupational levels. Marcia Freedman, *Labor Markets: Segments and Shelters* (Montclair, N.J.: Allanheld, Osmun, Publishers, 1976). For an overview of both approaches see Montagna, *Occupations and Society*, pp. 67–71, 79–83.

[32]Lester C. Thurow, *The Zero-Sum Society* (New York: Penguin Books, 1980), p. 18.

[33]Randall Collins, *Conflict Sociology* (New York: Academic Press, 1975), pp. 60–61. This point of view is similar to the Marxian, as expressed, for example, in Paul Goldman and Donald R. Van Houten, "Managerial Strategies and the Worker: A Marxist Analysis of Bureaucracy," *Sociological Quarterly*, 18 (1977): 100–125. A fundamental contrast between conflict theory and the Marxian perspective is that the former is nonutopian. Conflict theory assumes that material interests diverge among persons in all societies, capitalist or communist, and that these differing interests will not at some future time, or in some future society, wither away.

analyst's attention to empirically observable matters, power resources. A disadvantage is that the perspective is based on unverified assumptions about human nature.

If by now you are tempted to conclude that the process of income distribution is inadequately illuminated by theory, that conclusion is correct. So although nearly everyone has more than a passing concern with income, its allocation principles are dim. Shortcomings of theory, however, do not prevent a look at the income data shown below.

We saw earlier the distribution of people among occupations (Table 3-4). Now we look at their pay in Table 3-12. This shows the median

TABLE 3-12

Occupations and Median Weekly Earnings of Full-Time Workers, 1982

	Men	Women	All Full-Time Workers
Professional & technical	$489	$338	$411
Managers & officials	520	310	436
Clerical workers	337	236	247
Sales workers	397	222	326
Forepersons & skilled workers	380	232	370
Semiskilled workers	315	201	325
Laborers	256	208	250
Service workers	247	174	201
Farm workers	191	160	189
All occupations:	$370	$240	$308
Women's earnings as percent of men's:		65%	

Note: The earnings do not include fringe benefits, which may equal 20 to 30 percent of income.

Source: U.S. Department of Labor, Bureau of Labor Statistics, News, August 12, 1982, Tables 4 and 5.

weekly earnings of full-time workers. (Since the median divides a distribution in half, some people will earn more, and some less, than the median for an occupation indicates.) Professional and technical workers, and managers and officials earn the most, while farm workers and service workers, on average, earn the least. Moreover, in every comparison, women earn less than men in the same occupation. In these broadly defined occupational categories women tend to be in the lower-paying jobs—among professionals, for example, they are more often nurses and teachers than doctors or professors. As a rough measure of this, notice that women's median income is 65 percent of the men's. If we had included black and Hispanic women separately, we would find that they fare more poorly yet: black women's median income is about 60 percent of the men's, and Hispanic women's 57 percent. Similarly, black men's income, compared to the white men's median, is 78 percent, and for Hispanic men it is 75 percent.[34] Thus sex and race and, of course, education and age, play their parts in distributing people among occupations and allocating occupational earnings.

An intriguing study of people's opinions on income distribution found that "an equal distribution of earnings would be considered unjust."[35] Respondents in this research consistently stated that increments in education and occupation should yield higher earnings, but that responsibility for supporting a family should also be an important criterion. What is fair or just payment, then, is seen to hinge on a person's inputs (education, occupation) to the production of goods and services, and their family responsibilities.

A substantial share of the earnings differences between men and women is probably a holdover from the time when men were usually the sole, or at least primary, breadwinners for a family. To the extent that men and women are occupationally segregated, the "holdover" in earnings differences is likely to be tenacious. In the study mentioned above, respondents felt that family responsibilities should influence pay, but contrary to the historical differences which favor men, they believe that a fair distribution of earnings should favor married men *and* women with families to support.

Although the marriage bond is shakier than it used to be, marriage is still a popular institution, and though people may stay single longer, most do get married. Information on family income provides an overview of families as economic units. (Currently earned income, pensions or Social Security, unemployment compensation, interest and dividends, and welfare payments are all included in family income.) Table 3-13 shows median family income over the years 1947 to 1982. In terms of dollars received, family income tripled between 1947 and 1970, and then more than doubled from 1970 to 1982. But that, unfortunately, is only part of the story.

---

[34]U.S. Department of Labor, Bureau of Labor Statistics, *News* (August 12, 1982), Table 4. On the brighter side, black women college graduates' earnings are equal to their white counterparts, and if they have postgraduate education, their earnings exceed those of white women with similar education. On the other hand, black men with graduate or postgraduate education average only about 80 percent of their white counterparts' earnings: Janice N. Hedges and Earl F. Mellor, "Weekly and Hourly Earnings of U.S. Workers, 1967-78," *Monthly Labor Review*, 102 (1979): 36.

[35]Guillermina Jasso and Peter H. Rossi, "Distributive Justice and Earned Income," *American Sociological Review*, 42 (1977): 650.

When family income is adjusted for inflation (constant dollars), we notice that median family income almost doubled between 1947 and 1970, and then stayed at the 1970 level into 1982.[36] So over thirty-five years, median family income in constant dollars did not quite double. Wives increasingly worked over these years, and we can see one important reason for this in family income. The lower part of Table 3-13 shows that the two-earner family, with a median income of over $31,000, obviously has access to more of life's comforts than its single-earner counterpart with under $21,000. Taxes narrow this gap by about 30 percent, but this still leaves the two-earner family with a significant income advantage.

TABLE 3-13

Median Annual Family Income, 1947–1982

	Family Income	In Constant (1978) Dollars
1947	$3,031	$8,848
1950	3,319	8,991
1960	5,620	12,374
1970	9,867	16,569
1975	13,719	16,621
1978	17,640	17,640
1980	21,060	17,059
1982	23,423	16,866

1982 Median Annual Income of:

Families with just husband working	$20,748
Families with husband and wife working	$31,356
Families maintained by women	$11,372
Black families	$13,930
Hispanic families	$17,220

Note: The median income of Hispanic families exceeds that of black families because among Hispanics there is a tendency for more family members to work.

Sources: 1947–1978 data, U.S. Bureau of the Census, Money Income of Families and Persons in the U.S., 1978, Current Population Reports, Series P-60, no. 123 (Washington, D.C.: U.S. Government Printing Office, 1980), pp. 50, 51, 54; U.S. Department of Labor, Bureau of Labor Statistics, Employment and Earnings, 30 (January 1983): 65; Statistical Abstract of the U.S., 1982–83, pp. 431-32.

---

[36]A word of caution. Constant dollars are based on changes in the Consumer Price Index (CPI). The CPI does not reflect taxes, with the exception of direct sales taxes on purchases. Also, the CPI gives much weight (about 15 percent of the total index) to houses and cars and reflects their current purchase price, although hardly anyone buys a house or car every year. Starting in 1983, two CPIs will be constructed, one of which will include rent instead of house prices.

Another way of describing family income is shown in Table 3-14, along with the income of "unrelated individuals" (persons not living in a family related by marriage or blood). The percentage of different families (white, black, Hispanic) in each income category can be readily seen; the proportions living at the poverty level are indicated in the two bottom rows. Notice that over the period 1959–1980, the percentage of

TABLE 3–14

Money Income of Families and Unrelated Individuals, 1980
(in percent)

	White Families	Black Families	Hispanic Families	All Families	Unrelated Individuals
under $5,000	5%	17%	11%	6%	31%
$5,000 to 9,999	11	24	21	13	27
$10,000 to 14,999	14	17	19	14	18
$15,000 to 19,999	14	13	15	14	11
$20,000 to 24,999	14	10	11	14	7
$25,000 to 34,999	21	12	14	20	5
$35,000 to 49,999	14	6	6	13	1
$50,000 and over	7	2	3	7	—
Number (in millions)	52.7	7.6	3.2	63.5	27.1
Median income	$21,904	$12,674	$14,716	$21,060	$8,315
Percent in poverty:					
1959	15	48	n.a.	19	46
1980	8	29	23	10	23

Note: Poverty was officially defined as $8,385 in 1980 for a nonfarm family of four, and $4,184 for an unrelated individual; for 1959 the comparable income levels were $2,973 and $1,467. For nonurban families and individuals, the poverty line is about 15 percent below the urban level; additionally, the poverty line is adjusted for family size.

Unrelated individuals refers to persons not living in a household related by blood or marriage.

Sources: U.S. Bureau of the Census, Money Income and Poverty Status of Families and Persons in the United States, 1980, Current Population Reports, Series P-60, no. 127 (Washington, D.C.: U.S. Government Printing Office, 1981), pp. 14, 15, 29.

families in poverty has been about halved (the poverty cut-off levels are shown in the note to Table 3-14). But the proportions of families in poverty remain substantial at 29 percent among black families and 23 percent among Hispanics, while much lower among white families. The 23 percent of "unrelated individuals" who are poor is perhaps greater than one might expect and probably overstates the situation, since sizable numbers of these individuals do share their resources in a manner similar to families, though with less binding obligations. Over all, acute poverty has lost its hold on most families and individuals, but by no means has it disappeared, and for some population segments it remains a harsh daily reality.

As we saw, median family income in constant dollars is presently about twice the 1947 level. However, this still leaves open the question of the relative shares of income received. If the total income received by all families and individuals is considered as 100 percent, then it is possible to ask how that 100 percent is divided among them. Table 3-15 shows the results of that sort of analysis. Look at the first column: 5 percent of the

TABLE 3-15

Income of Families and Unrelated Individuals—Percent of Aggregate Income Received by Each Fifth and Highest Five Percent, 1947 and 1980

	All Families		Black Families		Unrelated Individuals	
	1947	1980	1947	1980	1947	1980
Lowest fifth	5	5	4	4	2	4
Second fifth	12	12	11	10	6	9
Third fifth	17	17	16	16	13	15
Fourth fifth	23	24	24	25	22	24
Highest fifth	42	42	45	45	57	47
Top 5 percent	18	15	16	16	19	19

Source: U.S. Bureau of the Census, *Money Income of Families and Persons in the U.S., 1978,* Current Population Reports, Series P-60, no. 123 (Washington, D.C.: U.S. Government Printing Office, 1980), pp. 63–65; U.S. Bureau of the Census, *Money Income and Poverty Status of Families and Persons in the United States, 1980,* Current Population Reports, Series P-60, no. 127 (Washington, D.C.: U.S. Government Printing Office, 1981), p. 15.

total income of all families in 1947 went to the poorest 20 percent (lowest fifth) of all families, whereas 42 percent went to the best-off 20 percent (highest fifth) of families. The second column reveals the situation in 1980: the lowest fifth of families still received 5 percent of all income, while the top fifth again received 42 percent. The data in Table 3-15 show a remarkable stability over the years—each fifth of families received just about the same share in 1980 that it received in 1947.[37] (The largest shift has been among unrelated individuals, with the lowest fifth doubling its share and the highest fifth losing about 18 percent of its share.) After making allowances for after-tax income, the sharply uneven distribution

---

[37]For an analysis of the first half century, see Gabriel Kolko, *Wealth and Power in America* (New York: Frederick Praeger, 1962).

of family income remains about the same since 1947.[38]

The economically cheery years of 1947–70 witnessed real dollar gains followed by the discomfort of stagnating income and steeply rising prices. Gains in real income are dependent on productivity increases to provide the basis for increases in real wages; otherwise pay raises are illusory because of rising prices. Segments of the work force may of course alter their relative earnings—organized workers, for instance, have gained income relative to the unorganized[39]—but when income increases outstrip firms' productivity gains, prices tend to move up in response to the added costs, with all segments of workers then caught in the wage-price squeeze.

Recent data on output per hour and hourly compensation in manufacturing illustrate the sticky problem. The first row of Table 3-16 reveals that increases in American output per hour are outpaced by hourly compensation, thereby pushing up unit labor costs (calculated by taking into account hourly output and compensation), and thus eventually prices. It can also be seen that this situation is not confined to the United States; in fact, our unit labor costs have risen less steeply than in all but two of the other countries listed. So where do we (and other nations) go from here to achieve increases in real wages and salaries? It appears clear that productivity gains in goods and services are required.[40]

Based on the postwar experience of the 1950s and 1960s, Americans had come to expect yearly improvement in real income. Since the 1970s, however, this expectation was frustrated by the sad fact that a single income may easily slip behind increases in the total cost of living, including taxes.[41] Thus, the incentive of outpacing the cost of living underlies the economic side of the growing popularity of two-earner families. But even when or if productivity gains prod real income to recover its former upward movement, there is little reason to expect the

---

[38]Miller and Form, *Industrial Sociology*, pp. 641–44.

[39]The impact of unionization is gauged by Marvin H. Kosters, "Relative Wages and Inflation," in Barbara Dennis, ed., *Proceedings of the Thirtieth Annual Winter Meeting* (Madison, Wisc.: Industrial Relations Research Association, 1978), pp. 193–207. For a description of differential income increases among occupational segments, see *Statistical Abstract of the U.S., 1979*, p. 421 and *1982–83*, p. 403. A useful discussion of occupational competition for rewards is George Ritzer's *Working* (Englewood Cliffs, N.J.: Prentice-Hall, 1977), chapter 8.

[40]If one is inclined toward the view that more should be done with transfer payments (e.g., welfare) to assist people on the lower rungs of the income ladder, it is realistic to assume that this can be accomplished with the least social friction when real incomes are rising, thus making the taxes that support transfer payments less disagreeable.

[41]George D. Stamas, "Real After-Tax Annual Earnings from the Current Population Survey," *Monthly Labor Review*, 102 (1979): 42—45; Paul Ryscavage, "Two Divergent Measures of Purchasing Power," *Monthly Labor Review*, 102 (1979): 25–30.

TABLE 3-16

Average Annual Rates of Change in Manufacturing Productivity,
Hourly Compensation, and Unit Labor Costs, 1960–1980

	Average Annual Percent Change					
	Output per hour		Hourly Compensation		Unit Labor Costs	
	1960–1973	1973–1980	1960–1973	1973–1980	1960–1973	1973–1980
United States	3.0	1.7	5.0	9.3	1.9	7.5
Canada	4.5	2.2	6.4	11.9	1.8	9.5
Japan	10.7	6.8	14.6	10.5	3.5	3.4
France	6.0	4.9	9.7	15.2	3.1	9.9
Sweden	6.7	2.1	10.1	13.8	3.5	11.2
West Germany	5.5	4.8	9.4	9.7	3.7	4.7
Italy	6.9	3.6	12.3	20.1	5.1	16.0
England	4.3	1.9	8.7	19.1	4.1	17.2

Source: Patricia Capdevielle and Donato Alvarez, "International Comparisons of Trends in Productivity and Labor Costs," Monthly Labor Review, 104 (December 1981): 15, 17, 19.

two-earner family to dwindle. It is an arrangement that has taken root in industrialized nations.[42]

As noted earlier, income, prestige, and job satisfaction are primary work outcomes. We focus now on prestige.

Prestige

Consider this scene. You are sitting around a table having coffee with two other people. Each of you contributes to the conversation, but the largest share of comments by two people, including yourself, are directed to the same individual. It is a good bet that the person to whom much of the conversation is directed has the highest prestige among these three people.

One more for instance. An assistant professor is walking down the hall one morning. Coming toward her is the department's chairperson, accompanied by an associate professor. Now to whom do you suppose the assistant professor will say "good morning," taking care to make eye contact? The reader might point out that the chairperson, though admittedly holding higher prestige, was orally saluted because of the potential to reward or punish; and that too would be true.

What is involved, then, is a sequence of elements: Power gives rise to privilege, and power and privilege create prestige. But why? Because, as Treiman put it, "There is no society where power is not accorded respect."[43] Or as another social analyst commented: "Empirical evidence strongly suggests that prestige. . . can largely be deduced from discussion of the distribution of power and privilege and their causes. . . ."[44]

Prestige hierarchies arise along these lines:[45] A society, once beyond the subsistence level of life, inevitably becomes occupationally

[42]In West Germany, France, and England, the labor-force participation rates of married women range between 44 and 50 percent; Sweden has the West's highest rate at 70 percent. A good review of data on working women in these countries and the U.S. is provided by Alice M. Yohalem ed., *Women Returning to Work* (Montclair, N.J.: Allanheld, Osmun, Publishers, 1980). In the Soviet Union, for comparison, about 85 percent of all working-age women are in the labor force; as it turns out, women there perform much of the heavy manual labor: Hedrick Smith, *The Russians* (New York: Ballantine Books, 1977), pp. 169, 174.

[43]Donald J. Treiman, *Occupational Prestige in Comparative Perspective* (New York: Academic Press, 1977), p. 21.

[44]Gerhard E. Lenski, *Power and Privilege* (New York: McGraw-Hill Book Co., 1966), p. 45.

[45]The logic sketched here essentially follows Treiman, *Occupational Prestige in Comparative Perspective*, pp. 5–24. With evidence Treiman argues that there is a common, worldwide occupational prestige hierarchy (p. 6) resting on similar occupational power.

differentiated. It is simply more efficient for full-time specialists to carry out tasks; their proficiency becomes much greater than that of nonspecialists. Differentiation of occupational functions then creates differences in control over scarce resources. These resources include combinations of (1) the knowledge and skill required to perform socially valued tasks, (2) control over economic resources on which others depend, and (3) authority to coordinate and define others' tasks. We see then that the division of labor gives rise to differences in power which ultimately foster prestige.

Prestige, which we can also think of as social standing or esteem, might not matter very much were it not for its consequences. Prestige inherently involves social ranking, creating layers of similarly ranked persons, or as the sociologist would say, social strata. The consequences are twofold, involving internal and external considerations.

By "internal" we mean subjective consequences, notably self-regard. It may be recalled that self-regard was mentioned earlier as a work outcome because occupational rank is often described as a fundamental determinant of self-regard.[46] (This follows from the premise that we see ourselves the way we think others see us.) But self-respect is a bit more complicated because people lead a "double life" which partially shields them from low self-regard:

> In the activities of daily life people have direct interactions with, or are indirectly exposed to, incumbents of positions who represent a very wide range of status. Visits to the doctor, inspections by the boss, newspaper and television implicate men in the overall status hierarchy. Yet much of life is experienced within the narrower span of status represented by relatives, colleagues at work, and friends. Analytically, then, there co-exist two contrasting status orders—two alternative frames of reference to anchor judgments of status—on the one hand the full range of occupational status in a community..., on the other the more circumscribed span of status represented by an immediate social circle.[47]

Now even if we assume that people have a "need" for, or certainly prefer, favorable responses from others, there is no reason why rank in the overall status system must always serve as the baseline for self-judgment. As long as the individual stays within the boundaries of "people like me," self-regard is not likely to suffer. But on venturing beyond a social circle, an individual is exposed to a range of others; the

---

[46]For instance, Talcott Parsons, "An Analytical Approach to the Theory of Social Stratification," in his *Essays in Sociological Theory* (Glencoe, Ill.: The Free Press, 1954), pp. 69–88; William F. Whyte, *Men at Work* (Homewood, Ill.: Dorsey Press, 1961), pp. 18–19; Edward B. Harvey, *Industrial Society* (Homewood, Ill.: Dorsey Press, 1975), p. 294.

[47]Curt Tausky, "Occupational Mobility Interests," *The Canadian Review of Sociology and Anthropology*, 4 (1967): 244.

discomfort of ego-deflation is then a risk.[48] I recall attending a sociological convention at which a small crowd had gathered around an author to comment on his paper. (At such gatherings everyone is provided a name tag with their university affiliation in large letters.) A teacher from a community college attempted some remarks, which were ignored by all; comments by another from a renowned university received polite attention and response. Prestige differences are nowhere easily discarded, not even by those who study them.

If you are a college student, frequent interaction with professors is unavoidable. Ordinarily, you are called by your first name but address the professor more formally. And if you go to his or her office, you may be kept waiting in the hall while the professor chats with a colleague or finishes some task. Indeed, an excellent rule of thumb in gauging status is to discover who can keep whom waiting. This points toward the second aspect of prestige, its external effects.

Internal consequences, it was noted, involve how people regard themselves in light of others' evaluations. External consequences involve social arrangements which reflect prestige differences. There will be no attempt here to exhaust the topic or the reader. We will only sample some major external consequences, social contact, and intimate relationships, bearing in mind that people's conceptions of prestige summarize elements which in everyday life bestow it: the *education* required to perform various *occupations* and the *income* associated with the occupations.[49]

A neighborhood is likely to house people of at least roughly similar status.[50] Although with the growth of suburbs there is less spatial segregation currently than there used to be, its rough outlines exist nonetheless. For instance, a study conducted in Providence, Rhode Island, found that 59 percent of the next-door neighbors of skilled blue-collar workers were also blue collar; among managers and professionals, 62 percent of their next-door neighbors were other managers and professionals.[51] If youngsters attend the local school, as most do, the

---

[48]Richard Sennett and Jonathan Cobb have written an entire book around this theme. In their view, status differences ravage the self-esteem of people in less highly regarded occupations: *The Hidden Injuries of Class* (New York: Vintage Books, 1973).

[49]Treiman, *Occupational Prestige in Comparative Perspective*, p. 115. Treiman also points out that "for the most part, the connections between educational requirements, income and prestige are similar throughout the world" (p. 115). However this might be (he offers fairly persuasive data), it is clear that the combination of education and income is a strong predictor of occupational prestige as measured in opinion surveys in the U.S.: Featherman and Hauser, *Opportunity and Change*, pp. 26–30.

[50]Kurt B. Mayer and Walter Buckley, *Class and Society* (New York: Random House, 1970), pp. 91–92.

[51]Calculated from data in Gavin Mackenzie, *The Aristocracy of Labor* (New York: Cambridge University Press, 1973), p. 159.

social composition of the neighborhood school can have a substantial impact on learning. (A lower-status child, in classrooms composed largely of similar children, will often perform poorly; if the other children are from more advantaged backgrounds, the child will perform better.)[52] Thus it is not only that housing is less or more elegant in different neighborhoods, but that more far-reaching patterns of life intrude.[53]

The long arm of social status reaches even to close relationships. Looking again at the study of Providence, almost exactly half of the friends of skilled workers were other craftsmen, and another 20 percent of friends were other blue-collar workers. Among the total pool of friends, then, only 30 percent were white-collar. The managers in the sample restricted their friendship choices more narrowly yet—86 percent of their friends were from the white-collar ranks.[54] Arrangements of this sort, it seems, are the prevailing pattern.[55]

The most intimate relationship, of course, is marriage. First we must notice that the overwhelming proportion of American marriages are intraracial: cross-racial marriage occurs in only 5 percent of all marriages.[56] And most marriages do not cut across Protestant, Catholic, and Jewish religious affiliation.[57] When to race and religion is added age, choice is further channeled. But status stretches across all these characteristics in the sense that within racial, religious, and age categories, the social status of prospective mates narrows choices.

When the fathers of marriage partners are divided into just two categories—blue-collar and white-collar—about 80 percent of marriages are *within* their fathers' category; if six or seven levels are used, this declines to 50 percent.[58] A direct look at brides' and grooms' first

---

[52]The finding that the social characteristics of schoolmates strongly influences academic achievement is based on a massive study of 600,000 children: James S. Coleman et al., *Equality of Educational Opportunity* (Washington, D.C.: U.S. Government Printing Office, 1966).

[53]Mayer and Buckley, *Class and Society*, chapter 5. For analyses of socialization patterns in different strata see: Melvin L. Kohn, *Class and Conformity* (Homewood, Ill.: The Dorsey Press, 1969); Urie Bronfenbrenner, "Recent Trends in American Socialization Patterns," in William Feigelman, ed., *Sociology Full Circle* (New York: Holt, Rinehart and Winston, 1980), pp. 82–93.

[54]Mackenzie, *The Aristocracy of Labor*, p. 153.

[55]Edward O. Laumann, *Prestige and Association in an Urban Community* (Indianapolis, Ind.: Bobbs-Merrill Co., 1966); and Laumann's *Bonds of Pluralism: The Form and Substance of Urban Social Networks* (New York: John Wiley & Sons, 1973).

[56]Alan C. Kerkhoff, "Patterns of Marriage and Family Formation and Dissolution," *Journal of Consumer Research*, 2 (1976): 262; also, Thomas P. Monahan, "An Overview of Statistics on Interracial Marriage in the United States," *Journal of Marriage and the Family*, 38 (1976): 223–31.

[57]About 80 percent of couples share the same religion: Kerkhoff, "Patterns of Marriage," p. 262.

[58]Bert N. Adams, *The Family* (Chicago: Rand McNally College Publishing Co., 1980), p. 235.

marriages discloses a similar pattern. Using education as an indicator of social ranking, it was found that among every hundred couples, forty husbands and wives were in the same educational level, thirty-eight were in adjacent levels, and twenty-two husbands and wives were two or more levels apart.[59] Educational levels in this study were quite finely divided into thirds within elementary school, high school, and college. Marrying someone in an adjacent educational level thus indicates, for instance, that a high school graduate wed someone with one or two years of college. Overall, 78 percent of these couples married either within their educational level or the level adjacent to it. Among black couples the same pattern, only slightly muted, held true for 73 percent of the marriages.[60] Thus men and women expecting a particular life-style and level of social esteem are attracted to each other and feel compatible.[61]

Since social relationships are so intertwined with occupational prestige, it is useful to see how people rank occupations when asked to do so. The most extensive research of this sort was carried out by the National Opinion Research Center (NORC) of the University of Chicago. In 1947 and again in 1963, ninety occupations were rated by asking respondents to judge each occupation's "general standing" as excellent, good, average, somewhat below average, or poor.

Several important and interesting findings emerged. First, judgments of occupational prestige were strikingly similar in 1947 and 1963. Moreover, on examining other studies conducted as early as 1925, it was determined that evaluations of occupational status have not significantly changed in the United States since 1925. Second, all sectors of the population rate occupations' standing in much the same way.[62] Based on these results, the researchers concluded that the structure of occupational prestige is very stable.

To facilitate analysis, the NORC had transformed respondents' judgments into numerical ratings,[63] and one finding was that ratings in 1947 and 1963 were nearly identical (the coefficient of correlation was .99). The procedure also generated an occupational prestige scale, which potentially ranged from 100 (highest prestige) to 20 (lowest prestige). The

[59]Hugh Carter and Paul C. Glick, *Marriage and Divorce* (Cambridge, Mass.: Harvard University Press, 1970), p. 116.

[60]Ibid.

[61]The assumption is nearly always made that a woman takes on the status of her husband, although research has barely probed this issue. For incisive comment, see Richard H. Hall, *Occupations and the Social Structure* (Englewood Cliffs, N.J.: Prentice-Hall, 1975), p. 254.

[62]Robert W. Hodge, Paul M. Siegel, and Peter H. Rossi, "Occupational Prestige in the United States, 1925–1963," *American Journal of Sociology*, 70 (1964): 286–302.

[63]A rating of "excellent" was assigned the numerical value of 100, "good" was given the value of 80, and so on. Since these assigned numerical values are arbitrary, the average scores for an occupation can not be interpreted as indicating precise differences between one score and other scores.

scale is shown in Table 3-17, with Supreme Court justice at the top of the ratings and shoe shiner at the bottom. There is good reason to have confidence in these findings. Other researchers have been able to predict NORC scores: Using combined measures of education and income, a very high correlation (.91) with NORC ratings was found.[64]

TABLE 3-17

NORC Prestige Scores of Ninety Occupations

Occupation	NORC Score	Rank	Occupation	NORC Score	Rank
U.S. Supreme Court			Sociologist	83	26
justice	94	1	Instructor in public		
Physician	93	2	schools	82	27.5
Nuclear physicist	92	3.5	Captain in the		
Scientist	92	3.5	regular army	82	27.5
Government scientist	91	5.5	Accountant for a		
State governor	91	5.5	large business	81	29.5
Cabinet member in			Public school		
the federal			teacher	81	29.5
government	90	8	Owner of a factory		
College professor	90	8	that employs		
U.S. representative			about 100 people	80	31.5
in Congress	90	8	Building contractor	80	31.5
Chemist	89	11	Artist who paints		
Lawyer	89	11	pictures that are		
Diplomat in the U.S.			exhibited in		
foreign service	89	11	galleries	78	34.5
Dentist	88	14	Musician in a		
Architect	88	14	symphony		
County judge	88	14	orchestra	78	34.5
Psychologist	87	17.5	Author of novels	78	34.5
Minister	87	17.5	Economist	78	34.5
Member of a board			Official of an		
of directors of a			international		
large corporation	87	17.5	labor union	77	37
Mayor of a large city	87	17.5	Railroad engineer	76	39
Priest	86	21.5	Electrician	76	39
Head of a			County agricultural		
department in a			agent	76	39
state government	86	21.5	Owner-operator of a		
Civil engineer	86	21.5	printing shop	75	41.5
Airline pilot	86	21.5	Trained machinist	75	41.5
Banker	85	24.5	Farm owner and		
Biologist	85	24.5	operator	74	44

[64]Peter M. Blau and Otis D. Duncan, *The American Occupational Structure* (New York: John Wiley & Sons, 1967), p. 120. See also note 49 in this chapter.

Occupation	NORC Score	Rank	Occupation	NORC Score	Rank
Undertaker	74	44	Garage mechanic	62	65.5
Welfare worker for a			Truck driver	59	67
city government	74	44	Fisherman who		
Newspaper			owns his own		
columnist	73	46	boat	58	68
Policeman	72	47	Clerk in a store	56	70
Reporter on a daily			Milk route man	56	70
newspaper	71	48	Streetcar motorman	56	70
Radio announcer	70	49.5	Lumberjack	55	72.5
Bookkeeper	70	49.5	Restaurant cook	55	72.5
Tenant farmer (one			Singer in a nightclub	54	74
who owns live-			Filling station		
stock and			attendant	51	75
machinery and			Dockworker	50	77.5
manages the			Railroad section		
farm)	69	51.5	hand	50	77.5
Insurance agent	69	51.5	Night watchman	50	77.5
Carpenter	68	53	Coal miner	50	77.5
Manager of a small			Restaurant waiter	49	80.5
store in a city	67	54.5	Taxi driver	49	80.5
A local official of a			Farm hand	48	83
labor union	67	54.5	Janitor	48	83
Mail carrier	66	57	Bartender	48	83
Railroad conductor	66	57	Clothes presser in a		
Traveling salesman			laundry	45	85
for a wholesale			Soda fountain clerk	44	86
concern	66	57	Sharecropper—		
Plumber	65	59	one who owns no		
Automobile			livestock or		
repairman	64	60	equipment and		
Playground director	63	62.5	does not manage		
Barber	63	62.5	farm	42	87
Machine operator in			Garbage collector	39	88
a factory	63	62.5	Street sweeper	36	89
Owner-operator of a			Shoe shiner	34	90
lunch stand	63	62.5			
Corporal in the					
regular army	62	65.5			

Source: Robert W. Hodge, Paul M. Siegal, and Peter H. Rossi, "Occupational Prestige in the United States, 1925–63," *American Journal of Sociology,* 70 (1964), Table 1, pp. 290–92. (By permission of the University of Chicago Press, copyright 1964.)

In sum, people make prestige judgments of others' occupations, with education and income providing the basic elements for such judgments. The prestige distinctions that result have a variety of consequences, some of which are "internal" to individuals and some "external" in their effect on social relationships. The impact of prestige is not a trivial matter and must be considered an important work outcome. All societies generate prestige systems; there is no reason to assume that their consequences are substantially different.[65]

This discussion of prestige was based mainly on data produced by social scientists adhering to commonly accepted standards of research. But some social scientists also step beyond their data in an attempt to gain insight into the human condition. What might such speculation suggest about prestige? Treiman, for instance, comments that "man is an evaluative animal, holding some objects, ideas, and attributes to be more worthy than others; the propensity for invidious distinctions is a fundamental aspect of human nature."[66] Gordon writes, "according to my hypothesis, the process of mutual evaluation is pervasive, continuous, and ineradicable by any cultural system...."[67] And in a sweeping surmise on privilege in all its aspects, Parkin says, "I do not seek an explanation of existing privileges in the past, because the past cannot give one: an explanation is to be found, if anywhere, in the nature of society and man himself."[68]

These notions go beyond the division of labor and its measurable consequences by locating the ultimate cause of social hierarchy within people themselves. Although these conceptions of human nature may quite possibly be on the right track, no one can say aye or nay to them on strictly empirical grounds—they are speculations by shrewd observers.

In the concluding part of this chapter, the third and final major work outcome, job satisfaction, will be examined.

Job Satisfaction

The number of studies on this topic is enormous, easily reaching into the thousands. (Work satisfaction and job satisfaction are used interchangeably in this literature, and will be here, too.) Much of the interest in work satisfaction has revolved around three issues: (1) the relationship between satisfaction and productivity, (2) the overall

[65]For useful writings on the consequences of status or "class" in command economies see Frank Parkin, *Class Inequality and Political Order* (New York: Praeger Publishers, 1971), especially pp. 137–59; Simon Leys, *Chinese Shadows* (New York: Penguin Books, 1978), particularly pp. 113–27; Joseph A. Kahl, "Cuban Paradox: Stratified Equality," in Irving L. Horowitz, ed., *Cuban Communism* (New Brunswick, N.J.: Transaction Books, 1981), pp. 331–54.

[66]Treiman, *Occupational Prestige in Comparative Perspective*, p. 19.

[67]Milton M. Gordon, *Human Nature, Class, and Ethnicity* (New York: Oxford University Press, 1978), p. 54.

[68]Parkin, *Class Inequality and Political Order*, p. 8.

amount or level of job satisfaction among the labor force, and (3) the connection between satisfaction and occupational characteristics.

Our interest in job satisfaction as a work outcome leads to concern with the last two issues. However, because it has remained such a central topic, the link between work satisfaction and productivity will also be discussed.

Productivity and Work Satisfaction

Systematic study of the relationship between productivity and job satisfaction can be traced to the famous Hawthorne studies of 1927 through 1932. A number of experiments were conducted, stimulated by the first, which produced a totally unexpected finding. In this initial study, illumination and productivity were examined. Lighting was increased and decreased in three departments, but no consistent relationship with productivity occurred. One department was then selected and divided into a test group and control group. Lighting for the test group was increased and decreased while kept constant for the control group. In the test group, productivity went up as illumination increased; yet, surprisingly, productivity went up equally in the control group. Another two groups were then set up, with lighting again kept constant in the control group, but decreased from initially bright illumination in the test group. Once again productivity in both groups increased. This prompted the researchers to a series of studies at the Western Electric Company's Hawthorne Plant in Chicago.[69]

Among the conclusions which emerged from the Hawthorne studies were that: (1) No person's behavior in an organization should be viewed as motivated primarily by economic or rational considerations; values, beliefs, and emotions are highly potent influences on behavior. (2) Groups in organizations are the carriers of values, beliefs, norms. Because people value their membership in work groups, such groups powerfully affect behavior. (3) An organization must distribute satisfactions to its members to gain their cooperation. Satisfaction is not the result of economic reward or physical comfort; rather, it is generated by a cohesive and emotionally supportive work group and its leader. (4)

---

[69]The studies are reported in F. J. Roethlisberg and William J. Dickson, *Management and the Worker* (Cambridge, Mass.: Harvard University Press, 1939); T. North Whitehead, *The Industrial Worker* (Cambridge, Mass.: Harvard University Press, 1939); Elton Mayo, *The Human Problems of an Industrial Civilization* (New York: The Macmillan Company, 1933); F. J. Roethlisberger, *Management and Morale* (Cambridge, Mass.: Harvard University Press, 1941), chapter 2.

A satisfied employee will be a more productive worker.[70] With these principles "human relations theory" was launched.

This perspective directly contradicted the theory and practice of "scientific management," which insisted that the primary motivational key to higher productivity was the pay envelope.[71] Work groups, according to scientific management, were naturally concerned with restricting output in order to protect themselves against increased production standards for the same pay. The solution was to tie pay to output, thus giving workers an incentive to produce more.

In human relations theory, *social man* inhabits our factories and offices; in scientific management's perception, *economic man* peoples the work place. New versions have emerged, but these contrasting views still furnish the themes around which motivational prescriptions are devised. From one perspective, motivation is aroused by self-interest oriented to protecting and enhancing the tangible features of work life such as pay, promotion opportunities, job security, vacations, and other benefits; alternatively, people are viewed as motivationally responsive to psychological stimuli such as supportive work groups, considerate leadership, participation in decisions, tasks which nourish self-actualization. (Although there is no inherent reason why these perspectives can not be blended, theorists usually advocate one or the other.)

The Hawthorne studies, of course, incorporated the "social man" point of view, with its accompanying assumption that employees' level of satisfaction strongly influences their productivity. Thus, if the worker is happy with his or her work mates, leaders, involvement in decisions, task, or whatever, the subjective feeling of satisfaction will lead to greater work effort. At first glance this may seem reasonable. But if you think about it for a moment, why should it be true? One possible, but hardly convincing, answer is that employees will work harder to display their gratitude to management. Another possibility is that engagement in a satisfying activity elicits deeper involvement with more intense concentration of effort. Although this is more plausible, it is most likely to yield better quality work but not more output. (For that, the old notions of tangible incentives are necessary—which of course implies

---

[70]Reanalyses of the Hawthorne data have raised serious doubts about the original interpretations: H. W. Parsons, "What Really Happened at Hawthorne?" *Science* 183 (1974): 922-32; Alex Carey, "The Hawthorne Studies: A Radical Criticism," *American Sociological Review*, 32 (1967): 403-16. Milder critiques are Henry Landsberger's *Hawthorne Revisited* (Ithaca, N.Y.: Cornell University Press, 1958); Reinhard Bendix and Lloyd Fisher, "The Perspectives of Elton Mayo," in Amitai Etzioni, ed., *Complex Organizations* (New York: Holt, Rinehart and Winston, 1962), pp. 113-26.

[71]Frederick W. Taylor, *Scientific Management* (New York: Harper and Row, 1947). See also the discussion and footnote 46 in the previous chapter.

that a combination of older and newer ideas is a sensible solution.) The point is that it is not easy to come up with a convincing reason why satisfaction should raise the effort to do more work.

Research has not been kind to the satisfaction-effort bond, despite its tenacious popularity as a key to productivity. As early as 1955, Brayfield and Crockett's review of research on morale and productivity concluded that "there is little evidence in the available literature that employee attitudes of the type usually measured in morale surveys bear any simple—or for that matter, appreciable—relationship to performance on the job."[72] Vroom examined data from twenty studies and found that the median correlation between satisfaction and performance was +.14. Vroom noted that "the median correlation of .14 has little theoretical or practical importance.... Obtained correlations are similar for analyses based on individuals and groups and do not seem to depend...on the occupation level of the subjects."[73] After reviewing a number of studies undertaken by the University of Michigan's Institute for Social Research, Kahn concluded:

> Indices of worker satisfaction were developed...which showed four well-defined dimensions of satisfaction: satisfaction with supervision, with the job itself, with the company as a whole, and with the extrinsic rewards of money, mobility, etc. None of these indices was significantly related to individual productivity.[74]

Using a large sample of 11,000 persons, Ronan, too, found that, in his words, "job attitudes have little relation to actual behaviors."[75]

We are thus left with the unavoidable conclusion that work attitudes have no clear or direct association with work effort. However, when a distinction is made between (1) the motivation to exert more or less effort at work, and (2) the motivation to remain in an organization or escape it, then the latter does show a relationship with work attitudes.

It seems that the effects of rules, behavioral routines imposed by technology,[76] accountability, ambition, and fear, constrain behavior

[72]Arthur H. Brayfield and James H. Crockett, "Employee Attitudes and Employee Performance," *Psychological Bulletin*, 52 (1955): 408.

[73]Victor H. Vroom, *Work and Motivation* (New York: John Wiley & Sons, 1964), p. 183.

[74]Robert H. Kahn, "The Prediction of Productivity," *Journal of Social Issues*, 12 (1956): 46.

[75]W. W. Ronan, "Individual and Situational Variables Relating to Job Satisfaction," *Journal of Applied Psychology Monograph* 54, Part 2 (1970): 20. See also Richard T. Mowday, Lyman W. Porter, and Richard M. Steers, *Employee-Organization Linkages* (New York: Academic Press, 1982), pp. 35-36. Edward Lawler and Lyman Porter have proposed reversing the commonly assumed direction of the relationship; they suggest that satisfaction is the result of work which has been fairly rewarded: "The Effect of Performance on Job Satisfaction," *Industrial Relations*, 7 (1967): 20-28.

[76]Technology and its behavioral consequences are carefully examined by Charles Perrow, *Organizational Analysis* (Belmont, Calif.: Wadsworth Publishing Co., 1970), pp. 80-89.

sufficiently to minimize measurable performance differences among people with differing attitudes. The various pressures of the work place thus limit the withdrawal of effort while at work. But another form of withdrawal is absenteeism and turnover. The evidence indicates that the less satisfied employees have higher rates of absenteeism and turnover, although the strength of the relationship differs among studies.[77] Individuals may desire to avoid a displeasing situation, but they can not always act on that desire: frequent absenteeism may lead to job loss while quitting the job may leave one without alternative employment. These sorts of conditions dampen the magnitude of the correlation between satisfaction and absenteeism or turnover, particularly in times of economic slump. Still, it is clear that people who dislike their work situations are more inclined to withdraw from them than those who are satisfied. However, this is very different from the idea that work attitudes are directly reflected in work performance.

What, then are the organizational advantages of programs designed to raise employees' satisfaction? If the research is correct, and it does make sense, productivity gains are likely to be disappointing, while lower absenteeism and turnover are more apt to occur, thereby benefiting operating costs and efficiency.[78]

It is important to be realistic about productivity. Meaningful output gains will not appear without recognizing that employees expect their better performance to yield tangible benefits such as improved job security and pay.[79] We will return to this theme in the final chapter.

---

[77]For an extensive review of the literature on satisfaction and turnover, and the conditions (mainly opportunities for other jobs) that affect the strength of the satisfaction-turnover relationship, see James L. Price, *The Study of Turnover* (Ames, Iowa: Iowa State University Press, 1977), pp. 79-87. Another in-depth review of the literature examines the satisfaction-turnover and satisfaction-absenteeism relationships with attention to the factors affecting the intensity of the relationships: Mowday, Porter, and Steers, *Employee-Organization Linkages*, pp. 78-79, 82-102 on absenteeism, pp. 110-131 on turnover. A solid study of the causes of absenteeism is provided in J. K. Chadwick-Jones, Nigel Nicholson, and Colin Brown, *Social Psychology of Absenteeism* (New York: Praeger Publishers, 1982).

[78]It is by no means clear, however, that managers worry much about absenteeism or turnover as cost factors: Ivar Berg, Marcia Freedman, and Michael Freeman, *Managers and Work Reform* (New York: The Free Press, 1978), p. 255 et passim.

[79]For instance, Mitchell Fein, "Motivation for Work," in Robert Dubin, ed., *Handbook of Work, Organization, and Society* (Chicago: Rand McNally College Publishing Co., 1976), pp. 465-530; Paul Champagne and Curt Tausky, "When Job Enrichment Doesn't Pay," *Personnel*, 55 (1978): 30-40; "U.S. Chamber of Commerce Finds Workers Want to Raise Productivity," *World of Work Report*, 5 (1980): 73, 79; David Macarov, *Worker Productivity: Myths and Reality* (Beverly Hills, Calif.: Sage Publications, 1982), chapters 4 and 10.

The Distribution of Work Satisfaction

Let us look now at the distribution of satisfaction, noticing first its level in the working population. In doing so, we immediately confront a contradiction. Many social scientists have painted a bleak picture of satisfaction; they have portrayed work as unpleasant, disliked, and alienating for most people outside the professions.[80] As will be seen, the data by no means confirm this dour view.

Before proceeding, it is necessary to be a bit more definite about the gauging of satisfaction. There are basically two ways this has been done: (1) One method assesses overall or "global" satisfaction. The respondent is asked to judge the total job experience. For example, "All things considered, how satisfied are you with your job?" Usually, four response alternatives are offered, ranging from "very satisfied" to "very dissatisfied." (2) Another approach has been to obtain judgments on "facets" or "dimensions" of the job such as work content, earnings, promotion opportunities, opportunities for skill development, and so forth. A respondent is presented with a list containing such items as "the work is interesting," "the job security is good," and is asked to select for each item from several response categories which typically range from "not at all true" to "very true."

Table 3-18 shows the responses to "global" work satisfaction queries over the years 1958–1982. (Answers falling within the satisfied response categories are combined.) Consistently over more than two decades, this crude but useful measure shows a large majority of people expressing favorable opinions about their jobs. The first two columns of Table 3-18 show that from 80 to 90 percent of men and women report satisfaction; there is virtually no difference between the sexes. In the last two columns, however, differences occur between the white and black respondents. In almost every year that the surveys were taken, the percentage of satisfied black workers is smaller than among white workers. But even so, the lowest figure for black workers is 76 percent. Although not shown in the table, the responses of younger workers resemble those of blacks,[81] whereas older workers have the highest

---

[80]See, for instance, Stanley Aronowitz, *False Promises* (New York: McGraw-Hill Book Co., 1973); Report of a Special Task Force to the Secretary of Health, Education and Welfare, *Work in America* (Cambridge, Mass.: MIT Press, 1973), especially pp. 13–28; Harold L. Sheppard and Neal Q. Herrick, *Where Have All the Robots Gone?* (New York: The Free Press, 1972); Harry Braverman, *Labor and Monopoly Capital* (New York: Monthly Review Press, 1974).

[81]For a well-reasoned discussion and data on age and job satisfaction, see James D. Wright and Richard F. Hamilton. They suggest that career stage rather than age accounts for the lower satisfaction of younger workers: "Work Satisfaction and Age," *Social Forces*, 56 (1978): 140–58.

TABLE 3-18

Satisfied Workers, 1958-1982

| Year of Survey | Wage and Salary Workers | | | |
	Men	Women	White	Black
1958	81%	n.a.	n.a.	n.a.
1962	84	81%	84%	76%
1964	92	n.a.	92	88
1969	88	81	86	77
1972	85	86	87	78
1975	90	87	89	85
1978	89	88	90	76
1980	85	83	84	87
1982	84	86	86	78

Note: Black includes other nonwhites. About 90 percent of this category is black workers.

Sources: Statistical Abstract of the United States, 1978 (p. 398) and 1981 (p. 387); 1982 responses were calculated from the National Opinion Research Center's General Social Survey (University of Chicago), 1982. The satisfaction data reported in the Statistical Abstract of the U.S. were derived from surveys by NORC and the Survey Research Center, University of Michigan. All samples are representative of the U.S. labor force. The surveys included between 850 and 1,500 persons responding to some version of the question, "How satisfied are you with your job?" The "very satisfied" and "fairly satisfied" responses are combined above.

proportions of satisfied workers (around 90 percent) over the span of these surveys. Overall, then, the findings in these surveys do not confirm an attitudinal revolt against work.

Occupations and Work Satisfaction

In a 1982 nationwide survey, NORC asked men and women: "On the whole, how satisfied are you with the work you do—would you say you are very satisfied, moderately satisfied, a little dissatisfied, or very dissatisfied?" The answers people gave are shown in Table 3-19. Again most respondents were either very or moderately satisfied. Looked at another way, if the two response categories indicating dissatisfaction are combined, we see that among the semiskilled, unskilled, and service workers, about one out of five is dissatisfied. In the other occupational categories, dissatisfaction ranges between 8 and 13 percent. These are all quite modest rates of dissatisfaction.

Higher rates of discontent—or what has been called the "blues"—become more visible when the nature of the task itself is more closely examined. One such study asked white male blue-collar workers about the amount of variety, autonomy, and responsibility in their jobs.

TABLE 3–19

"Global" Work Satisfaction and Occupations, 1982

(in percent)

Work Satisfaction	Professionals, Technicians	Managers, Administrators	Sales Workers	Clerical Workers	Skilled Workers	Semiskilled Workers	Unskilled Workers	Service Workers
Very satisfied	53%	63%	61%	43%	46%	37%	39%	38%
Satisfied	35	28	27	42	43	41	40	42
Dissatisfied	7	5	8	8	6	16	12	13
Very dissatisfied	4	3	2	5	3	6	9	5
Don't know or no answer	1	1	2	2	2	—	—	2
Total	100%	100%	100%	100%	100%	100%	100%	100%
	N = 174	N = 97	N = 49	N = 189	N = 127	N = 129	N = 58	N = 130

Source: Computed from data collected by the National Opinion Research Center (University of Chicago) in their General Social Survey, 1982. This national sample is representative of the working population eighteen years of age and over. Respondents were asked: "On the whole, how satisfied are you with the work you do?"

The job dimensions were combined in a summary score ranging from 1 to 4, with 4 indicating much variety, autonomy, responsibility, and 1 indicating the opposite. The "blues" were assessed by four questions on satisfaction with the job and its rewards.[82] As Table 3-20 shows, higher

TABLE 3-20

The "Blues" Among Male Blue-Collar Workers and Task Attributes
(in percent)

Task attributes: variety, autonomy, responsibility		Workers with the "blues"	Workers without the "blues"	Total	N
Much	4	15	85	100%	71
	3	20	80	100	101
	2	35	65	100	89
Little	1	50	50	100	82

Source: Calculated from data on pp. 19 and 29 of Harold L. Sheppard and Neal Q. Herrick, *Where Have All the Robots Gone?* (New York: The Free Press, 1972).

scores on the job attributes index are related to lower rates of the blues. Of the men in jobs that they felt provided little variety, autonomy, and responsibility, 50 percent were measured as having the blues. Interestingly, other studies, using different measures of satisfaction and of task attributes, also seem to find that discontent hovers close to 50 percent among people performing the most repetitive, routine, and fragmented tasks.[83] When the various studies using different ways of assessing tasks and satisfaction are considered jointly, they point to a substantial rate of discontent among individuals engaged in highly repetitive work.

In 1972–73 the University of Michigan's Institute for Social Research conducted a national "quality of employment" survey in which nearly 1,500 employed persons were interviewed. Among the issues the respondents were asked about were questions that probed satisfaction with facets of their jobs. One approach to unscrambling these data is shown in Table 3-21. It is organized around the idea that satisfaction is a result of the degree of *importance* individuals attach to various job facets, and the extent to which these job facets are perceived as *present* (available) in the work setting. For every job facet item, importance was measured by four response categories ranging from "it is very important

---

[82]Sheppard and Herrick, *Where Have All the Robots Gone?*, pp. 18–19, 29.
[83]A number of such studies are reviewed in Curt Tausky and E. Lauck Parke, "Job Enrichment, Need Theory, and Reinforcement Theory," in Dubin, ed., *Handbook of Work, Organization, and Society*, p. 541.

TABLE 3-21

Satisfaction with Job Facets

Job Facets:	Importance	Importance Rank	Presence	Mean Difference	Difference Rank
Professional, Technical, Managerial					
Extrinsic	3.39	3	2.83	−.56	1
Intrinsic	3.61	1	3.52	−.09	3
Resource Adequacy	3.57	2	3.20	−.37	2
Convenience	2.70	5	3.11	+.41	5
Relations with coworkers	3.24	4	3.38	+.14	4
Clerical & Sales Workers					
Extrinsic	3.53	2	2.93	−.60	1
Intrinsic	3.41	3	3.18	−.23	2
Resource Adequacy	3.57	1	3.42	−.15	3
Convenience	2.97	5	3.17	+.20	5
Relations with coworkers	3.33	4	3.40	+.07	4
Blue-Collar Workers					
Extrinsic	3.56	2	2.82	−.74	1
Intrinsic	3.33	4	2.89	−.44	2
Resource Adequacy	3.58	1	3.31	−.27	3
Convenience	3.15	5	3.01	−.14	4
Relations with coworkers	3.44	3	3.39	−.05	5

Source: Calculated from data collected by the 1972–1973 Quality of Employment Survey, Institute for Social Research, University of Michigan. Importance of each job facet was measured by multiple items, as was presence. Importance ratings range from "very important" to "not at all important," and presence ratings range from "very true for my job" to "not at all true," with four response categories for both, providing an index of importance and presence ranging from 4 ("very important" or "very true") to 1 ("not at all important" or "not at all true"). Total respondents = 1,479. A different version of this table is in Jon E. Walker and Curt Tausky, "An Analysis of Work Incentives," *Journal of Social Psychology*, 116 (February 1982): 32–33.

to me" to "it is not at all important to me," and presence offered four response categories ranging from "this is very true of my job" to "this is not at all true of my job" The importance and presence ratings thus potentially ranged from 4 (high) to 1 (low). The job facets include:[84]

Extrinsic elements—pay, job security, fringe benefits, opportunity for promotion.

Intrinsic elements—interesting work, challenge, chance to develop abilities, autonomy.

Resource adequacy—adequacy of supervision, equipment, authority and information to get job done.

Convenience—convenient travel to work, enough time to do work, free from conflicting demands, can air problems on the job.

Relations with co-workers—friendly, helpful co-workers, chance to make friends.

Table 3-21 shows the mean (average) importance and presence ratings of the job facets, their mean differences (importance minus presence, hence a minus sign indicates a "deficit" and a plus sign indicates that the importance of a job facet is matched or exceeded by its presence), and difference rank. To see how the table can be interpreted, let us look at some of its information. We can observe that the convenience job facet is rated as least important by each of the three occupational groups shown, and that relations with co-workers follows closely. The presence of these factors also rather closely matches or exceeds the desire for them. This is indicated by the last column, difference rank. It also shows that extrinsic elements hold first rank in all three occupational groupings. Although extrinsic benefits are second or third in the importance rankings, extrinsic benefits show the largest "deficit" or difference between importance and presence. The nature of the job itself, the intrinsic job facet, shows the next largest deficit for all but the higher white-collar workers. Notice that only they give the intrinsic job facet importance rank one, whereas this facet slips to third and fourth place among the rest. Finally, resource adequacy has an importance ranking of one or two among all groups, and shows a moderate deficit with presence.

What does this mean for satisfaction? First, the magnitude of the deficits between the importance of a job facet and its presence is large

---

[84]The methods and findings of the original survey are in Robert P. Quinn and Linda J. Shepard, *The 1972–73 Quality of Employment Survey* (Ann Arbor, Mich.: Institute for Social Research, University of Michigan, 1974). The job facet questions are shown on pp. 63–68.

enough in several instances to signal discontent. This is apparent for extrinsic benefits: Members of every occupational grouping want more material rewards than they are receiving. However, the gap between desire for more extrinsic rewards and their presence is greatest among blue-collar workers. Extrinsic benefits are, then, one important source of discontent in general, but most seriously among blue-collar workers. The intrinsic job facet also shows up as a source of dissatisfaction, most strongly among blue-collar workers, moderately among clerical and sales workers, but hardly at all among higher white-collar workers. The other job facets trail off to relatively small differences between importance and presence. In sum, this look at job facets shows wide dissatisfaction with extrinsic rewards and dissatisfaction with intrinsic benefits among blue-collar workers. But a word of caution is necessary on the intensity of discontent with these job facets. The average "presence" ratings do not disclose a roar of discontent; the ratings are closer to a loud grumble, but the grumble is there.[85]

Lastly, one other approach to job satisfaction deserves attention. It asks respondents whether or not they would choose the same kind of work they are presently doing if they could begin their work lives again. This variation on the conventional global satisfaction question yields dramatically different responses from people doing certain kinds of work, as Table 3-22 shows. Satisfaction can be seen to range from a high of 93 percent to a low of 16 percent, with professionals on the higher end of this range, unskilled workers at the lower end, and others in between. For many people, then, the status, pay, tasks, and so on believed to accompany work other than what they are doing look attractive. So if they could start over, they might aim higher. This approach thus registers the discomfort people may feel about their location, roles, and rewards in the occupational structure.

We have looked at work satisfaction in a number of ways. Depending on the data one selects, it is quite possible to conclude either that discontent is pervasive or that the large majority of jobholders are content. The truth, as usual, lies somewhere between such opposite claims. At the most abstract level of satisfaction—the global "all things considered" level—a very large proportion of people are satisfied. They

---

[85]For other recent job facet studies, see, for example, Bernard J. White, "The Criteria for Job Satisfaction: Is Interesting Work Most Important?" *Monthly Labor Review*, 100 (1977): 30–35; James D. Wright and Richard F. Hamilton, "Education and Attitudes Among Blue-Collar Workers," *Sociology of Work and Occupations*, 6 (1979): 59–83; Wright and Hamilton, "Work Satisfaction and Age"; Barry Gruenberg, "The Happy Worker," *American Journal of Sociology*, 86 (1980): 247–71; Beatrice Walfish, "Workers Report Wage, Benefit Problems," *World of Work Report*, 4 (1979): 17, 20–21.

TABLE 3–22

Workers Who Would Choose Same Kind of Job Again
(in percent)

Occupation	Would Choose Same Kind of Work Again
Professional and white-collar	
Urban university professors	93%
Mathematicians	91
Physicists	89
Biologists	89
Chemists	86
Firm lawyers	85
School superintendents	85
Lawyers	83
Journalists (Washington correspondents)	82
Church university professors	77
Solo lawyers	75
White-collar workers (nonprofessional)	43
Skilled trades and blue-collar	
Skilled printers	52
Paper workers	42
Skilled auto workers	41
Skilled steelworkers	41
Textile workers	31
Blue-collar workers (cross section)	24
Unskilled steelworkers	21
Unskilled auto workers	16

Source: Adapted from Robert L. Kahn, "The Work Module: A Proposal for the Human-
ization of Work," in James O'Toole, ed., Work and the Quality of Life (Cambridge, Mass.:
The MIT Press, 1974), Table 9.1, p. 204. (By permission of the publisher.) These data are a
composite of several studies.

are saying, in essence, "with my education, my skills, the job market for
people like me, my job is OK." More pointed research, however, reveals
that as extrinsic and intrinsic job elements decrease, discontent increases.
In this light, job satisfaction exhibits a hierarchical distribution roughly
parallel with occupational prestige. Pulling all this together, one might
say that people can be and are simultaneously satisfied and dissatisfied
with their jobs[86]—satisfied overall with the job, yet discontented with
specific features of it, and increasingly so toward the lower rungs of the
occupational ladder.

---

[86]The notion that satisfaction and dissatisfaction may occur simultaneously was
originally suggested by Frederick Herzberg. My emphasis is on the different levels of
abstraction in which satisfaction and dissatisfaction occur, whereas Herzberg views
satisfaction and discontent as separate reactions to distinct job facets: "One More Time:
How Do You Motivate Employees?" Harvard Business Review, 46 (1968): 53–62.

Having now examined several major work outcomes, we notice that people's attempts to change their work outcomes are a major source of job quits, job changing, and conflict. These topics are discussed in the following chapter.

OVERVIEW

The U.S. labor force included more than 110 million persons in 1982. Men's labor-force participation has been quite stable for many years; women have dramatically increased their involvement. Between 1940 and 1982, the women's participation rate more than doubled. In contrast to just twenty years ago, neither the presence of young children nor husbands with good incomes substantially reduce women's participation. The reasons for women's increased entry into the labor force are cultural and economic: To have a job has come to represent favorable traits, while the earnings of a wife, together with her husband's, provides significantly higher income than a single-earner family enjoys. Currently, in about half of our families, both husband and wife work.

Since the turn of this century, white-collar jobs more than tripled as a proportion of all jobs. Women, however, are concentrated in clerical and sales jobs. Nearly 45 percent of women workers are in just these two categories. Also in this century, the service sector has markedly expanded; it now includes more than 70 percent of the labor force.

Unemployment has been an increasingly serious and persistent problem since the 1970s. Unemployment is highest among the young, especially blacks, and the less educated. The problem of unemployment has emerged in all Western industrialized nations, along with inflation.

Between the late 1940s and 1970, median family income doubled. But due to price increases, family income has stayed at the 1970 level in actual purchasing power. Without the increase in two-earner families, inflation would have taken a larger bite and median family income would have shrunk between 1970 and 1982.

People are connected to work by its outcomes. Although there are a number of outcomes, pay, prestige, and job satisfaction are the primary ones. Each of these major outcomes displays a hierarchical pattern. The distribution of work outcomes is ultimately based on occupational power. Work outcomes are unequally allocated in all large-scale societies, and their consequences for shaping social interaction patterns are similar.

4. Changing Work Outcomes

Unless illness, children, or a lucky lottery ticket intervene, a large chunk of many people's lives—about forty-five years or so—is invested in work. From executive suite to shop floor, the factor shared by working men and women is their concern with attaining work outcomes, protecting them, and when possible, improving them.

This way of looking at why people go to work draws on conflict theory (described in chapter 3) and suggests this conceptual framework: People are attached to work by its outcomes. Our culture encourages work, and economic necessity ordinarily demands it. For most persons, therefore, work is the only available path to desired ends. Additionally, people will resist a decrease in the level of work outcomes; they much prefer to increase their income, prestige, and job satisfaction. Since satiation with these benefits rarely occurs, individuals and groups compete for them. The forms of competition include individual occupational mobility and collective action by labor unions.

This perspective thus incorporates individuals and groups by highlighting their similar goals—to obtain, protect, and improve work outcomes. And it alerts us to the seemingly inevitable tensions and frictions in the work place that result from frustrated hopes for better work outcomes.

In the previous chapter we examined income, prestige, and job satisfaction, focusing on their existing distribution among the labor force. In this chapter we look at activities which, if all goes well, raise the level of these work outcomes. We begin with occupational mobility and then move on to labor unions.

OCCUPATIONAL MOBILITY

Intragenerational Mobility and Labor Turnover

Let us first define a few terms, starting with *intragenerational occupational mobility*. This refers to occupational shifts within a person's working life. Mobility may be *upward* to a better job, *downward* to a poorer job, or *lateral* (outcomes stay about the same). Labor turnover involves *separations* from a firm brought on by quits and layoffs, and *accessions* which include new hires and recalls of workers who had been laid off.

Economic growth stimulates labor turnover and sluggishness retards it. One might thus expect lower turnover rates now than say, in 1970; and to some degree this is true. The amount of turnover in our economy, however, is still high. One reason is the many young persons and mature women who have entered the labor force. They often start in jobs that happen to be available and then seek better ones. And many firms scale employment up or down in response to product demand. As the definition of turnover indicates, both voluntary quits and imposed layoffs generate turnover.

To get some idea of the extent of turnover, we can notice that in 1981 about 15 percent of the entire manufacturing work force quit their jobs and another 20 percent were laid off, while around 38 percent were new hires or recalls. That is certainly a lot of turnover. But it is somewhat less in other industries. Although the data are more fragmentary, it seems that on average the annual separation and accession rates are both closer to 25 percent.[1]

Considering the extent of turnover, it is not surprising that the average (median) length of time that employees work for the same employer has been going down. It is now just five years for men and half that for women. Among younger workers it is even shorter. Even for workers age fifty-five to sixty-five, the age group with the longest tenure, the average is only eleven years.[2] A study in the late 1940s found that people typically

---

[1]Data on turnover are clearest for manufacturing. This information is collected and tabulated by the Department of Labor. For turnover trends in manufacturing from 1971 through 1981, see *Employment and Earnings*, 29 (1982): 109 and 114. Comparative turnover data among several industries are shown in James L. Price, *The Study of Turnover* (Ames, Iowa: Iowa State University Press, 1977), p. 63; and Richard T. Mowday, Lyman W. Porter, and Richard M. Steers, *Employee-Organization Linkages: The Psychology of Commitment, Absenteeism, and Turnover* (New York: Academic Press, 1982), pp. 108-9. Outside of manufacturing, turnover rates must be treated cautiously.

[2]Francis W. Horvath, "Job Tenure of Workers, 1981," *Monthly Labor Review* 105 (1982): 35. For a discussion of the "initial," "trial," and "stable" stages of work life, see Delbert C. Miller and William H. Form, *Industrial Sociology* (New York: Harper and Row, 1980), pp. 198-256.

changed jobs about seven times during their working years;[3] currently, the corresponding number of moves is probably closer to ten.

To what do these job changes lead? If people were laid off or quit, do they do better or worse on the next job? We can obtain a rough picture of what happens by looking at those persons who shift occupation when they change jobs. A national survey conducted for the Census Bureau gathered information on this question from 56,000 respondents in 1978. The data were then projected to the whole labor force. The basic findings are shown in Table 4-1. All the people represented in it were job changers, either by moving to another employer or remaining with the same employer (actually nine out of ten had changed employers): These job changers account for nearly 12 percent of the employed labor force in 1978.

Job changers' occupations in 1977 are shown in the numbered columns. Their subsequent destination in 1978 can be seen in the rows of occupations. The number heading each column corresponds to the number preceding each occupational title. For example, look at column 1. It tells us that among persons who held professional or technical jobs in 1977, 50 percent found other professional-technical jobs in 1978, 16 percent became managers, 7 percent went into sales, and so forth. Notice that many job changers find work in the same occupation, but there is also much upward and downward movement. For an overall, albeit crude, indicator of the total shifts up and down, movement from white-collar to blue-collar occupations, and the opposite, was calculated. This revealed that among job leavers with white-collar occupations in 1977, about 22 percent were in blue-collar occupations in 1978; among people doing blue-collar work in 1977, 28 percent had moved to white-collar jobs in 1978. (Since only very few persons had moved out of or into agricultural work, they were not included.) The general tendency among these job changers is toward a moderate upward shift.

The data in Table 4-1 are consistent with other studies that trace job changers over longer time spans. Rather clearly, the net effect of job changing is upward occupational mobility.[4] But perhaps the most striking aspect of job changing is simply that there is so much of it.

[3]Seymour M. Lipset and Reinhard Bendix, *Social Mobility in Industrial Society* (Berkeley, Calif.: University of California Press, 1959), p. 153.

[4]Robert M. Hauser and David L. Featherman, *The Process of Stratification* (New York: Academic Press, 1977), pp. 96–97; Otis D. Duncan, David L. Featherman, and Beverly Duncan, *Socio-Economic Background and Achievement* (New York: Seminar Press, 1972), pp. 206–7; U.S. Department of Labor, Employment and Training Administration, R and D Monograph No. 24, 1976, *Years for Decision*, pp. 44–45; A. J. Jaffe, *The Middle Years*, Special Issue of *Industrial Gerontology* (September 1971), p. 50; James L. Stern and David B. Johnson, *Blue- to White-Collar Job Mobility* (Madison, Wisc.: Industrial Relations Research Institute, University of Wisconsin, 1968), especially pp. 17–18.

TABLE 4-1

Occupational Mobility, 1977–1978
(in percent)

Occupation in January 1978	Occupation in January 1977								
	1	2	3	4	5	6	7	8	9
1 Professional, technical	50%	13%	9%	10%	7%	3%	5%	7%	8%
2 Managerial	16	39	22	10	10	5	5	6	9
3 Sales workers	7	14	20	6	2	3	3	8	3
4 Clerical workers	11	12	18	52	6	9	9	20	7
5 Skilled workers	6	7	9	4	37	19	26	7	11
6 Semiskilled workers	3	9	9	7	23	42	25	14	24
7 Unskilled workers	2	1	4	2	7	8	19	6	14
8 Service workers	5	5	8	9	6	9	6	32	9
9 Farm workers	—	—	—	—	1	2	2	—	15
Total	100%	100%	100%	100%	100%	100%	100%	100%	100%
Number (in thousands)	955	775	667	1685	888	1579	551	1123	181

Source: Calculated from data in U.S. Department of Labor, Bureau of Labor Statistics, Occupational Mobility During 1977, Special Labor Force Report No. 231, 1980, Table 4.

Compared, for instance, to Japanese employees, American workers (and
those of Western Europe) are much less firmly attached to a specific
employer,[5] and the employer is also less committed to retaining the
employees.

Related to job changing and occupational mobility is geographic
mobility. We cannot know for sure how much geographic movement is
caused by job changing, but a very substantial amount undoubtedly is. A
survey sponsored by the Bureau of the Census found that in a five-year
period (1975–1980) about half of all working-age heads of families had
moved. Most, however, had moved to another dwelling within the same
county or state; only one out of five went out of state.[6]

It was mentioned earlier that younger workers change jobs most
frequently. It turns out that younger family heads also make the most
long-distance moves, especially if their income is low.[7] It is therefore the
younger and poorer families that are the most likely to seek opportunities
for better jobs in more distant locations.

Intergenerational Occupational Mobility

Intergenerational occupational mobility refers to occupational
movement between generations, such as fathers and sons. Studies of
intergenerational mobility attempt to answer these questions: Is there as
much upward and downward mobility now as in earlier years? And what
are the patterns of movement between occupational origins and
destinations? Researchers also attempt to explain intergenerational
mobility with sophisticated statistical techniques that make visible the
variables most closely associated with occupational movement.

Before going further, let us notice that the process of intergenerational
occupational mobility can be activated in two ways. First, new
occupations may be created or existing ones multiplied. When many of
these occupations are higher-level, opportunities for upward mobility
increase. In short, if there is growth in the number of more highly
rewarded occupations, people must be found to fill the positions.
Second, mobility can occur (even with scant occupational growth) if
there is circulation of occupation holders from one generation to
another—when occupations are allocated among people according to

[5]Ronald Dore, *British Factory—Japanese Factory* (Berkeley, Calif.: University of
California Press, 1973), pp. 308–11; Ernest van Helvoort, *The Japanese Working Man*
(Vancouver, B.C.: University of British Columbia Press, 1979), pp. 29–32.

[6]U.S. Bureau of the Census, Current Population Reports, Series P-20, No. 368,
Geographical Mobility: March 1975 to March 1980 (Washington, D.C.: U.S. Government
Printing Office, 1981), p. 32.

[7]Ibid., pp. 40–41.

"meritocratic" criteria (such as educational credentials), thereby reducing occupational inheritance. People then compete for advantageous occupations by competing for access to appropriate credentials.

Industrialized societies have fostered occupational mobility in both these ways. The growth of white-collar occupations and credentials attainment have been the main currents, although some groups have been less touched by them than others. In the United States, women and blacks were less likely to compete for the credentials that opened the doors to higher-level occupations, or if they did attain the credentials, could not as readily as white males get past the doorkeepers. The evidence, however, rather clearly indicates that black males in particular are becoming more fully incorporated into the mainstream of intergenerational occupational mobility.

Now we step back to one of the questions mentioned at the beginning of this discussion of intergenerational mobility, and briefly summarize the attempts to uncover the variables most closely related to mobility.

Intergenerational Mobility Explanatory Variables

The most thorough recent analysis of variables that "explain" intergenerational mobility is based on a national sample of nearly 21,000 men between twenty and sixty-four years of age in 1973.[8] Statistical (regression) analysis showed that among white sons, their level of education and fathers' occupation had the strongest favorable impacts on mobility, with education by far the most important. There were also, however, variables that *reduced* mobility chances: farm origins, and large families.[9] For black sons, the findings only slightly, but revealingly, differ. Sons' education does not have quite as much impact on occupational placement, while their fathers' education plays a greater role in mobility than does their fathers' occupation, and broken homes reduce mobility chances a great deal more than among white sons from broken families.[10]

Let us, for a moment, look more closely at the impact of education on white and black men. Among both, it is certainly the single most potent variable in occupational placement, but somewhat less so among black men. This indicates some difficulty in using schooling for occupational advancement, which signals institutional discrimination. On the brighter

---

[8]David L. Featherman and Robert M. Hauser, *Opportunity and Change* (New York: Academic Press, 1978).

[9]Ibid., p. 339.

[10]Ibid.

side, the data unambiguously point to the increasingly stronger linkage of education and occupation among black males. This can be seen in these data in two respects. First, a comparison with a similar survey in 1962 shows that only ten years later, in 1973, the importance of education for occupational placement had greatly increased. Second, comparisons among age groups in the 1973 survey show that among the youngest group (age twenty-five to thirty-four) the impact of education on occupation among black males is close to their white age-peers, whereas among older black men (age fifty-five to sixty-four) education had a much more muted impact than among their white age-peers.[11] Whether one looks back in time, from one survey to another, or compares age groups in the same survey, schooling and occupational advancement have become more tightly connected among black men, indicating a clear though gradual decrease in blocked mobility opportunities.

For convenience, those elements that increase the chances for mobility are listed below with a plus sign, and those that decrease mobility chances are shown with a minus sign:

+ education of son (lengthier elevates occupational placement)
+ education of father (lengthier enhances son's occupational placement)
+ occupation of father (higher improves son's chances for higher occupation)
− broken family (weakens mobility chances especially among black sons)
− farm origin (weakens mobility chances more strongly among white sons)
− number of siblings (the more, the weaker is mobility)

Because the sons' education is so pivotal to mobility, it is useful to notice that the variables most highly related to education are, in order of importance, fathers' occupation and fathers' education.[12]

In discussing the elements that help or hinder occupational mobility, it has probably not escaped the reader that nothing was said of women. However, with the exception of farm origin (which does not diminish women's mobility), working women's mobility is statistically explainable with the same set of variables that apply to men. Put another way, when mobility does occur, the same set of variables is operating.[13]

[11]Ibid., pp. 338–39.
[12]Hauser and Featherman, *The Process of Stratification*, p. 275.
[13]Ibid., pp. 208 and 212. This does not deny that women's social status benefits, or suffers, from that of their husbands; it only tells us that women's occupational placement is statistically related to the same variables that influence men's occupational locations.

Finally, a word on the rather bloodless way the elements in this explanatory scheme were treated, for example, father's occupation or education. It should be recognized that these variables are "indicators" which represent a very complex set of relationships between family members, involving parents' influence on offspring (socialization). The results of the socialization process are then reflected in statistical relationships among variables which are more directly and conveniently measurable. Indicators are a common and helpful method to penetrate complex relationships, but it is well to remember that they represent an underlying dense social reality. Recall that "number of siblings" was listed as a variable that hindered mobility. As an exercise in social analysis, you may wish to consider the handicaps that this variable represents.

Intergenerational Mobility Data

Let us look now at some data. For men, we will notice first the large-scale survey of 21,000 respondents mentioned earlier. Fortunately, some reasonably good data on women's occupational mobility are also available. These will be examined a bit later.

Table 4-2 shows sons' occupations in 1973 and their fathers' occupations. (The latter was defined as the occupation held by the father when the son was sixteen years old.) A substantial amount of movement is evident, the net result of which is that there is more upward than downward mobility. Since the 289 cells in this detailed table might be discouraging, the importance of these patterns suggests their display with less detail.

Broad occupational groups are shown in Table 4-3. (The groups are defined in the note to the table.) Intergenerational mobility, as measured in 1973, appears in the upper part of the table. For comparison, mobility as measured more recently is shown in the lower part of the table.[14]

The table shows that in 1973, sons of upper nonmanual fathers were most likely to remain there—nearly 60 percent did. The largest share of lower nonmanual sons either stayed there (17 percent) or moved up (45 percent). Among the sons of upper manual fathers, over 40 percent moved up, while fewer than 30 percent moved down. And well over half of the sons of lower manual fathers moved up. These patterns indicate much more upward than downward mobility: Over twice as many sons moved up as moved down.

---

[14]These mobility patterns were constructed from data in the NORC's General Social Survey, 1980 and 1982. The two surveys were combined to provide 555 employed adult sons who reported their fathers' occupations.

TABLE 4–2

Mobility from Father's Occupation to Son's Occupation: Men Age 21–64 in 1973
(in percent)

Father's Occupation	1	2	3	4	5	6	7	8	9	10	11	12	13	14	15	16	17	Total
								Son's 1973 Occupation										
1 Professionals, self-employed	12.6	32.5	18.0	5.9	3.4	3.4	2.5	3.3	4.9	3.3	3.2	3.3	1.4	0.7	1.0	0.5	0.3	100%
2 Professionals, salaried	3.6	34.6	15.1	4.5	1.4	7.3	2.2	4.7	6.0	3.0	4.3	4.1	5.3	1.0	2.0	0.7	0.2	100
3 Managers	3.4	23.0	24.9	7.9	3.2	5.3	3.7	4.2	5.7	2.4	4.9	4.2	3.8	0.5	2.0	0.4	0.4	100
4 Salesmen, other	3.7	21.2	21.0	12.5	2.5	6.1	2.9	4.2	6.1	2.5	5.2	4.1	4.4	0.5	2.3	0.2	0.6	100
5 Proprietors	2.7	16.6	19.9	7.9	8.0	5.9	2.9	5.7	5.4	5.1	3.8	5.6	5.5	1.0	2.1	1.2	0.5	100
6 Clerks	1.4	22.3	16.4	4.2	2.0	10.5	2.0	6.4	5.7	4.5	5.4	6.0	7.6	1.3	3.4	0.5	0.4	100
7 Salesmen, retail	4.2	13.6	15.8	8.2	6.6	8.7	4.6	5.7	7.9	2.7	5.5	5.4	6.6	1.4	2.2	0.6	0.0	100
8 Craftsmen, manufacturing	1.1	16.4	11.1	4.6	2.5	7.3	1.8	13.4	8.7	4.1	5.2	6.4	12.5	1.5	2.7	0.5	0.2	100
9 Craftsmen, other	0.8	15.1	11.7	4.0	2.9	7.6	2.3	8.6	12.7	5.1	5.8	7.9	9.6	1.4	3.4	0.8	0.3	100
10 Craftsmen, construction	0.7	11.6	12.1	3.1	4.2	6.1	1.7	6.4	9.2	15.2	5.1	7.4	9.1	1.0	4.4	0.8	0.9	100
11 Service	1.3	12.3	10.5	3.1	3.3	8.3	2.1	6.4	8.8	4.9	10.8	8.8	11.6	2.0	5.1	0.2	0.4	100
12 Operatives, other	0.6	10.0	9.3	2.6	2.7	8.1	1.6	8.6	10.5	5.5	6.1	14.3	12.0	1.5	5.1	0.6	0.8	100
13 Operatives, manufacturing	0.9	11.2	8.8	2.7	2.6	7.5	1.9	12.5	8.0	4.8	5.9	7.4	19.5	3.0	2.8	0.5	0.2	100
14 Laborers, manufacturing	0.9	7.0	7.9	2.5	2.6	5.6	1.8	10.4	8.2	7.6	5.0	10.2	18.7	5.8	4.6	0.4	0.7	100
15 Laborers, other	0.8	7.0	8.7	2.1	2.8	6.5	1.4	8.5	8.7	6.5	8.2	11.3	15.8	2.0	8.3	0.4	0.9	100
16 Farmers	0.7	7.0	8.2	2.1	3.4	4.0	1.7	7.0	8.0	7.2	6.0	8.4	12.9	2.4	5.2	12.4	3.3	100
17 Farm laborers	0.4	4.4	4.4	1.5	2.4	4.8	1.3	10.1	8.7	6.5	7.1	11.2	16.1	3.5	7.4	4.2	6.2	100

Source: David L. Featherman and Robert M. Hauser, Opportunity and Change (New York: Academic Press, 1978), p. 535, Table E.5. (By permission of the publisher.) Total N = 19,913.

TABLE 4-3

Mobility from Father's Occupation to Son's Occupation
(in percent)

Father's Occupation	Upper Nonmanual	Lower Nonmanual	Upper Manual	Lower Manual	Farm	Total
			Son's Occupation in 1973			
Upper Nonmanual	59	11	13	16	1	100%
Lower Nonmanual	45	17	16	21	1	100
Upper Manual	31	12	28	28	1	100
Lower Manual	23	12	24	40	1	100
Farm	16	9	23	37	15	100
			Son's Occupation in 1982			
Upper Nonmanual	51	12	18	17	2	100%
Lower Nonmanual	44	20	12	24	—	100
Upper Manual	24	11	38	27	—	100
Lower Manual	21	11	21	46	1	100
Farm	14	7	27	31	21	100

Note: Occupation groups are: upper nonmanual: professional and technical workers, managers and officials, nonretail sales workers; lower nonmanual: proprietors, clerical and retail sales workers; upper manual: craftsmen and foremen; lower manual: service workers, semiskilled workers (operatives), laborers except farm; farm: farmers and farm managers, farm laborers and foremen.

Sources: 1973 data are from David L. Featherman and Robert M. Hauser, *Opportunity and Change* (New York: Academic Press, 1978), p. 89, Table 3.14. (By permission of the publisher.) Total N = 20,850. 1982 mobility was calculated from data collected by the National Opinion Research Center (University of Chicago) in their General Social Survey. Total N = 555.

By 1982, mobility patterns had changed. Fewer upper nonmanual sons stayed there, whereas nearly half skidded down. And the sons of fathers in other occupational groups were more likely to stay in their fathers' occupational groups, while fewer moved up. A bird's eye view of these recent findings on mobility looks like this:

Nonmovers	38%
Movers	62
up	36
down	26

Our troubled economy is mirrored in these data. Compared to 1973, the 1982 data show less upward occupational movement, increased non-movement and more downward shifts. On balance, however, there is still significantly more upward than downward mobility.

Now let us look at women's mobility. In 1955 through 1966, the

NORC conducted six surveys on women's mobility. Each respondent was asked about her father's occupation when she was sixteen years old, or when she was a child. One study combined these surveys which together include nearly 2,400 adult working women.[15] The upper part of Table 4-4 shows women's mobility as measured in 1955–1966. The lower part of this table describes the mobility patterns drawn from recent NORC research.[16]

TABLE 4–4

Mobility from Father's Occupation to Daughter's Occupation
(in percent)

Father's Occupation	Daughter's Occupation in 1955–1966					
	Upper Nonmanual	Lower Nonmanual	Upper Manual	Lower Manual	Farm	Total
Upper Nonmanual	36	42	2	20	—	100%
Lower Nonmanual	24	51	—	24	—	100
Upper Manual	15	44	2	39	—	100
Lower Manual	13	32	3	51	1	100
Farm	18	25	1	49	7	100
	Daughter's Occupation in 1982					
Upper Nonmanual	39	46	1	14	—	100%
Lower Nonmanual	39	35	2	24	—	100
Upper Manual	15	43	5	36	1	100
Lower Manual	14	37	2	47	—	100
Farm	22	22	1	52	3	100

Note: The occupational categories are the same as in Table 4–3 (see note to Table 4–3).
Sources: 1955–1966 calculated from data in Peter DeJong, Patterns of Intergenerational Occupational Mobility of American Females (San Francisco: R & E Associates, 1977), p. 125, Table 1. The data are combined from six NORC studies conducted in 1955 through 1966: total N = 2,371. Data for 1982 were calculated from information collected by the National Opinion Research Center (University of Chicago) in their General Social Survey: total N = 648.

The data on women's mobility indicate that upward movement has increased, compared to the earlier period, and that downward shifts have decreased. The daughters of fathers in every occupational group were more likely to reach upper nonmanual positions now than formerly, and less likely to go into lower manual occupations. Nevertheless, the

---

[15]Peter DeJong, Patterns of Intergenerational Occupational Mobility of American Females (San Francisco: R & E Research Associates, 1977), p. 125.
[16]The mobility data were calculated from findings in the NORC's General Social Survey, 1980 and 1982. These two surveys were combined and provided 648 adult working women who reported their fathers' occupations.

concentration of women in the lower nonmanual (clerical and sales) jobs, persisted without much change over the years.

A summary of the 1982 data on women's mobility looks like this (for convenience the comparable information on men is repeated in the parentheses):

Nonmovers	27% (38%)
Movers	73 (62%)
up	40 (36%)
down	33 (26%)

Seen this way, although women's downward mobility exceeded the men's, women were more likely to shift out of their fathers' occupational groups and move up: 40 percent moved up compared to 36 percent of the men. But the majority (63 percent) of these upward moves were into clerical and sales work. Women's upward mobility chances have discernibly improved in relation to earlier years; their occupational destinations, however, are often still the lower nonmanual dead-end jobs. The flow of women into these jobs is so strong and persistent that even a vigorous economy would probably not alter women's mobility patterns dramatically or soon.

In their summary of mobility trends, two leading analysts concluded that:

> In this century, there has been essentially no trend in the relative mobility chances of American men whose fathers held differing occupations.... This striking lack of trend has been documented in...analyses of intergenerational occupational mobility tables for the period from about 1910 to 1970....[17]

And in 1973 much the same can be said.[18] In light of findings on the early 1980s, however, it appears that men's opportunities for upward mobility have recently weakened. In contrast, women's chances for upward movement have moderately improved.

Intergenerational and intragenerational mobility are the primary routes to gains in work outcomes by individuals through personal actions. Another means of raising work outcomes involves the association of people in organized groups, which can bring collective pressure to bear on issues of work outcomes. We look next, then, to unions and the laws that legitimate them. Because of the importance of unions, the topic will be discussed in some detail.

---

[17]Hauser and Featherman, *The Process of Stratification*, p. 169.
[18]Featherman and Hauser, *Opportunity and Change*, p. 93.

UNIONS AND COLLECTIVE BARGAINING

Although we take unions and collective bargaining for granted, their legitimacy under our laws is of relatively recent origin. For the largest share of the world's workers these activities are still either not permitted or stunted. Outside North America and Western Europe, collective bargaining is found in a comparatively few nations.[19] In the rest, unions are either absent altogether—as in China, Indochina, and the major OPEC countries—or so tightly controlled by government that the unions resemble an arm of the state—as in Russia, Cuba, Eastern Europe. and most of South America.

The reasons for suppressing or controlling unions involve power and economics. Autonomous unions represent a challenge to the concentration of power in a government's hands, as the recent suppression of Polish unions unmistakably illustrates.

In addition to the power issue, but tied to it, is the economic dimension. The amounts of money invested in different sectors of an economy are directly determined by government if the economy is not open to organized demands for wage hikes and consumption goods. Organized pressure for such gains can be avoided if unions are prohibited or tightly regulated. Clearly, we should not expect a reversal of current policies toward unions in nations with a history of centralized power.

In stark contrast, labor unions achieved acceptance by the governments of Western countries. As was mentioned earlier, the framework of law that protects unions in the United States came into being relatively recently. Collective bargaining had a precarious existence until the appropriate laws were passed. Before turning directly to unions, let us get an overview of this legislation.

Basic Labor Law

The Sherman Antitrust Act of 1890 prohibited any contract, or combination of business interests in restraint of foreign or domestic trade. This was often interpreted by the courts as applying to people associated in a union, as well as employers. The authority of the courts to dissolve "combinations" posed a serious threat to existing unions and their activities.

---

[19]These include, for example, Japan, Israel, Australia, New Zealand, India, South Africa, Panama, Guyana, and Greenland. For a more complete listing, see Michael Kidron and Ronald Segal, *The State of the World Atlas* (New York: Simon and Shuster, 1981), 42.

To provide some protection to unions, the Clayton Act (1914) was passed. It declared that the antitrust laws are not to be "construed to forbid the existence and operations of labor...organizations...from lawfully carrying out the legitimate objects thereof...." Frequently, however, the courts still held that although unions as such were not illegal, their use of illegal tactics in a labor dispute could be ended by issuing an injunction—a court order prohibiting a certain action. As late as the early 1930s, employers obtained hundreds of injunctions to stop organizing activities, picketing, boycotts, and strikes.

Then the pendulum began to swing in the other direction with the passage of the Norris-LaGuardia Act in 1932. It accomplished what the Clayton Act feebly began—halting interference by courts in labor disputes. Unions were now effectively shielded from injunctions: in a precedent-setting case brought to the Supreme Court, the Norris-LaGuardia Act was held to mean that unions were protected from antitrust legislation.[20] But the protection of union activities is one thing; recognition of unions by employers is another. For this, further legislation was needed. It appeared in the Wagner Act.[21]

The Wagner Act (or National Labor Relations Act) was adopted in 1935. In it Congress established the framework of our present labor-management relations. The Wagner Act prohibits employers from interfering with employees' rights to organize and bargain collectively, or refusing to bargain with representatives of the employees. And the act set up procedures for employees to choose collective bargaining representatives. To administer and enforce the act, the National Labor Relations Board was created. It is currently guided by the Wagner Act and two later laws, the Taft-Hartley and Landrum-Griffin Acts.

The Wagner Act prohibited employers from specific actions, and Taft-Hartley (1947) added prohibitions of certain union activities, among which are:

1. Attempting to cause an employer to discriminate against an employee because of his membership or nonmembership in a labor organization, with the exception of union-shop agreements;[22]
2. Refusing to bargain in good faith with an employer;

---

[20]For a discussion of the Sherman, Clayton, and Norris-LaGuardia acts, see Sar A. Levitan, "An Appraisal of the Antitrust Approach," *The Annals*, 33 (1961): 108–18.

[21]Useful reviews of labor law are: U.S. Department of Labor, Bulletin 262, *Federal Labor Laws and Programs* (Washington, D.C.: U.S. Government Printing Office, 1971); Howard Anderson, *Primer of Labor Relations* (Washington, D.C.: The Bureau of National Affairs, 1980).

[22]Union shop refers to a contract under which an employer may hire any worker, but the new employee must join the union within a specified time and remain a member; otherwise the employer is obligated to discharge the employee. See also footnote 28.

3. Encouraging employees to stop work in order to compel an employer to assign particular work to members of the union instead of to members of another union (*jurisdictional strike*);
4. Encouraging employees to stop work in order to compel an employer to stop doing business with any other firm (*secondary boycott*).

Unions had strongly opposed the passage of Taft-Hartley, voicing particular objections to the prohibition of secondary boycotts and the *closed shop*. The closed shop, a contractual agreement under which an employer can hire only workers who are already members of the union, became an illegal arrangement, as seen in point (1) above. The combination of prohibitions, it was feared by unions, would weaken them. All in all, this has not turned out to be nearly the problem originally anticipated. Nor are the provisions of Taft-Hartley always strictly applied. We can see that in construction, for instance, the jurisdictional strike is not uncommon, and in trucking and construction the closed shop remains alive.[23]

A dozen years after Taft-Hartley, the Landrum-Griffin Act (Labor-Management and Disclosure Act) was prompted by congressional hearings that uncovered shady practices among a number of unions. The act guarantees certain rights to union members and imposes specific obligations on union officers. Among the obligations are that each labor organization must file its procedures and annual financial records with the secretary of labor, and this information must be disclosed to union members. Further, union members were given a "bill of rights" which includes:

— The equal right to attend meetings and vote at meetings;
— Protection from increases in dues except under specified procedures, for example, secret ballots at a meeting, or mailed referendum;
— The right to inspect collective bargaining agreements;
— The guarantee of fair election of officers, including a reasonable opportunity to nominate candidates.

Of course, no set of laws can prevent all wrongdoing, but the Landrum-Griffin Act has helped to reduce abuses of power by union

---

[23]Jack Barbash, "Collective Bargaining: Contemporary American Experience," in Gerald G. Somers, ed., *Collective Bargaining: Contemporary American Experience* (Madison, Wisc.: Industrial Relations Research Association, 1980), pp. 561–63. Paradoxically, the weakened position of unions in construction and trucking is due to their success in gaining restrictive work rules, and boosting wages and fringes to levels that created opportunities for nonunionized firms to capture increasing shares of the markets for construction and trucking.

officials.[24] Nevertheless, in comparison to Europe, our record of abuses is seemingly more abundant.[25]

With the Wagner, Taft-Hartley, and Landrum-Griffin acts as guides, the National Labor Relations Board (NLRB) administers a large body of rules and decisions.[26]

The NLRB

The NLRB's jurisdiction covers labor-management relations that affect interstate commerce. The NLRB may reject a case if in its view interstate commerce is not substantially involved; in those instances, the statutes of individual states are in effect. Specifically excluded from the NLRB's jurisdiction are federal employees, state and local public-sector employees, domestic servants, and agricultural laborers. The NLRB has two principal functions: (1) to prevent and remedy unfair labor practices by unions or employers, and (2) to conduct elections by secret ballot among employees to determine if they wish to be represented by a union.

Who is an "employee"? Much hinges on this because the NLRB protects only the bargaining rights of persons defined as employees. Under the NLRB's rules, individuals performing supervisory duties are

---

[24]For a review of the union practices which gave impetus to the Landrum-Griffin Act, and the subsequent enforcement of the act, see Benjamin Aaron, "Regulation of Internal Union Relations," and W. Willard Wirtz, "Union Morals," in E. Wight Bakke, Clark Kerr, and Charles W. Anrod, eds., *Unions, Management and the Public* (New York: Harcourt, Brace & World, 1967), pp. 677–81, and 682–83, respectively. Some corrupt practices involved employers' payments to union officials in exchange for favorable wage agreements, labor peace, and nonenforcement of certain provisions of the collective bargaining contract. As one student of these matters pointed out, in no industry "is there a public record of substantial employer opposition to the works of the corrupt. . . . In most cases there was only collaboration or silence." John Hutchinson, "The Anatomy of Corruption in Trade Unions," *Industrial Relations*, 8 (1969): 144.

[25]Derek C. Bok and John T. Dunlop, *Labor and the American Community* (New York: Simon and Schuster, 1970), pp. 65–69.

[26]Several other major acts are not administered by the NLRB. The Federal Wage and Hour Law (Fair Labor Standards Act of 1938, and amendments) sets a minimum wage, and requires overtime pay at one and a half times the regular rate for over forty hours in a week—professional, executive, and administrative employees are exempt. The secretary of labor administers this act. Title VII of the Civil Rights Act of 1964 prohibits discrimination by employers and labor unions on the grounds of race, color, sex, and national origin. The Equal Employment Opportunity Commission, appointed by the president with senate approval, administers the act, although the NLRB enforces the act among unions. The Occupational Safety and Health Act (OSHA) of 1970 created a new agency for carrying out the act's purpose: "to assure so far as possible every working man and woman in the Nation safe and healthful working conditions and to preserve our human resources." Health and safety standards and their enforcement are overseen by the Occupational Safety and Health Review Commission. This sketches only several highlights of the many federal laws bearing on work. Obviously, the NLRB is joined by others in a patchwork of legislation and rulings.

excluded and thus unprotected. A supervisor is defined as a person who has the authority to hire, fire, transfer, reward, and discipline, *or* effectively recommend such actions. In short, the responsibility to exercise authority over other employees disqualifies one from the right to bargain collectively. In a recent case, for instance, the NLRB ruled that the faculty of Yeshiva University exercised supervisory authority in hiring, firing, pay increases, promotion, and other administrative matte, s. The university, therefore, was not required by law to recognize the faculty union; the university administration might, if it so wishes, negotiate with the union, but need not do so. (Since the Yeshiva faculty are in a private university and are not state employees, the case was within the NLRB's jurisdiction.)

To give some idea of the nature and scope of NLRB rulings, a sample of the board's decisions is described below:[27]

— An employer may not discharge a union member for violating a rule not enforced among other employees.
— If an employee was unlawfully discharged, the employee must be reinstated with back pay.
— Mandatory bargaining topics include: seniority and discharge provisions, union security[28] and dues collection, vacations, wages, bonuses, merit raises, pension and insurance plans, rest breaks and lunch periods, safety rules, production quotas.
— During a strike over economic demands, an employer may hire replacements. However, the employer can not discriminate against the strikers when job vacancies occur after the strike has ended.
— Employees may be discharged for strikes in violation of collective bargaining contracts.
— Picketing in such numbers that nonstrikers are barred from entering a work place is not lawful, nor are threats of injury to nonstriking employees.
— Employers must bargain "in good faith" and may not refuse to discuss union proposals or refuse to provide the union with information it needs for informed bargaining.

---

[27]The examples are drawn mainly from the useful *Primer of Labor Relations*, pp. 19 ff.
[28]Union security refers to union membership provisions in a contract. The main types of union security clauses are: *closed shop*—the employer may hire only members of a specific union (barred under Taft-Hartley, however); *union shop*—the employer may hire any persons, but they must join the union within a specified time, usually within thirty days; *agency shop*—an employee may choose not to join the union, although a fee must be paid to the union for its services. Twenty states (mainly in the South and Southwest) have "right-to-work" laws that prohibit most forms of union security arrangements, including the agency shop.

To bring a case before the NLRB, an employer or union must file an unfair labor practices charge with the board. A ruling will then be made after a hearing. If either party to the ruling does not comply with it, the NLRB uses the courts to enforce its decisions; an NLRB decision may also be appealed in the federal courts, all the way to the Supreme Court.

With its rulings on labor practices, and responsibility for conducting union representation and decertification elections through its field offices, the NLRB has a major role in America's industrial relations system.

Unions

In 1778 journeyman printers in New York City combined to form a union which demanded a wage increase, and received it; and in 1886 a number of craft unions formed the forerunner of the present American Federation of Labor (AFL).[29] As these examples illustrate, unions have been around for a long time. However, shaky legal ground kept their actions open to challenge until changes in the political climate of the 1930s prodded enactment of the Wagner Act. The road to organizing was paved but still bumpy.

Over the years, union membership went up and then down. Looking at membership as a proportion of the nonagricultural labor force shows these percentages:[30]

1930	12%
1935	13
1940	27
1945	36
1955	33
1965	30
1975	29
1980	25

Organized labor's share of the nonagricultural work force tripled between 1930 and the postwar 1940s. A gradual decline in union membership then began and has not been reversed.

---

[29]A good historical overview of union activities is presented in U.S. Department of Labor, *Important Events in American Labor History, 1778-1978* (Washington, D.C.: U.S. Government Printing Office, 1979).

[30]U.S. Department of Labor, Bureau of Labor Statistics, *Directory of National Unions and Employee Associations, 1979*, Bulletin No. 2079 (Washington, D.C.: U.S. Government Printing Office, 1980), pp. 59-60; Bureau of Labor Statistics, *News* September 18, 1981, p. 2.

These data, spanning the years 1930 through 1980, are revealing because they include "employee associations." Members of the National Education Association, Newspaper Guild, Airline Pilots Association, American Nurses Association, and so on are counted as white-collar unionists. As the proportion of blue-collar workers declined, professional, technical, and other white-collar employees would either enter the ranks of the organized, or organized employees would inevitably represent a declining proportion of workers. Unionization (or its "associational" equivalent) has had some marked success among professionals and near-professionals in the public sector—teachers, social workers, postal workers, firefighters, and policemen. In the private sector, however, professionals and other white-collar employees have been much less willing to join unions.

The rapid growth of employment in the public sector, accompanied by new state laws that permit collective bargaining, provided the elements that favored unions' organizing efforts. The expansion of the public sector, however, has at a minimum been braked, and therefore will not provide the infusion of new union members that it has in the recent past. A long-time student of such matters noted that "Public-sector bargaining represents a collective-bargaining breakthrough which is, for its time, comparable in historical importance to the first collective bargaining 'revolution' of the 1930's. But public-sector expansion and its union population seem to be slowing down earlier than did the private sector in an analogous stage."[31]

Unions have so far not been able to reverse the gradual erosion of their share of American employees. It may be recalled that just one of every four nonagricultural employees is now a union member: Among these, only a relatively small proportion are in white-collar occupations—mainly in the public sector—whereas 75 percent are manual workers.[32]

American unions have been more successful in organizing blue-collar workers than their French, British, and West German counterparts, but have done more poorly than Swedish and Australian unions.[33] In the white-collar private sector, however, unions in the United States lag behind.[34]

---

[31]Barbash, "Collective Bargaining," p. 574.
[32]U.S. Department of Labor, *Directory of National Unions and Employee Associations, 1979*, p. 67.
[33]Barbash, "Collective Bargaining," p. 572.
[34]Hugh A. Clegg, *Trade Unionism Under Collective Bargaining* (Oxford: Basil Blackwell, Ltd., 1976), p. 12. A fine collection of papers on this topic is in Adolph Sturmthal, ed., *White-Collar Trade Unions* (Urbana, Ill.: University of Illinois Press, 1966).

Collective Bargaining

Collective bargaining, American style, is essentially an adversary relationship. Each side of the negotiations—with labor representatives literally on one side of a table and management negotiators on the other—attempts to get as much as it can from the other side while giving away as little as possible. Thus, labor asks for more money, expanded insurance programs, more paid holidays, and so forth, while management tries to yield as little as possible in terms of financial costs and control over work. Labor initially demands far more than it really expects to receive, while management offers substantially less than it will finally give. Each side thus attempts to gauge the true intentions of the other: What will labor really settle for, and what is management really prepared to offer? If the negotiations do not result in a satisfactory outcome, the negotiations may break off and result in a strike or lockout (temporarily closing down a business to put economic pressure on the employees). If the negotiations are successful, the membership of the union must still approve the proposed contract.

The contract negotiation process has worked rather well. Strikes are not the usual result and actually account for little time lost, typically less than one-quarter of one percent of total working time per year.[35] Still, the ultimate threat of resort to strike or lockout looms large in bringing the parties to compromise their demands and reach a contract settlement. Although public employee strikes are in all but eight states prohibited by law, and for essential services (fire, police) barred in every state,[36] this has not noticeably deterred firemen and policemen, or social workers and teachers from threatening to strike and sometimes doing so. In the end, bargaining is a power relation, and the terms of the agreement reflect that fact.

------

[35]The most strike activity was in 1946, with over 1 percent of total work time lost to strikes. Other high rates occurred in 1952 and 1959, with about .5 percent of work time lost in work stoppages. Between 1960 and 1979, only 1970 saw more than .25 percent of work time lost in strikes: U.S. Department of Labor, Bureau of Labor Statistics, "Work Stoppages," Summary 80-12 (December 1980), Table 1, p. 3. See also the classic analysis by Arthur Kornhauser, Robert Dubin, and Arthur M. Ross, eds., *Industrial Conflict* (New York: McGraw-Hill Book Co., 1954), pp. 3-22.

Although the U.S. has not lost large amounts of time to strikes, our record is worse than that of most other industrialized countries: Everett M. Kassalow, "Industrial Conflict in Europe and the United States," in Barbara B. Dennis, ed., *Proceedings of the Thirtieth Annual Winter Meeting* (Madison, Wisc.: Industrial Relations Research Association, 1977), pp. 113-22.

[36]Thomas A. Kochan, "Dynamics of Dispute Resolution in the Public Sector," in Benjamin Aaron, Joseph R. Grodin, and James L. Stern, eds., *Public-Sector Bargaining* (Madison, Wisc.: Industrial Relations Research Association, 1979), pp. 154-55.

The core sections of a negotiated agreement cover wages, hours, and working conditions. However, a great deal more is included in the contract, for instance, pensions, seniority provisions, cause for suspension and discharge, warnings, work rules, grievance handling, and contract renewal procedures. (Two pages of a contract are shown in Figure 4-1; the complete agreement ran to over 300 pages.) A contract is thus a complex document which can easily generate disagreement over its interpretation. Disputes arising over violation of a contract—lack of proper warning before suspension, for example—may give rise to a *grievance*.

FIGURE 4-1

Two Pages of a Contract

---

the time limits prescribed in Articles 14.2 and 14.3, the grievance may be appealed in the next stage of the procedure.

14.15 It is understood that the procedure outlined in Section 14.2 does not preclude the Foreman and the Employee from discussing any matter.

14.16 Notwithstanding the procedure herein provided, any grievance may be submitted to arbitration at any time by agreement between the Union's Staff Representative and the Company's Field Administrator.

14.17 Grievances resolved in Section 14.2 shall be considered resolved without precedent and shall not be used in the discussion of other grievances or arbitration cases.

ARTICLE 15—SUSPENSION AND DISCHARGES

Purpose

15.1 This article sets up special procedures for the prompt review and disposition of complaints involving the suspension or discharge of employees who have completed their probationary periods.

Initial Suspension

15.2 An employee shall not be discharged immediately. When the company concludes that an employee's conduct may justify discharge, or suspension for more than five working days, he will be so notified and immediately suspended initially for a period of six working days pending determination by the company.

Hearing and Grievance Procedure

15.3 During the six-day initial suspension period the employee may request a hearing before the plant manager or his designated representative, which hearing shall be granted within the six-day suspension period. If he chooses, the employee may be accompanied by a union grievance committeeman. At the

FIGURE 4–1 continued

hearing the company will state the offense and the facts concerning the case.

Within one working day after the hearing or within one working day after the end of the initial six-day suspension period if the employee does not request a hearing, the company will state in writing to the employee and the union that the six-day suspension is affirmed, modified, extended, revoked, or converted into a discharge. If the employee wishes to appeal the company's decision, he may, within two working days after notice of the decision, file a grievance at the second stage of the grievance procedure; if no such grievance is filed within this two-day period, the company's decision will be final.

Suspension of 5 Days or Less

15.1 Suspension of five working days or less may be taken up as grievances provided such grievances are filed and presented at the second stage of the grievance procedure within five working days from the beginning of the suspension period.

Reinstatement

15.5 If a suspension or discharge should be revoked by the company or not sustained in arbitration proceedings, the company will reinstate the employee without loss of seniority or accredited service and he will be made whole, without any offset for outside earnings. A lesser settlement may be agreed to by the employee, grievance committee and local management.

Notification

15.6 In all cases of suspension, the company will notify the union immediately if possible, but in no case later than the next day.

Discipline Records

15.7 Copies of disciplinary write-ups will be promptly given to the employee involved in the action and the president of the local union.

All disciplinary write-ups, except those involving suspensions of six (6) days or more, will be removed from the employee's personnel history folder after a period of one (1) year from the date of issuance of such discipline and thereafter shall not be relied upon for any purpose, by either party, excepting as may be necessary for processing and handling of complaints or charges filed outside of this agreement.

ARTICLE 16—LOCAL SUPPLEMENTS, CUSTOMS AND PRACTICES

16.1 This agreement supersedes all preceding written local agreements and supplements which were executed under the provisions of section 16.2 of the basic agreement dated March 16, 1950 as amended. Provisions contained in local

---

Source: Contract negotiated between American Can Company and United Steelworkers of America, for the period February 1974 to March 1977. The full text of the Agreement was 312 pages.

Contract negotiations and grievances are the two major focal points of disputes. To the degree that such disputes can be resolved under agreed-upon rules, the system of collective bargaining will churn out solutions rather than strikes. To a considerable extent, labor's loss of pay, and the employer's loss of profits, impose restraints on private-sector disputes because strikes are costly affairs. In the public sector, labor of course also loses pay in a work stoppage, and "management" foregoes the services labor provides; labor is therefore under pressure to settle, as is management if the public's convenience (transportation), health (sewage, garbage, municipal hospitals), or safety (fire, police) would be affected. So dispute resolution mechanisms are desirable to all parties. The American system of dispute resolution is built on contract rules that often call for mediation or arbitration.

Mediation is a process in which a third party makes proposals for resolving an impasse. The proposals are not binding, so the mediator must attempt to persuade the parties to accept them. A government agency, the Federal Mediation and Conciliation Service, employs mediators to aid in contract negotiation. Much of the mediators' work is at times of crisis bargaining, in the weeks and days just before a strike or lockout could erupt. Each year, the Federal Mediation and Conciliation Service assists in thousands of contract negotiations.

Arbitration, in contrast to mediation, is binding. In the public sector, in the event of an impasse, eighteen states require arbitration of contracts among their uniformed services (police, prison guards, firefighters), and several states require arbitration of all state and local public employee contract impasses.[37] Most states, however, require *fact-finding* as a contract resolution device. The fact finder is a neutral third party who looks into the facts of the disputed issues and makes recommendations. The fact finder's proposals are not binding.

Fact-finding, mediation, and arbitration, are important settlement procedures in the public sector. Few private-sector contracts go beyond requiring fact-finding or mediation in contract negotiation.

Arbitration, however, is used widely in both the public and private sectors as the final step in grievance handling.[38] Before resorting to an arbitrator, the foreman and shop steward (a worker delegated to handle complaints), as the first step, must attempt to resolve the complaint immediately. If the grievance remains unsettled, the next step is a union-management committee; if that does not resolve the issue, the grievance

---

[37]Kochan, "Dynamics of Dispute Resolution in the Public Sector," p. 154.
[38]Harold W. Davey, "Arbitration," in Bakke, Kerr and Anrod, eds., *Unions, Management and the Public*, pp. 323–29. Since the 1950s, about 90 percent of contracts require arbitration as the final step in grievance disputes.

may be pushed upward three or four times to committees composed of increasingly higher-level union and management officials. If the parties still can not settle the grievance, a third party, acceptable to both labor and management, is selected to rule on the dispute. The arbitrator interprets the contract to determine whose claim is valid. The contract, in this sense, is the law of the work place, and the arbitrator interprets this law and applies it.

Grievance handling is perhaps the most successful facet of labor-management relations under collective bargaining. (American-style grievance practices are not used outside North America. European unions, typically, have left local grievance processes outside their specific areas of concern and focus on collective bargaining at the national or regional industry level.)[39] Contract negotiations have proven less susceptible to such smooth settlement. With so much at stake, the parties are understandably reluctant to turn to arbitration or forego threats of strike or lockout. Nevertheless, as we saw, the overwhelming number of contract negotiations end successfully, without an open clash. There are now about 160,000 separate contracts in force,[40] and most of them were peacefully concluded.

Does unionism pay? Generally, yes. What is harder to answer is how much it benefits union members. Since an answer to "how much" depends on comparison between union and nonunion wages (and benefits), we should notice that union wages also affect nonunion employers. They too may follow along, at least roughly, in order to avoid unions. But it does appear that among employees doing approximately similar work, over the past twenty years there has been a 5 to 20 percent wage advantage in the private sector for union versus nonunion pay, with the low side of this estimated advantage for unionized federal workers and state and local public employees.[41]

Multi-year contracts, which most now are, might of course exert a drag on union wages. In a period of rapidly rising prices, the multi-year contract's wages may lag behind in the second and third years of the typical agreement, since wage increases usually decrease by about 1 percent in each year of a multi-year contract (say 8 percent increase the first year, 7 percent the second, and so on). On the other hand, COLA

[39]Oliver Clarke, "The Development of Industrial Relations in European Market Economies," in Barbara B. Dennis, ed., *Proceedings of the Thirty-Third Annual Meeting* (Madison, Wisc.: Industrial Relations Research Association, 1980), pp. 167–73.

[40]Barbash, "Collective Bargaining," p. 583.

[41]Marvin Kosters, "Relative Wages and Inflation," in Dennis, ed., *Proceedings of the Thirtieth Annual Winter Meeting*, p. 200; Daniel P. Mitchell, "The Impact of Collective Bargaining on Compensation in the Public Sector," in Aaron, Grodin, and Stern, eds., *Public-Sector Bargaining*, pp. 136, 141.

(cost-of-living adjustment) provisions recoup some of the lag. Over half of contracts now include COLA clauses and, on average, they yield 60 percent of the annual rise in the Consumer Price Index.[42]

To get a closer look at union and nonunion workers' gains in the private sector, we can compare the wage and benefit increases obtained in 1980:[43]

Unionized workers	10.4%
manufacturing	11.1
nonmanufacturing	9.8
Nonunion workers	8.6
manufacturing	8.7
nonmanufacturing	8.5

The average wage and benefit gain was thus over 10 percent among organized workers, compared to under 9 percent for the unorganized: The difference amounted to a 17 percent advantage in favor of unionized workers. In the organized public sector, the average 1980 increase in wages and benefits was slightly over 9 percent for federal workers, and just about reached 7 percent among state and local employees.[44]

People join unions to secure and improve their wages and benefits, and avoid arbitrary discharge or favoritism in all its forms.[45] Overall, the voice of unions has been audible in the work place.

The intent of labor law and the processes of fact-finding, mediation, and arbitration is the peaceful settlement of potentially conflicting interests. On the face of it, this may seem a good thing, and it is, but not always. Negotiated peace between a labor union and management may represent the taming of conflict, perhaps bought at too high a price. The problem is that if management yields to demands for costly settlements, labor peace is usually achieved by passing the settlement terms on to society. Barbash, a sympathetic and sensible observer of unions, put it this way: "how should the state intervene to minimize the inflationary effects of collective bargaining in the light of the demonstrated inefficiency of previous interventions to this end?" Unfortunately,

---

[42]U.S. Department of Labor, Bureau of Labor Statistics, *News*, January 26, 1981, pp. 1-2.

[43]Calculated from data in U.S. Department of Labor, Bureau of Labor Statistics, *Current Wage Developments*, April 1981, Table 10, p. 41.

[44]U.S. Department of Labor, Bureau of Labor Statistics, *Current Wage Developments*, February 1981, p. 38. Federal employee gains are from *Current Wage Developments*, January 1981, p. 41. The 9 percent increase is an estimate based on the average increase for non-executive-level federal workers.

[45]E. Wight Bakke, "To Join or Not to Join," in Bakke, Kerr, and Anrod, eds., *Unions, Management and the Public*, pp. 85-92.

neither he nor others offer a good answer to either that question or another Barbash posed: "What should be done about public-sector strikes which (a) disrupt or threaten public order and health, and (b) defy the law in a manner amounting to mass civil disobedience?"[46]

These issues are serious and difficult—serious because they ripple out to affect so many people, and difficult because their solution would require the willingness to defer gains. Most people, however, have their own families to provide for and the bills keep coming. The issue, really, is how to reconcile self-interest with the public interest. To that there is no easy answer.

Finally, let us notice that American unions, in contrast to their West European counterparts, do not have much interest in "co-determination."[47] Co-determination places worker representatives on company boards of directors—as in West Germany, Sweden, and Holland—usually as one-third of a board's members. Legislation, backed by unions, requires such worker representation. Additionally, most European countries also require "works councils." Production workers and white-collar employees, in rough proportion to their number in a firm, serve on these councils, which have consultative rights on matters affecting labor.

Neither membership on boards of directors nor works councils have been an attractive idea on this side of the Atlantic. Union members and labor leaders in the United States hold the conviction that their aims can best be achieved through existing forms of collective bargaining. And, perhaps most significant, there is scant ideological support among either labor leaders or union members for going beyond current forms of representation through unions.

OVERVIEW

Two major ways in which people attempt to improve work outcomes are through individual action and collective activity. Individuals may change jobs, with the expectation that there will be some advantages to the change. Overall, a moderate upward movement (intragenerational mobility) is discernible among job changers. Individuals may also alter their work outcomes, compared to their fathers' outcomes (intergenerational mobility). Educational credentials are the single most

---

[46]Barbash, "Collective Bargaining," p. 587.

[47]Ted Mills, *Industrial Democracy in Europe: A 1977 Survey* (Washington, D.C.: American Center for the Quality of Work Life, 1978), pp. 20–28; Daniel Zwerdling, *Democracy at Work* (Washington, D.C.: Association for Self-Management, 1978), pp. 165–80.

important element in gaining a higher socioeconomic status than one's father, or slipping downward. Again, there is a net upward movement between generations; women's upward mobility, however, is weaker than men's, when occupational mobility between generations is examined.

Protecting and enhancing work outcomes by collective representation through unions was firmly legitimated in the mid-1930s with the Wagner Act. Under the act, nonsupervisory employees have the right to organize, and employers are required to bargain in good faith with the employees' chosen representatives. About one out of every four members of the labor force is currently in a union or union-like association. The evidence indicates that organized workers' pay and benefits are generally favorable compared to nonorganized employees. Collective bargaining, during the life of a contract, temporarily rests specific labor-management concerns; old concerns, along with new ones, are then taken up once more in the next round of bargaining.

The public interest is necessarily affected by collective bargaining, since generous wage settlements or work stoppages affect the public's consumption dollars, convenience, and sometimes even health and safety. The dilemma is that in a situation of conflicting goals, it is impossible to devise laws that simultaneously benefit everyone. All societies generate conflicting interests—the difference is that in some its expression is protected, while in others it is suppressed.

5. Epilogue

RETROSPECT

As late as the eighteenth century, over 90 percent of people everywhere lived by farming. In the Western world, the long-lived manorial system of self-sufficient production eventually came to coexist with the craft and merchant guilds that developed in medieval towns. The land, however, was still the source of livelihood for all but the relatively few town dwellers. The putting-out system gradually displaced guilds, although cottage industry was always only a meager supplement to rural families' agricultural incomes.

With the rise of industrialization—initially in Britain and then spreading to western Europe and the United States—the factory mode of production altered the location and means of livelihood of the millions of people drawn into towns to find work. Within the brief span of a hundred years, the industrialized Western nations became dotted with large urban centers of manufacturing, commerce, and finance. In the United States the pace of industrialization was heady indeed, compressed into a remarkably few decades. Spurred in the 1860s by the Civil War's enormous appetite for manufactured goods, American industry made up for lost time and in the early 1890s equaled the combined output of England, France, and Germany.[1]

---

[1] Herbert G. Gutman, *Work, Culture and Society in Industrializing America* (New York: Vintage Books, 1977), p. 33. The period 1860–1890 was also a time of monumental immigration. In these decades America's population grew from 31 million to 63 million. In the peak years, 1860–1870, the population soared an astounding 27 percent. The magnitude of immigration and its impact are examined in Hilda H. Golden's *Urbanization and Cities* (Lexington, Mass.: D. C. Heath and Co., 1981), pp. 202–7.

Among non-Western countries, only Japan took the path of industrialization. After the revolution of 1868, the new government made industrialization a primary national goal.

Along with industrialization standards of living rose. The relatively abrupt increase of material goods is neatly captured in Daniel Bell's summary:

> From the earliest times, back to two thousand years before Christ, down to the eighteenth century there was no very great change in the standard of life of the average man living in the civilized centres of earth. But with the combination of technical efficiency and capital accumulation, mankind had discovered the "magic" of "compound interest," of growth building on growth.... Think of this in terms of material things—houses, transport and the like.[2]

The populations of industrialized countries today enjoy a standard of living immensely higher than those of nonindustrialized nations. The world's population of 4.5 billion people is projected to reach over 6 billion by the year 2000, and about 80 percent of them will inhabit the poorest countries in the nonindustrialized regions of Asia, Latin America, and Africa.[3] That is the scenario if current trends in population growth and economic disparities persist between the prosperous and poor nations. There is presently little reason to assume that this dour projection is not essentially correct. Industrialization of the poorest regions will be slow at best, and improving their living standards will depend on restraining population growth.

UTOPIA IS ELUSIVE

It is no coincidence that industrialization in the nineteenth century was accompanied by the call for social reform. For the first time in human history it was possible to imagine material abundance; the central problem was its distribution. This is at the core of Karl Marx's critique of capitalism: As an engine to drive investment and production, capitalism was unsurpassed; its fatal flaw, however, according to Marx, was the unequal access to material goods, which would inevitably result in great luxury for some and poverty for most. Only an entirely different type of economy was capable of overcoming such deep-rooted inequality—an economy with common ownership of the means of production and the distribution of output according to need.

The Marxist critique of capitalism has had a discernible impact in two important respects: The effect has been intellectual in the sense that it has

---

[2]Daniel Bell, *The Coming of Post-Industrial Society* (New York: Basic Books, Inc., 1975), pp. 459–60.

[3]Gus Speth, "Resources and Society: The Global 2000 Report," *National Forum*, 61 (1981): 34–35.

attracted reform-minded persons in some academic and labor circles (particularly in Europe), and political in the sense that leaders of revolutions in Russia, China, and Cuba used Marxist doctrine to gain broad-based support among local populations. (Perversely refusing to confirm Marx's theory of revolutionary locations, economic conditions favored, and still do, revolutions in agriculturally based societies rather than highly industrialized nations.)

Marx was a profoundly pessimistic thinker on economic matters. However, the doom and gloom he anticipated for industrialized countries that failed to overthrow capitalism did not come about. Over the long haul, living standards rose steeply, in large part because industrial productivity increased enormously, and to some extent because organized labor made its voice heard on the issue of wages. Russia, the nation with the longest record of a nationalized, command economy (the means of production are controlled by government) has a GNP roughly half that of the United States, and its standard of living for the average wage earners is about one-quarter of ours.[4] Marx sketched the outlines of an economy that freed people from material scarcities and a political system that ended the repression of man by man when the private ownership of the means of production was ended. Very few observers would claim that this vision has materialized or is on its way to embodiment in the U.S.S.R. or other command economies.

The point is not that a government-managed economy is in all respects inferior to an economy based on privately owned enterprise—indeed, in the Soviet Union the fear of unemployment, for example, is not nearly as common as in the U.S.[5]—but as a system for stocking stores with agricultural and manufactured goods, the government-managed economy has a far poorer record. I mentioned job security, since that is an especially serious concern, and it is not difficult to find other problems—urban decay, crime, poverty among the elderly and minorities, weak public transportation systems, and so on. Despite all this, it is still true that most people in the United States (and the West in general, plus Japan) enjoy a standard of living that is not matched elsewhere. Although the utopian vision of plenty for all has not become reality in command economies, it is also the case that our ability to

---

[4]Robert W. Campbell, *The Soviet-Type Economies* (Boston: Houghton Mifflin Co., 1974), pp. 103, 105. For a penetrating discussion of the situation of Soviet and East European workers, see Seymour M. Lipset, "Industrial Proletariat in Comparative Perspective," in Jan F. Triska and Charles Gati, eds., *Blue Collar Workers in Eastern Europe* (Boston: Allen and Unwin, 1981), pp. 29–42.

[5]Hedrick Smith, *The Russians* (New York: Ballantine Books, 1976), p. 90; Paul Hollander, *Soviet and American Society* (New York: Oxford University Press, 1973), p. 232.

produce material goods has not yielded utopia either. Economic systems, then, are less an answer to all problems than they are alternative means of providing bread and washing machines. Command economies provide the material stuff of life less amply than economies based on privately held firms.

The primary reason is that in a command economy, such as the Soviet Union's, centrally determined quotas provide an incentive just to meet the quota; if the quota is met, everyone can look forward to a steady job and a bonus. Production plans and output goals are too well insulated from the marketplace. Profitability, in contrast, is more rough and tumble. If people will pay for something, provide it; if a higher price can be gained, ask for it; if a higher wage is thinkable, demand it; if the company is overstaffed, lay people off. The play of self-interest is scarcely constrained. Perhaps that is what is really meant by the notion of "free enterprise." In the command economy, self-interest is active also, but is channeled along lines that satisfy the planners that the economic blueprint is being followed. That is a fundamental difference, so it is not at all surprising that our firms churn out a huge variety and amount of goods, because a profit can be made, while the command economy cranks out goods more sparingly.

Most of us prefer to consume more rather than less, and we grumble unless our incomes permit increasingly higher consumption, or as one would say in polite company, improve our standard of living. Yet that goal may, in the absence of socially unifying ethical restraints, stimulate unbridled egoism.

Ordinarily we are disturbed by the political limitations under which people live in, let me call it, a *command society*, such as the Soviet Union. Mass communications, schools, youth groups are all in the service of the state; the aim is to create a like-thinking populace that loyally supports the regime and its programs. This sort of systematic attempt to indoctrinate and control is deeply troubling to Westerners. But perhaps we miss the crucial point in our hurry to pass moral judgment—the Soviets have something we lack. Some of the propaganda, indoctrination, socialization—call it what you like— inevitably affects the beliefs of citizens exposed daily to it, from cradle to grave. The message is: "Work hard for the benefit of society, be disciplined, be loyal, trust your leaders. Communism is the wave of the future. It is morally superior to the decadent West." And accompanying this is the heavy hand of the censors. Their task is to prevent information critical of the regime from reaching the population.

The result is not only awareness of an official ideology (to which lip service must be given), but also at least the kernel of a set of values, an ethic, that provides the individual with a life purpose and meshes that purpose with societal ends.

In the U.S. (and the West generally), in contrast, we are daily bombarded with criticism of leaders, policies, institutions. (I am *not* saying that criticism is necessarily unwarranted, only that it is present.) This too inevitably rubs off in bits and pieces, contributing to the detachment of individuals from society. Consider the missing element of a value system that contrains egoism and links the individual to a collective purpose, and the dilemma can be seen.

Daniel Bell's observation reveals the heart of this situation:[6]

By the middle of the twentieth century capitalism sought to justify itself. . .by the status badges of material possessions and by the promotion of pleasure. The rising standard of living and the relaxation of morals became ends in themselves as the definition of personal freedom. . . .[The] system is completely mundane, for any transcendent ethic has vanished. . . .Material goods provide only transient satisfaction or an invidious comparison over those with less. . . .The lack of a rooted moral belief system is the cultural contradiction of the society, the deepest challenge to its survival.

Similarly, Peter Berger noted:[7]

. . .socialism continues to activate profound, even mythic, aspirations for community and solidarity. . . .Capitalism has been singularly unsuccessful in coping with this category of human needs.

The absence of shared values that bond people to each other and to society is, it seems, a more deep-seated dilemma than the more familiar social ills to which the media usually direct attention. The fragility of a society devoted to personal satisfaction does suggest concern for its longevity.

Individualism has been an effective mechanism for generating material goods, but it leaves people ethically adrift and the society peculiarly vulnerable to individuals' denial of the obligation to restrain egoism in its collective behalf. Relations between the individual and society may seem a bit far afield from concern with work life, but if one thinks about it, our everyday world of work also reflects an egocentric ethos, or its derivative, located in groups. It is visible in the mistrust between employees and employers, and is most clearly apparent in union-management relations. Union-management relations are essentially a

---

[6]Bell, *The Coming of Post-Industrial Society*, pp. 477–78, 480.
[7]Peter L. Berger, *Pyramids of Sacrifice* (Garden City, N.Y.: Anchor Books, 1976), p. 63.

form of legitimized conflict in which each side pursues its interests without regard for the public. Moreover, it is not unreasonable to believe that adversarial work relationships—whether acted out by organized or unorganized employees—do not help to boost productivity or quality.

In the fiercely competitive markets of the 1980s, the ability to compete in international trade with attractively priced, high-quality products, has become crucial; jobs, taxes, and national self-confidence are at stake. Notice, for instance, that Xerox's share of sales dollars for copiers in the American market plummeted from 96 percent in 1970 to 46 percent in 1980.[8] The dominant position of Xerox was eroded by good lower-priced copiers produced in Japan. Contributing to Xerox's problems was poor planning by management, which failed to anticipate and counter foreign competitors' inroads on the market. Personnel cuts at all levels became part of Xerox's response strategy. "We have too much manpower generally in the company," said President David Dearns, "and we've got to drive up productivity at a much faster rate."[9] In the unionized sector, a similar short-sightedness afflicted executives and labor leaders in such basic industries as steel and autos: During the 1970s, prices climbed, along with wage costs, while the competition from overseas gained momentum.

It would be overstating the case to propose that improved employee-organization relations are all that is needed to improve our competitive position—but that would certainly be a very substantial help. Table 3-16 showed that U.S. productivity increases for the period 1973–1980 dropped far behind Japan's. In 1980 the situation grew worse: U.S. manufacturing productivity declined, whereas Japan registered a 6.2 percent gain. If we look back to 1960 through 1973, we still find a large difference. Over that span of years American manufacturing productivity rose at an annual average rate of slightly more than 3 percent, while the corresponding rate in Japan was over 10 percent.

An obvious and intriguing question arises: What are they doing that might be beneficial in the U.S. context? Apparently there are some practices that are well worth considering, and these practices, it turns out, aim toward minimizing the loss of productive human energy that so easily occurs with adversarial relations. The Japanese have somehow created work relationships that have more of a collaborative quality. Let us see what that "somehow" is by taking a bird's-eye view of Japanese work arrangements and culture.

---

[8]"The New Lean, Mean Xerox," *Business Week*, October 12, 1981, p. 126.
[9]Ibid., p. 128.

A GLANCE AT JAPAN

The taken-for-granted beliefs and behaviors among the members of a society are the result of lengthy exposure to others who hold the beliefs and encourage the behaviors. In the terminology of the social sciences, the social definition of values and behavior appropriate to situations is labeled "culture." If there are deep ethnic divisions in a society, substantial immigration from culturally different areas of the world, marked rural-urban or social class differences in outlook and behavior, the notion of a uniform cultural canopy is certainly less applicable than to a more homogeneous society, such as Japan, which ranks low on these indicators of diversity. Japan, moreover, does not leave to chance the cultural upbringing of its youth.

The ministry of education prepares detailed curriculum guidelines for all courses in all schools, through grade twelve, including "ethics" courses.[10] Educators, appointed by the ministry, select four or five textbooks for every subject in each course. These "approved" books are used nationwide. The intent is to provide similar materials to all students.

Comparing U.S. and Japanese educational assumptions, Vogel comments:[11]

> Japanese travelling to French Canada, Belgium, New York and other areas with dual cultures are surprised that minority groups are required to know so little of the dominant culture and language. In their view it is ultimately damaging to minority groups not to provide and require the same high level of training as that of the majority,...for without it minority groups ...would not be able to compete effectively in the marketplace....The Japanese...have more confidence in training the entire population to meet a high level of educational standards.

Aside from the interesting observation that Japanese education is geared to a more equal achievement standard than ours, Vogel points to a more subtle cultural phenomenon: the lack of assumptions by teachers about incapacitating individual differences. Whereas American teacher training makes a virtue of accommodating diversity in students' learning abilities, the Japanese teacher is more disposed to see virtue in disciplined study among all students so that even the slowest reaches a reasonably demanding standard.

---

[10]For a summary of Japan's educational practices, see Ezra Vogel, *Japan as Number One* (New York: Harper Colophon Books, 1980), pp. 167–83.
[11]Ibid., p. 179.

Japanese culture emphasizes collective ends. Groups and group goals are primary, whereas individuals' inclinations are de-emphasized. Loyalty to a membership group is the major requirement for gaining others' respect.[12]

Japanese Productivity Inducements

In the work setting this cultural emphasis has become embedded in specific personnel practices among large firms as well as government bureaus. People who enter a company in a given year are usually promoted as a group, rather than singling out especially meritorious persons. The company is paternalistic, providing dormitories and housing allowances, family allowances, food commissaries, day care and medical facilities, vacation hotels, group travel arrangements.[13]

The larger and more successful firms offer these benefits, while the smaller ones attempt to approximate them. Over and above all this are two particularly significant personnel practices: permanent employment and the bonus system.

In the larger companies both managers and workers, after a probationary period, receive the status of permanent employee. (This is not, however, a contractual, legally binding arrangement.) In the 1960s a number of smaller firms were able to offer permanent employment to key personnel. Estimates vary, but it appears that around 35 percent or so of the work force has permanent employment. (Women are excluded from this employment arrangement, although discharging any employee is avoided by all firms whenever possible.)[14] Permanent or lifetime employment means just that: The employee has assured job security. We will return to this after looking at the bonus system.

The average Japanese wage is approximately half of the U.S. wage, but only for direct base wages. On top of this go the various benefits already mentioned, and twice yearly bonuses which equal between 75 to 100 percent of the base wage.[15] The size of the semi-annual bonus is

[12]Chie Nakane, *Japanese Society* (Berkeley, Calif.: University of California Press, 1970), chapters 1–2.

[13]Ernest van Helvoort, *The Japanese Working Man* (Vancouver, B.C.: University of British Columbia Press, 1979), pp. 99–104.

[14]Ibid., p. 35. Firms with permanent employment still have substantial flexibility by also using personnel more easily dismissed: (1) temporary employees, who are hired with the understanding that they are temporary; (2) workers brought into a company by labor contractors for a specific time period; and (3) satellite firms, which perform work for a larger firm under a contract or as a subsidiary. Robert Cole, *Japanese Blue Collar* (Berkeley, Calif.: University of California Press, 1971), pp. 37–40; Ronald Dore, *British Factory-Japanese Factory* (Berkeley, Calif.: University of California Press, 1973), pp. 31–33.

[15]Vogel, *Japan as Number One*, pp. 138–39; van Helvoort, *The Japanese Working Man*, p. 95; Lester C. Thurow, *The Zero-Sum Society* (New York: Penguin Books, 1981), p. 84.

determined by a firm's profitability for the six months preceding the bonus. So economically successful firms distribute bigger bonuses while those that fare less well give smaller bonuses.[16]

Permanent employment and the bonus system create a tight bond between employees and their companies. These twin policies mesh workers' self-interest with organizational goals of productivity and high quality. It is to the employees' advantage to contribute to a firm's prosperity because that assures secure employment and a larger bonus. It is also to the company's advantage to train its members, since the investment in training will not be lost through turnover; and it is to the workers' advantage to develop their skills because doing so contributes to the enterprise's success.

This framework contrasts sharply with our approach to industrial relations. The threat of job loss is often present, and we prefer that income be clearly specified beforehand, usually over a two- or three-year period in unionized firms, without prudent regard for market conditions unless bankruptcy is in sight. Moreover, productivity increases may weaken job security (fewer people can do the work) and has no clear or direct bearing on employees' incomes. Skill development through training is risky for the firm (our labor turnover is high), while for the employee, more highly developed skills may or may not be recognized through heightened job security or a fatter paycheck. All in all, management and employees too often jockey for short-term advantages and too rarely pursue the same goals for everyone's long-run benefit.

Personnel practices in Japan are designed to minimize adversarial relations. Permanent employment and the bonus system generate a situation in which it is in the individual's self-interest to contribute energy, intelligence, and loyalty to the enterprise. Each employee has a stake in the firm's future because each will benefit from its prosperity or experience disadvantages if it falters. Concern with productivity and quality is directly encouraged by the situation and reinforced within work groups because the lazy or noncooperative worker's behavior is damaging to work mates. The Japanese way of doing work fosters cooperation with the goal of productivity improvement; it is a tough system to compete against.

Lessons From Japan

It is not possible to transplant Japan's cultural patterns, nor would we necessarily wish to do so. Although it is true that their cultural emphasis

---

[16]Japanese firms are unionized along the lines of "company unions," only loosely affiliated in confederations. These company unions, however, are very active in negotiating the relative shares of the total bonus payout to different levels of employees.

on loyalty to one's employer and work group contributes to high productivity, so do secure employment and hefty bonuses by integrating workers' interests with company success. In the words of economist Lester Thurow:[17]

> Every worker has an incentive to maximize productivity by welcoming technical change, learning new skills, and contributing to industrial teamwork in a way that makes U.S. employers envious. Faced with the same incentives, U.S. workers would respond in the same way.

That is precisely what we can learn from Japan: provide the incentives that make productivity gains important to all members of a firm. Both common sense and evidence support this idea. The U.S. General Accounting Office in a recent study of thirty-six firms with productivity sharing programs found that they outperformed companies without such programs. Productivity sharing plans resulted in substantial output gains, more take-home pay for employees, and reduced labor costs in the range of 8 to 29 percent.[18] The plans differed, but had in common frequent bonuses, elimination of individual incentives, and employee involvement in suggesting ways to improve productivity. Over half of the firms with productivity sharing programs were unionized; but in all instances labor-management relations improved, and absenteeism and turnover declined.

Perhaps the most revealing American success story is Lincoln Electric. Since 1934 Lincoln Electric has had remarkably high productivity, low turnover, and excellent labor relations.[19] Its founder, James F. Lincoln, laid down these principles, and stuck to them:

1.   Protect every employee's job security. More productivity must not harm the employee.
2.   Increased productivity must result in greater take-home pay and more job security.
3.   Pass along reduced costs to the consumer, to strengthen the company in the marketplace and thus add to job security.
4.   Reinvest the company's earnings to improve the plant and Lincoln's competitive position.

---

[17]Thurow, *The Zero-Sum Society*, p. 84.

[18]"Sharing the Gains," *World of Work Report* 6 (1981): 64; "Productivity Sharing Plans Can Cut Costs, Boost Productivity," *World of Work Report*, 6 (1981): 77–78.

[19]For a report on Lincoln Electric, see Mitchell Fein, "Motivation for Work," in Robert Dubin, ed., *Handbook of Work, Organization, and Society* (Chicago: Rand McNally College Publishing Co., 1976), pp. 510–15.

The pace of work at Lincoln is as fast as anywhere in the world. Lincoln's workers do not fear that high output will lead to job cuts; instead, they look forward to larger bonuses. Since 1934, Lincoln has distributed each year to every employee a bonus ranging from 26 percent of annual pay to 100 percent. Fein noted in his report on Lincoln Electric that its employees have the world's highest earnings, and that Lincoln is nevertheless able to sell its products worldwide in competition with lower paid foreign labor. "If the Lincoln experience can be established in other companies, high productivity increases can be accomplished.... Unleashing the will to work does not require new equipment or plant facilities—only the desire of workers to reach goals."[20]

It seems that Lincoln's policies are strikingly similar to Japanese firms' practices, and in both, everyone has benefited. A number of other U.S. companies—IBM, Intel, Rockwell, Hewlett-Packard, Dayton-Hudson—have independently developed Japanese-type practices, and it has paid off.[21] Employees are willing to work more energetically, develop their skills, stick with a firm, and work cooperatively, *if* there are incentives that make doing so in their interest.

USEFUL BUT STILL WEAK REFORMS

Some American work places have installed various plans intended to make work more pleasant (job enrichment), more involving (participation), or convenient (flexible work hours) in order to raise productivity and reduce absenteeism and turnover. Some observers, perhaps gilding the lily, refer to such programs as "empowerment" because decisions regarding tasks or work hours are given over to employees or at least shared with them.[22] Let us look briefly at these reforms.

Much has been written on job enrichment, although the number of workers in such programs is only a tiny fraction of our working population.[23] Job enrichment, also called job redesign, gives the worker some say over the sequence in which the steps in a task are accomplished, and discretion regarding the steps necessary to complete a task. Enrichment essentially involves the creation of a "whole task" with

---

[20]Ibid., p. 513.

[21]William Ouchi, *Theory Z* (Reading, Mass.: Addison-Wesley Publishing Co., 1981).

[22]Gale Miller, *It's a Living* (New York: St. Martin's Press, 1981), pp. 248–83. Miller presents a good overview of this approach to work reform and its assumptions.

[23]One estimate gives the number as under 5,000: Report of a Special Task Force to the Secretary of Health, Education and Welfare, *Work in America* (Cambridge, Mass.: MIT Press, 1973), p. 103.

some variety in the work routine. On the plant floor a worker might assemble the whole control panel of an automatic washing machine, then test the panel, and if necessary, make appropriate corrections. Enrichment in the office might require a clerk to process a whole application for insurance. In both cases (they are drawn from actual programs) very short, fragmented tasks—taking from one minute to five—were redesigned into modules taking as long as thirty minutes.[24] Nearly all reports on enrichment programs, not surprisingly, are based on relatively successful experiences that will not embarrass a firm or the consultants involved in the program. Interestingly, data on a program that collapsed (the participants opted out) indicate that it failed because workers' added responsibilities were not reflected in the pay scheme.[25]

Social scientists have urged employee participation in work decisions for nearly three decades. The recommended forms vary from informal consultation between supervisors and workers to formalized "linking-pin" relations in which each supervisor presents the decisions of his or her work group to the next higher organization level.[26] Although interest in "traditional" participation schemes has persisted,[27] much of the current attention has focused on "Quality Control (Q-C) Circles." It is no exaggeration to say that Q-C Circles have become the fastest growing organizational fad pushed by consulting firms. Some version of the Q-C Circle is now present in hundreds of U.S. companies, including such

---

[24]For a review of literature and cases see Curt Tausky and E. Lauck Parke, "Job Enrichment, Need Theory, and Reinforcement Theory," in Dubin, ed., *Handbook of Work, Organization, and Society*, pp. 531-65; also J. Richard Hackman and Greg R. Oldham, *Work Redesign* (Reading, Mass.: Addison-Wesley Publishing Co., 1980). In Sweden, Volvo has incorporated work teams in some of its assembly operations. Teams of five to seven people assemble a whole motor; the team members divide the work among themselves in any way they prefer, including taking turns assembling the whole motor. K. G. Karlsson, *The Volvo Kalmar Plant* (Stockholm: The Rationalization Council SAF-LO, 1976). A good review of job redesign in Western Europe is presented in Lisl Klein, *New Forms of Work Organization* (New York: Cambridge University Press, 1976).

[25]Paul J. Champagne and Curt Tausky, "When Job Enrichment Doesn't Pay," *Personnel*, 55 (1978): 30-40.

[26]On such schemes and related data, see: Arnold S. Tannenbaum, *Control in Organizations* (New York: McGraw-Hill Book Co., 1968); Rensis Likert, *New Patterns of Management* (New York: McGraw-Hill Book Co., 1961).

[27]For instance, David G. Bowers, *Systems of Organization: The Management of the Human Resource* (Ann Arbor, Mich.: University of Michigan Press, 1976); Paul E. Mott, *The Characteristics of Effective Organizations* (New York: Harper and Row, 1972; Paul Bernstein, *Workplace Democratization: Its Internal Dynamics* (Kent, Ohio: Kent State University Press, 1976). The latter book also discusses and offers data on the most significant form of participation—worker-owned enterprises. They are relatively scarce, however. Bernstein focuses on sixteen plywood firms in the Pacific Northwest. Their economic performance, not surprisingly, has been quite good, since bonuses based on profitability boost workers' incomes and the value of their stock in the enterprise is increased by productivity gains.

firms as American Airlines, Honeywell Corporation, General Motors, and Metropolitan Life Insurance Company.[28]

The Q-C Circle concept comes from Japan, which in turn drew on statistical techniques for assessing quality and productivity popularized by W. E. Deming, an American professor of statistics. To learn these methods is not an overwhelming chore, but it does require a company's investment in employee training. The larger Japanese firms have made this investment (recall the practices of permanent employment and bonuses, which encourage such investment and workers' willingness to learn).

American Q-C Circles are much less statistically oriented, although they are formed on similar lines and with similar goals: the work group and its supervisor uncovering production or quality problems and coming up with solutions. Typically, a management team then evaluates the suggestions and approves or disapproves them. The large majority of Q-C Circles here and in Japan have been organized among blue-collar workers although a number of American firms are trying them among office workers and technical specialists.

Robert Cole, a shrewd observer of the Q-C Circle movement, notes that most of the U.S. Q-C Circles have existed for less than two years, so evaluating them on the basis of such a short experience is risky. However, indications of problems, he goes on to say, are already apparent: In some unionized firms, the circles are seen as an attempt to increase productivity without sharing the rewards, or as a way to gain workers' loyalty at the union's expense. Circle activities are often conducted after working hours, and American employers are not always ready to offer overtime pay (in Japan that is not necessary). Q-C Circle members are at times reluctant to make suggestions, and middle management has sometimes been less than enthusiastic about endorsing and facilitating the formation of Q-C Circles.[29]

These difficulties reflect the underlying problem to which Cole points:[30]

In large-scale Japanese organizations, management has been able to...use peer pressure on the shop floor to encourage workers to join and participate in circle activities. In the United States, given the adversary

[28]Robert E. Cole, "QC Warning Voiced by U.S. Expert on Japanese Circles," *World of Work Report*, 6 (1981): 49; Fritz K. Plous, Jr., "The Quality Circle Concept: Growing by Leaps and Bounds," Ibid., p. 25; New York Stock Exchange, *People and Productivity: A Challenge to Corporate America* (New York: N.Y.S.S.E., 1981), p. 26.
[29]Cole, "QC Warning Voiced by U.S. Expert on Japanese Circles," pp. 50–51.
[30]Ibid., p. 50.

relationships that predominate between management and labor, it is
difficult to mobilize such pressures. The circles are often seen as one more
in a series of management gimmicks designed to hustle the workers.

We will return to adversarial relationships in a moment, since the success
of potentially useful innovative programs hinges on reshaping these
relations.

Flexible work hours, or "flexitime," has also received a good deal of
attention. The specific purpose of flexitime is the reduction of tardiness
and absenteeism: By making work hours more convenient, people will
not need to be late for work or take a whole day off to see a doctor or
attend to other errands. About 10 percent of American workers have
flexible schedules, according to a survey sponsored by the Bureau of the
Census.[31]

Flexitime works like this:

> The fixed daily schedule, during which everyone is expected to work, is
> designated as "core time." This period commonly is 4 to 6 hours in
> length....A "flexible band" of up to several hours during which a worker
> can elect to begin work at any time replaced a specific starting time.
> Similarly, a specific quitting time is replaced by a band of several hours
> following core time.[32]

Just how flexible a schedule may be varies widely. There are differences
in the span of core hours and flexible bands on both sides (starting and
quitting times) of the core; and under some programs, employees can
carry "debit" hours for one day and make them up the next day or
within the week.[33] Flexitime programs have been used mainly among
managers, sales personnel, and clerical workers. Flexible schedules are
rarely applied to production jobs because whenever a set of tasks is so
highly interdependent that all workers must be present at the same
time—as on an assembly line—flexitime is not suitable. To use flexitime,
the work itself would have to be reorganized with an eye toward

---

[31]U.S. Department of Labor, Bureau of Labor Statistics, *News*, February 24, 1981, p. 1.

[32]Janice N. Hedges, "Flexible Schedules: Problems and Issues," *Monthly Labor Review*,
100 (1977): 62. Some companies have used a quite different form of alternative work
schedule, the compressed work week. For example, Prudential Insurance Company, at its
computing center, has twelve-and-a-half hour shifts working three days a week, Monday,
Tuesday, and Wednesday, or Thursday, Friday, and Saturday, with employees rotating
shifts every two weeks: Jill C. Lotto, "At Prudential: A Ten Year Track Record in New
Work Schedules," *World of Work Report*, 6 (1981): 90, 92. Only about 2 percent of full-
time American workers, however, have compressed workweeks of four days or less. U.S.
Department of Labor, Bureau of Labor Statistics, *News*, February 24, 1981, Table 1.

[33]In Europe, flexitime provisions are less restrictive because overtime pay requirements
are less controlled by laws. Thus a worker may make up "debit" hours in a following week
or even another month.

minimizing task interdependence, perhaps by forming work teams which used flexitime within each team (as, for example, at Saab's assembly plant in Sweden).[34]

Having looked now at several innovative programs, how might they be assessed? The typical results of these programs are that job enrichment improves quality, but without much if any impact on quantity. Some Quality Control Circles have uncovered production problems; yet, workers' interest in participating in Q-C Circles has often been less than enthusiastic and eliciting suggestions has proven difficult. Flexitime has aided in decreasing tardiness while more modestly reducing absenteeism.[35]

CHALLENGE AND RESPONSE

The programs we have reviewed have promise, but fall short of coming to grips with the underlying dilemma of adversarial relationships. Until that problem is resolved, no scheme is likely to extend its effects beyond rather restrained improvements. Adversarial relations are not handily detectable in strike statistics; their results are usually more subtle because they inhibit concern with higher productivity and better quality. There is, it seems to me, no mystery about the personnel policies that are sufficiently potent to stimulate substantial gains in cooperation. With the twin policies of secure jobs and profit sharing,[36] the perception of a shared fate emerges. Without such a perception, adversarial relations will most likely persist.

It is doubtful, however, that we can collectively continue to afford the results of antagonistic relations—sluggish or nonexistent productivity increases accompanied by wage and price boosts. This is not merely gloomy speculation. There are, unfortunately, solid reasons for

---

[34]In Saab's plant in Trollhattan, Sweden, seven-member teams perform their work within a specified period; within that time, the work teams schedule their own members' time. The work to be done comes from a pool called a "buffer." After a team finishes its task, the partly completed car goes into another buffer ready for the next team to do its task. At Trollhattan the teams repair their own machinery and monitor quality. Incentive pay of about twenty-two cents per hour is provided to team members for the added responsibilities: "Team Assembly at Saab," *World of Work Report*, 6 (1981): 94–95.

[35]Edward E. Lawler, "Job Design and Employee Motivation," in Richard Steers and Lyman W. Porter, eds., *Motivation and Work Behavior* (New York: McGraw-Hill Book Co., 1975), pp. 417–40, especially pp. 422–23 for a summary of quality and quantity effects; Cole, "QC Warning Voiced by U.S. Expert on Japanese Circles," p. 50; Hedges, "Flexible Schedules: Problems and Issues," p. 63.

[36]As of 1980, only 15 percent of production workers and 20 percent of professional and administrative employees worked under profit-sharing plans. U.S. Department of Labor, Bureau of Labor Statistics, *News*, June 26, 1981, p. 9.

suggesting that collaboration among all parties to raise productivity is now a necessity.

Foreign competition in U.S. markets and abroad, particularly by Japan, presents a very serious challenge to our industries. The Japanese are able to manufacture a wide variety of good products—steel, cars, watches, cameras, textiles, copiers, calculators, and so on—at lower cost than we can. This feature of life will not melt away.[37] It is a challenge that must be recognized.[38] Additionally, in this era of multinational companies, alternative locations for factories and labor are administratively quite feasible. If it is financially advantageous to do so, multinationals, including U.S.-based ones, can produce in Mexico, Taiwan, or other places and import finished or semi-finished products to the American market. The alternative locations are available; work can be done elsewhere.

These considerations may sound harsh, but they address the world in which we live. It is a turbulent world of relatively new political and economic forces, which we are reluctant to acknowledge fully. In view of the economic challenge confronting us, the necessary response is to fashion policies that raise productivity. Unlike bees or ants, humans are not born with an instinct that energizes cooperative productive activity. Our imperfect substitute for this instinctual prompting is socially constructed and takes the form of inducements to perform work and do so in particular ways. Organizationally, this is visible in reward systems.

Due to individual variability of responses, no plan will yield exactly its intended results. But we can all benefit by understanding that collaboration in raising productivity certainly would be much more common if the appropriate incentives were present. With enhanced job security and participation in profits, more cooperative and productive work places are indeed possible. If we continue on the path of adversarial relations we will all pay the penalty in higher prices, shrinking markets, and lost jobs. It is now time to try another approach.

---

[37]By way of comparison, Japan's population of 115 million people is roughly half that of the United States. At the end of the Allied occupation in 1952, Japan's GNP was less than a fifth as large as ours; by the late 1970s it equaled nearly 50 percent of ours and almost matched the Soviet Union's. It has been estimated that if present trends continue, Japan's GNP could exceed America's early in the next century: Vogel, *Japan as Number One*, pp. 10–21.

[38]If the reader believes that a solution might be to raise our import tariffs or impose severe import quotas, consider for a moment why this would not be useful. An important factor in dampening price increases is foreign imports; blocking imported goods would weaken that unpleasant but effective stimulus to more efficient, cost-conscious production. We would do ourselves long-run harm for a short-term gain if "protectionism" became national policy.

Bibliography

Aaron, Benjamin. "Regulation of Internal Union Relations." In E. Wight Bakke, Clark Kerr, and Charles W. Anrod, ed., *Unions, Management and the Public*. New York: Harcourt, Brace & World, 1967.

Adams, Bert N. *The Family*. Chicago: Rand McNally, 1980.

Anderson, Howard. *Primer of Labor Relations*. Washington, D.C.: The Bureau of National Affairs, 1980.

Andreski, Stanislas. *Military Organization and Society*. Berkeley, Calif.: University of California Press, 1968.

Antonio, Robert J. "Domination and Production in Bureaucracy." *American Sociological Review*, vol. 44 (1979), pp. 895–912.

Aronwitz, Stanley. *False Promises*. New York: McGraw-Hill, 1973.

Ashton, T. S. *The Industrial Revolution*, revised edition. New York: Oxford University Press, 1969.

Bailyn, Lotte. "Accommodation of Work to Family." In Robert and Rhona Rapoport, eds., *Working Couples*. New York: Harper and Row, 1978.

Bakke, E. Wight. "To Join or Not to Join." In E. Wight Bakke, Clark Kerr, and Charles W. Anrod, eds., *Unions, Management and the Public*. New York: Harcourt, Brace & World, 1967.

Barbash, Jack. "Collective Bargaining: Contemporary American Experience." In Gerald G. Somers, ed., *Collective Bargaining: Contemporary American Experience*. Madison, Wis.: Industrial Relations Research Association, 1980.

Bell, Daniel. *The Coming of Post-Industrial Society*. New York: Basic Books, 1975.

Bendix, Reinhard, and Lloyd Fisher. "The Perspectives of Elton Mayo." In Amitai Etzioni, ed., *Complex Organizations*. New York: Holt, Rinehart & Winston, 1962.

Berg, Ivar. *Industrial Sociology*. Englewood Cliffs, N.J.: Prentice-Hall, 1979.
_____, Marcia Freedman, and Michael Freeman. *Managers and Work Reform*. New York: Free Press, 1978.
Berger, Peter. *Pyramids of Sacrifice*. Garden City, N.Y.: Anchor Books, 1976.
Bernstein, Paul. *Workplace Democratization: Its Internal Dynamics*. Kent, Ohio: Kent State University Press, 1976.
Best, Geoffrey. *Mid-Victorian Britain, 1851–1875*. New York: Schocken Books, 1972.
Blau, Peter M., and Otis D. Duncan. *The American Occupational Structure*. New York: John Wiley, 1967.
Bok, Derek C., and John T. Dunlop. *Labor and the American Community*. New York: Simon and Schuster, 1970.
Bowers, David G. *Systems of Organization: The Management of the Human Resource*. Ann Arbor: University of Michigan Press, 1976.
"Brain Drain." *World of Work Report*, vol. 5 (1980), p. 24.
Braudel, Fernand. *Capitalism and Material Life, 1400–1800*, trans. Miriam Kochan. New York: Harper and Row, 1973.
Braverman, Harry. *Labor and Monopoly Capital*. New York: Monthly Review Press, 1974.
Brayfield, Arthur H., and James H. Crockett. "Employee Attitudes and Employee Performance." *Psychological Bulletin*, vol. 52 (1955), pp. 284–290.
Bronfenbrenner, Urie. "Recent Trends in American Socialization Patterns." In William Feigelman, ed., *Sociology Full Circle*. New York: Holt, Rinehart and Winston, 1980.
Bureau of the Census. *Historical Statistics of the United States, Colonial Times to 1970*, Bicentennial Edition, Part 2. Washington, D.C.: U.S. Government Printing Office.

Campbell, Robert W. *The Soviet-Type Economies*. Boston: Houghton-Mifflin, 1974.
Carneiro, Robert L. "A Theory of the Origin of the State." *Science*, vol. 169 (1970), pp. 733–738.
Carter, Hugh, and Paul C. Glick. *Marriage and Divorce*. Cambridge, Mass.: Harvard University Press, 1970.
Chadwick-Jones, J. K., Nigel Nicholson, and Colin Brown. *Social Psychology of Absenteeism*. New York: Praeger, 1982.
Champagne, Paul, and Curt Tausky. "When Job Enrichment Doesn't Pay." *Personnel*, vol. 55 (1978), pp. 30–40.
Chandler, Alfred D., Jr. "The Structure of American Industry in the Twentieth Century: A Historical Overview." In Edwin J. Perkins, ed., *Men and Organizations*. New York: G. Putnam's Sons, 1977.
Childe, Gordon V. *What Happened in History*. Baltimore: Penguin Books, 1964.
Clarke, Oliver. "The Development of Industrial Relations in European Market Economies." In Barbara B. Dennis, ed., *Proceedings of the Thirty-Third Annual Meeting*. Madison, Wis.: Industrial Relations Research Association, 1980.

Clawson, Dan. *Bureaucracy and the Labor Process*. New York: Monthly Review Press, 1980.

Clegg, Hugh A. *Trade Unionism Under Collective Bargaining*. Oxford: Basil Blackwell, 1976.

Cole, Robert E. *Japanese Blue Collar*. Berkeley: University of California Press, 1971.

_____. "QC Warning Voiced by U.S. Expert on Japanese Circles." *World of Work Report*, vol. 6 (1981), pp. 49–51.

Coleman, James S. *Power and the Structure of Society*. New York: W. W. Norton, 1974.

_____, et al. *Equality of Educational Opportunity*. Washington, D.C.: U.S. Government Printing Office, 1966.

Collins, Randall. *Conflict Sociology*. New York: Academic Press, 1975.

Connor, James E., ed. *Lenin on Politics and Revolution, Selected Writings*. New York: Pegasus Books, 1968.

Damus, Joseph. *The Middle Ages*. Garden City, N.Y.: Image Books, 1968.

Davey, Harold W. "Arbitration." In E. Wight Bakke, Clark Kerr and Charles W. Anrod, eds., *Unions, Management and the Public*. New York: Harcourt, Brace & World, 1967.

Davies, R. W. "Economic Planning in the USSR." In Morris Bornstein, ed., *Comparative Economic Systems*. Homewood, Ill.: Richard D. Irwin, 1979.

Davis, Howard. "Employment Gains of Women by Industry, 1968–78." *Monthly Labor Review*, vol. 103 (1980), pp. 3–9.

Davis, John P. *Corporations*. New York: Capricorn Books, 1961.

Davis, Kingsley, and Wilbert Moore. "Some Principles of Stratification." *American Sociological Review*, vol. 10 (1945), pp. 242–249.

Davis, Louis E., and Albert B. Cherns, eds. *The Quality of Working Life*, Volume Two. New York: Free Press, 1975.

DeJong, Peter. *Patterns of Intergenerational Occupational Mobility of American Females*. San Francisco: R & E Research Associates, 1977.

Didrichsen, Jon. "The Development of Diversified and Conglomerate Firms in the United States, 1920–1970." In Edwin J. Perkins, ed., *Men and Organizations*. New York: G. Putnam's Sons, 1977.

Doeringer, Peter B., and Michael J. Piore. *Internal Labor Markets and Manpower Analysis*. Lexington, Mass.: D. C. Heath, 1971.

Dore, Ronald. *British Factory—Japanese Factory*. Berkeley: University of California Press, 1973.

Dubin, Robert. "Power, Function, and Organization." *Pacific Sociological Review*, vol. 6 (1945), pp. 16–24.

_____, ed. *Handbook of Work, Organization, and Society*. Chicago: Rand McNally, 1976.

Duncan, Otis D., David L. Featherman, and Beverly Duncan. *Socio-Economic Background and Achievement*. New York: Seminar Press, 1972.

Fakhry, Ahmed. *The Pyramids*. Chicago: University of Chicago Press, 1961.

Featherman, David L., and Robert M. Hauser. *Opportunity and Change*. New

York: Academic Press, 1978.

Fein, Mitchell. "Motivation for Work." In Robert Dubin, ed., *Handbook of Work, Organization, and Society*. Chicago: Rand McNally, 1976.

Freedman, Marcia. *Labor Markets: Segments and Shelters*. Montclair, N.J.: Allanheld Osmun, 1976.

Ginzberg, Eli, and Hyman Berman. *The American Worker in the Twentieth Century*. New York: Free Press of Glencoe, 1964.

Goldman, Paul, and Donald R. Van Houten. "Managerial Strategies and the Worker: A Marxist Analysis of Bureaucracy." *Sociological Quarterly*, vol. 18 (1977), pp. 100–125.

Gordon, Milton M. *Human Nature, Class, and Ethnicity*. New York: Oxford University Press, 1978.

Gruenberg, Barry. "The Happy Worker." *American Journal of Sociology*, vol. 86 (1980), pp. 247–271.

Gutman, Herbert. *Work, Culture and Society in Industrializing America*. New York: Vintage Books, 1977.

Hackman, J. Richard, and Greg R. Oldham. *Work Redesign*. Reading, Mass.: Addison-Wesley, 1980.

Hall, Richard H. *Occupations and the Social Structure*. Englewood Cliffs, N.J.: Prentice-Hall, 1975.

Hall, Walter P., and Robert G. Albion. *A History of England and the British Empire*. New York: Ginn, 1953.

Harvey, Edward B. *Industrial Society*. Homewood, Ill.: Dorsey Press, 1975.

Hauser, Robert M., and David L. Featherman. *The Process of Stratification*. New York: Academic Press, 1977.

Hausman, Leonard J., et al., eds. *Equal Rights and Industrial Relations*. Madison, Wis.: Industrial Relations Research Association, 1977.

Hedges, Janice N. "Flexible Schedules: Problems and Issues." *Monthly Labor Review*, vol. 100 (1977), pp. 62–74.

_____, and Earl F. Mellor. "Weekly and Hourly Earnings of U.S. Workers, 1967–78." *Monthly Labor Review*, vol. 102 (1979), pp. 31–40.

Herzberg, Frederick. "One More Time: How Do You Motivate Employees?" *Harvard Business Review*, vol. 46 (1968), pp. 53–62.

Hill, Martha S., and Mary Corcoran. "Unemployment Among Family Men: A 10-year Longitudinal Study." *Monthly Labor Review*, vol. 102 (1979), pp. 19–23.

Hodge, Robert W., Paul M. Siegel, and Peter H. Rossi. "Occupational Prestige in the United States, 1925–63." *American Journal of Sociology*, vol. 70 (1964), pp. 286–302.

Hodson, Randy, and Robert L. Kaufman. "Economic Dualism: A Critical Review." *American Sociological Review*, vol. 47 (1982), pp. 727–39.

Hollander, Paul. *Soviet and American Society*. New York: Oxford University Press, 1973.

"Hominid Bones: Old and Firm at 3.75 Million." *Science News*, vol. 108 (1975), p. 292.

Horvath, Francis W. "Job Tenure of Workers, 1981." *Monthly Labor Review*, vol. 105 (1982), pp. 34–36.

Hutchinson, John. "The Anatomy of Corruption in Trade Unions." *Industrial Relations*, vol. 8 (1969), pp. 135–150.

Jacoby, Henry. *The Bureaucratization of the World*. trans. Evaline Kanes. Berkeley, Calif.: University of California Press, 1973.

Jaffe, A. J. *The Middle Years*. Special issue, *Industrial Gerontology* (1971).

Jasso, Guillermina, and Peter H. Rossi. "Distributive Justice and Earned Income." *American Sociological Review*, vol. 42 (1977), pp. 639–51.

Kahl, Joseph A. "Cuban Paradox: Stratified Equality." In Irving L. Horowitz, ed., *Cuban Communism*. New Brunswick, N.J.: Transaction Books, 1981.

Kahn, Robert L. "The Prediction of Productivity." *Journal of Social Issues*, vol. 12 (1956), pp. 41–49.

Kanter, Rosabeth M. *Men and Women of the Corporation*. New York: Basic Books, 1977.

Karlsson, K. G. *The Volvo Kalmar Plant*. Stockholm: The Rationalization Council SAF-LO, 1976.

Kassalow, Everett M. "Industrial Conflict in Europe and the United States." In Barbara B. Dennis, ed., *Proceedings of the Thirtieth Annual Winter Meeting*. Madison, Wis.: Industrial Relations Research Association, 1977.

Kerkhoff, Alan C. "Patterns of Marriage and Family Formation and Dissolution." *Journal of Consumer Research*, vol. 2 (1976), pp. 261–275.

Kidron, Michael, and Ronald Segal. *The State of the World Atlas*. New York: Simon and Schuster, 1981.

Klein, Lisl. *New Forms of Work Organization*. New York: Cambridge University Press, 1976.

Kochan, Thomas A. "Dynamics of Dispute Resolution in the Public Sector." In Benjamin Aaron, Joseph R. Grodin, and James L. Stern, eds., *Public-Sector Bargaining*. Madison, Wis.: Industrial Relations Research Association, 1979.

Kohn, Melvin L. *Class and Conformity*. Homewood, Ill.: Dorsey Press, 1969.

Kolko, Gabriel. *Wealth and Power in America*. New York: Frederick Praeger, 1962.

Kornhauser, Arthur, Robert Dubin, and Arthur M. Ross, eds. *Industrial Conflict*. New York: McGraw-Hill, 1954.

Kosters, Marvin H. "Relative Wages and Inflation." In Barbara Dennis, ed., *Proceedings of the Thirtieth Annual Winter Meeting*. Madison, Wis.: Industrial Relations Research Association, 1978.

Kranzberg, Melvin, and Joseph Gies. *By the Sweat of Thy Brow*. New York: G. P. Putnam's Sons, 1975.

Kreps, Juanita M., and R. John Lieper. "Home Work, Market Work, and the

Allocation of Time." In Juanita M. Kreps, ed., *Women and the American Economy*. Englewood Cliffs, N.J.: Prentice-Hall, 1976.

LaFay, Howard. "Ebla." *National Geographic*, vol. 154 (1978), pp. 730–759.

Landsberger, Henry. *Hawthorne Revisited*. Ithaca, N.Y.: Cornell University Press, 1958.

Laumann, Edward O. *Prestige and Association in an Urban Communtiy*. Indianapolis: Bobbs-Merrill, 1966.

_____. *Bonds of Pluralism: The Form and Substance of Urban Social Networks*. New York: John Wiley, 1973.

Lawler, Edward E. "Job Design and Employee Motivation." In Richard Steers and Lyman W. Porter, eds., *Motivation and Work Behavior*. New York: McGraw-Hill, 1975.

_____, and Lyman Porter. "The Effect of Performance on Job Satisfaction." *Industrial Relations*, vol. 7 (1967), pp. 20–28.

Lenski, Gerhard E. *Power and Privilege*. New York: McGraw-Hill, 1966.

_____, and Jean Lenski. *Human Societies*. New York: McGraw-Hill, 1982.

Levitan, Sar A. "An Appraisal of the Anti-trust Approach." *The Annals*, vol. 33 (1961), pp. 108–118.

Lewis, W. H. *The Splendid Century: Life in the France of Louis XIV*. Garden City, N.Y.: Anchor Books, 1957.

Leys, Simon. *Chinese Shadows*. New York: Penguin Books, 1978.

Likert, Rensis. *New Patterns of Management*. New York: McGraw-Hill, 1961.

Lipset, Seymour M. "Industrial Proletariat in Comparative Perspective." In Jan F. Triska and Charles Gati, eds., *Blue Collar Workers in Eastern Europe*. Boston: Allen and Unwin, 1981.

_____, and Reinhard Bendix. *Social Mobility in Industrial Society*. Berkeley: University of California Press, 1959.

Lotto, Jill C. "At Prudential: A Ten Year Track Record in New Work Schedules." *World of Work Report*, vol. 6 (1981), pp. 90–92.

Macarov, David. *Worker Productivity: Myths and Reality*. Beverly Hills, Calif.: Sage Publications, 1982.

Mackenzie, Gavin. *The Aristocracy of Labor*. New York: Cambridge University Press, 1973.

Mantoux, Paul. *The Industrial Revolution in the Eighteenth Century*. New York: Harper and Row, 1961.

Mayer, Kurt B., and Walter Buckley. *Class and Society*. New York: Random House, 1970.

Mayo, Elton. *The Human Problems of an Industrial Civilization*. New York: Macmillan, 1933.

Meyer, John W. "The Effects of Education as an Institution." *American Journal of Sociology*, vol. 83 (1977), pp. 55–77.

Miller, Delbert C., and William H. Form. *Industrial Sociology*. New York: Harper and Row, 1980.

Miller, Gale. *It's a Living*. New York: St. Martin's Press, 1981.

Mills, Ted. *Industrial Democracy in Europe: A 1977 Survey*. Washington, D.C.: American Center for the Quality of Work Life, 1978.

Mitchell, Daniel P. "The Impact of Collective Bargaining on Compensation in the Public Sector." In Benjamin Aaron, Joseph R. Grodin and James L. Stern, eds., *Public-Sector Bargaining*. Madison, Wis.: Industrial Relations Research Association, 1979.

Monahan, Thomas P. "An Overview of Statistics on Interracial Marriage in the United States." *Journal of Marriage and the Family*, vol. 38 (1976), pp. 223-231.

Montagna, Paul. *Occupations and Society*, New York: John Wiley, 1977.

Montgomery, David. "American Labor, 1865-1902." *Monthly Labor Review*, vol. 99 (1976), pp. 10-17.

Moore, Kristina A., and Isabel V. Sawhill. "Implications of Women's Employment for Home and Family Life." In Ann H. Stromberg and Shirley Harkess, eds., *Working Women*. Palo Alto, Calif.: Mayfield, 1978.

Mott, Paul E. *The Characteristics of Effective Organizations*. New York: Harper and Row, 1972.

Mowday, Richard T., Lyman W. Porter, and Richard M. Steers. *Employee-Organization Linkages: The Psychology of Commitment, Absenteeism, and Turnover*. New York: Academic Press, 1982.

Nakane, Chie. *Japanese Society*. Berkeley: University of California Press, 1970.

"The New Lean, Mean Xerox." *Business Week* (October 12, 1981), pp. 126-132.

"New Species of Man." *Science News*, vol. 115 (1979), p. 36.

Oldenbourg, Zoe. *The Crusades*, trans. Anne Carter. New York: Pantheon Books, 1966.

Ouchi, William. *Theory Z*. Reading, Mass.: Addison-Wesley, 1981.

Parkin, Frank. *Class Inequality and Political Order*. New York: Praeger, 1971.

Parsons, H. W. "What Really Happened at Hawthorne?" *Science*, vol. 183 (1974), pp. 922-932.

Parsons, Talcott. "An Analytical Approach to the Theory of Social Stratification." In his *Essays in Sociological Theory*. Glencoe, Ill.: Free Press, 1954.

Perrow, Charles. *Organizational Analysis*. Belmont, Calif.: Wadsworth, 1970.

Pfeiffer, John E. *The Emergence of Society*. New York: McGraw-Hill, 1977.

Pirenne, Henri. *A History of Europe*, trans. Bernard Miall. New York: University Books, 1955.

Plous, Fritz K., Jr. "The Quality Circle Concept: Growing by Leaps and Bounds." *World of Work Report*, vol. 6 (1981), pp. 25-27.

Polanyi, Karl. *The Great Transformation*. Boston: Beacon Press, 1957.

Price, James L. *The Study of Turnover*. Ames, Iowa: Iowa State University Press, 1977.

"Productivity Sharing Plans Can Cut Costs, Boost Productivity." *World of*

Work Report, vol. 6 (1981), pp. 77-78.

Report of a Special Task Force to the Secretary of Health, Education and
   Welfare. *Work in America*. Cambridge, Mass.: MIT Press, 1973.
de Riencourt, Amaury. *Sex and Power in History*. New York: Dell, 1974.
Ritzer, George. *Working*. Englewood Cliffs, N.J.: Prentice-Hall, 1977.
Robbins, Michael. *The Railway Age in Britain*. Baltimore, Md.: Penguin Books,
   1965.
Roethlisberger, F. J. *Management and Morale*. Cambridge, Mass.: Harvard
   University Press, 1941.
_____, and William J. Dickson. *Management and the Worker*. Cambridge,
   Mass.: Harvard University Press, 1939.
Ronan, W. W. "Individual and Situational Variables Relating to Job
   Satisfaction." *Journal of Applied Psychology Monograph*, vol. 54, Part 2
   (1970), pp. 1-31.
Rosenstein-Rodan, Paul N. "The Modernization of Industry." In Myron
   Weiner, ed., *Modernization*. New York: Basic Books, 1966.
Rothschild, K. W. *The Theory of Wages*. New York: Augustus Kelley, 1967.
Ryscavage, Paul. "More Wives in the Labor Force Have Husbands with Above-
   Average Incomes." *Monthly Labor Review*, vol. 102 (1979), pp. 40-42.
_____. "Two Divergent Measures of Purchasing Power." *Monthly
   Labor Review*, vol. 102 (1979), pp. 25-30.

Saint-Simon. *The Age of Magnificence: Memoirs of the Court of Louis XIV*,
   trans. Sanche de Gramont. New York: Capricorn Books, 1964.
Schumpeter, Joseph. *Capitalism, Socialism, and Democracy*. New York: Harper
   and Brothers, 1950.
Seligman, Ben B. *The Potentates*. New York: Dial Press, 1971.
Sennett, Richard, and Jonathan Cobb. *The Hidden Injuries of Class*. New York:
   Vintage Books, 1973.
"Sharing the Gains." *World of Work Report*, vol. 6 (1981), p. 64.
Sheppard, Harold L., and Neal Q. Herrick. *Where Have All the Robots Gone?*
   New York: Free Press, 1972.
Smelser, Neil J. *Social Change in the Industrial Revolution*. Chicago: University
   of Chicago Press, 1959.
Smith, Adam. *The Wealth of Nations*. New York: Random House, Modern
   Library Edition, 1937.
Smith, Hedrick. *The Russians*. New York: Academic Press, 1977.
Speth, Gus. "Resources and Society: The Global 2000 Report." *National Forum*,
   vol. 61 (1981), pp. 34-35.
Stamas, George D. "Real After-Tax Annual Earnings from the Current
   Population Survey." *Monthly Labor Review*, vol. 102 (1979), pp. 42-45.
Stern, James L., and David B. Johnson. *Blue- to White-Collar Job Mobility*.
   Madison: Industrial Relations Research Institute, University of Wisconsin,
   1968.
Sturmthal, Adolph, ed. *White-Collar Trade Unions*. Urbana: University of
   Illinois Press, 1966.

Tannenbaum, Arnold S. *Control in Organizations.* New York: McGraw-Hill, 1968.
Tausky, Curt. "Occupational Mobility Interests." *The Canadian Review of Sociology and Anthropology,* vol. 4 (1967), pp. 242-249.
_____. "Meaning of Work Among Blue Collar Men." *Pacific Sociological Review,* vol. 12 (1969), pp. 49-55.
_____. *Work Organizations: Major Theoretical Perspectives.* Itasca, Ill.: F. E. Peacock Publishers, 1978.
_____, and E. Lauck Parke. "Job Enrichment, Need Theory and Reinforcement Theory." In Robert Dubin, ed., *Handbook of Work, Organization, and Society.* Chicago: Rand McNally, 1976.
Taylor, Frederick W. *Scientific Management.* New York: Harper and Row, 1947.
"Team Assembly at Saab." *World of Work Report,* vol. 6 (1981) pp. 94-95.
Thompson, E. P. *The Making of the English Working Class.* New York: Pantheon Books, 1964.
Thurow, Lester C. *The Zero-Sum Society.* New York: Penguin Books, 1980.
Tilgher, Adriano. *Homo Faber: Work through the Ages,* trans. Dorothy Fisher. Chicago: Henry Regnery, Gateway Edition, 1958.
Tuchman, Barbara W. *A Distant Mirror.* New York: Alfred A. Knopf, 1978.
Tumin, Melvin. "Some Principles of Stratification: A Critical Analysis." *American Sociological Review,* vol. 18 (1953), pp. 387-394.

United Nations. *The Determinants and Consequences of Population Trends,* Vol. I. New York: United Nations, Sales No. E. 71. XIII. 5, 1973.
U. S. Bureau of the Census. Current Population Reports, Series P-20, No. 368, *Geographical Mobility: March 1975 to March 1980.* Washington: U. S. Government Printing Office, 1981.
"U. S. Chamber of Commerce Finds Workers Want to Raise Productivity." *World of Work Report,* vol. 5 (1980), pp. 73 and 79.
U. S. Department of Labor. Bulletin 262, *Federal Labor Laws and Programs.* Washington, D.C.: U. S. Government Printing Office, 1971.
_____. Bureau of Labor Statistics, *U. S. Workers and Their Jobs: The Changing Picture.* Washington, D.C.: U. S. Government Printing Office, 1976.
_____. *A Century of Change in Boston Family Consumption Patterns.* Washington, D.C.: Bureau of Labor Statistics, Regional Report No. 79-5, 1979.
_____. *Important Events in American Labor History, 1778-1978.* Washington, D.C.: U. S. Government Printing Office, 1979.
_____. Bureau of Labor Statistics, Bulletin No. 2079, *Directory of National Unions and Employee Associations, 1979.* Washington, D.C.: U. S. Government Printing Office, 1980.
_____. Bureau of Labor Statistics, *Perspectives on Working Women,* (June, 1980).

van Helvoort, Ernest. *The Japanese Working Man.* Vancouver: University of British Columbia Press, 1979.

Vogel, Ezra. *Japan as Number One*. New York: Harper Colophon Books, 1980.
Vroom, Victor H. *Work and Motivation*. New York: John Wiley, 1964.

Walfish, Beatrice. "Workers Report Wage, Benefit Problems." *World of Work Report*, vol. 4 (1979), pp. 17, 20–21.
Walker, Jon E., and Curt Tausky. "An Analysis of Work Incentives." *Journal of Social Psychology*, vol. 116 (1982), pp. 27–39.
Ware, Norman. *The Industrial Worker, 1840–1860*. Chicago: Quadrangle Books, 1964.
Weber, Max. *The Protestant Ethic and the Spirit of Capitalism*, trans. Talcott Parsons. New York: Charles Scribner's Sons, 1958.
_____. *The Theory of Social and Economic Organization*, trans. A. M. Henderson and Talcott Parsons. New York: Free Press, 1964.
Westcott, Diane N. "Blacks in the 1970's: Did They Scale the Job Ladder?" *Monthly Labor Review*, vol. 105 (1982), pp. 29–38.
White, Bernard J. "The Criteria for Job Satisfaction: Is Interesting Work Most Important?" *Monthly Labor Review*, vol. 100 (1977), pp. 30–35.
White, Lynn, Jr. *Medieval Technology and Social Change*. London: Oxford University Press, 1962.
Whitehead, T. North. *The Industrial Worker*. Cambridge, Mass.: Harvard University Press, 1939.
Whyte, William F. *Men at Work*. Homewood, Ill.: Dorsey Press, 1961.
Wilensky, Harold. *The Welfare State and Equality*. Berkeley, Calif.: University of California Press, 1975.
Wirtz, W. Willard. "Union Morals." In E. Wight Bakke, Clark Kerr, and Charles W. Anrod, eds., *Unions, Management and the Public*. New York: Harcourt, Brace & World, 1967.
Wittfogel, Karl. *Oriental Despotism*. New Haven: Yale University Press, 1957.
Wolf, Eric R. *Peasants*. Englewood Cliffs, N.J.: Prentice-Hall, 1966.
Wolfbein, Seymour. *Work in American Society*. Glenview, Ill.: Scott, Foresman, 1971.
Wright, James D., and Richard F. Hamilton. "Work Satisfaction and Age." *Social Forces*, vol. 56 (1978), pp. 1140–1158.
_____. "Education and Attitudes Among Blue-Collar Workers." *Sociology of Work and Occupations*, vol. 6 (1979), pp. 59–83.

Yellowitz, Irwin. *The Position of the Worker in American Society, 1865–1896*. Englewood Cliffs, N.J.: Prentice-Hall, 1969.
Yohalem, Alice M., ed. *Women Returning to Work*. Montclair, N.J.: Allanheld, Osmun, 1980.
Young, Anne M. "Educational Attainment of Workers, March 1981." *Monthly Labor Review*, vol. 105 (1982), pp. 52–55.

Zwerdling, Daniel. *Democracy at Work*. Washington, D.C.: Association for Self-Management, 1979.

Index

Absenteeism: 96, 143
Adversarial relations: *See* egoism
Agricultural revolution: 5-7
Alexander the Great: conquest of
  Sumeria, 10; conquest of Egypt,
  11
American system: interchangeabil-
  ity of parts, 44
Andreski, Stanislaus: 19n56
Antonio, Robert J.: on taxes in
  Rome, 14
Ashton, T.S.: on industrial revolu-
  tion, 1n1, 31n6

Bakke, E. Wight: 130n45
Barbash, Jack: on public-sector
  unions, 124; on state intervention in union affairs, 130-31
Bell, Daniel: on living standards,
  134; on belief systems, 137
Bendix, Reinhard: 108n3
Berg, Ivar: on defining industrialization, 31; on underutilization
  of workers, 61n15

Berger, Peter L.: on social engi-
  neering, 52; on social cohesion,
  137
Bernstein, Paul: on employee
  ownership, 144
Best, Geoffrey: on Victorian En-
  gland, 36, 38, 40
Blau, Peter: 90
Braudel, Fernand: on heating in
  Middle Ages, 26n70
Braverman, Harry: 25n67, 97n80
Brayfield, Arthur H.: study of
  satisfaction and productivity, 95

Canals: in England, 33-34; in
  U.S., 44
Champagne, Paul J.: on collapse of
  a job enrichment program, 144
Child labor: 37-38
Childe, V. Gordon: on hunter-
  gatherers, 4; on Sumeria, 8-9
Clarke, Oliver: 129n39
Clawson, Dan: on foremen's au-
  tonomy, 49

Footnotes are indexed with page reference, the letter *n*, and the footnote number, example
19n56 is page 19, footnote 56.

Clegg, Hugh A.: 124n34
Cole, Robert E.: on quality circles, 145-46
Coleman, James S.: 46n40
Collective bargaining: in England, 40-41. *See also* labor unions
College graduates: by race and sex (table), 63. *See also* education
Collins, Randall: on conflict theory, 77n33
Concentration of production: in agriculture, 46; in industry, 47-49
Conflict theory: on wages, 77-78; on changing work outcomes, 106
Crockett, James H.: study of satisfaction and productivity, 95

Davey, Harold W.: 128n37
Davis, Kingsley: on occupational rewards, 76
DeJong, Peter: on women's occupational mobility (table), 116
Didrichsen, Jon: 48
Domestic servants: in England, 40. *See* occupations
Domestic system: *See* putting-out
Dore, Ronald: 110n5
Dubin, Robert: on functional importance, 76n29, 40n21, 96n79, 125n35
Duncan, Otis D.: 90

Economic allocation: principle of, 52
Education: *See* college graduates; occupational mobility; Japan
Egoism: 137-38; and adversarial relations, 145-48
Egypt: 11-14

Factory system: origins, 26, 31-32; in U.S., 44

Featherman, David L.: on education and occupation, 60, 108n4; on mobility, 111-12, 117
Fein, Mitchell: 142
Ford, Henry: 49-50
Form, William H.: 64, 65, 83n38, 107n1

Geographic mobility: 110
Ginzberg, Eli: on work hours, 51
Golden, Hilda H.: on immigration to U.S., 133n1
Goldman, Paul: 77n33
Gordon, Milton M.: on the propensity to evaluate, 92
Guild system: 21-22; merchant guilds, 23; craft guilds, 23-24; decline of guilds, 24
Gutman, Herbert: 2n3, 44n31, 133n1

Hall, Richard H.: on women's status, 89n61
Hamilton, Richard F.: on age and work satisfaction, 97n81; education and work attitudes, 103n85
Harvey, Edward B.: 86n46
Hauser, Robert M.: on education and occupation, 60, 108n4; on intergenerational mobility, 111-12, 117
Hawthorne studies: 93-94
Herrick, Neal Q.: study of work satisfaction and task attributes (table), 100
Herzberg, Frederick: on work satisfaction and dissatisfaction, 104n86
Hodge, Robert W.: study of occupational prestige, 89n62, (table), 90-91
Hollander, Paul: 135n5
Hominids: 3

Human relations: theory of, 94
Hunting-gathering: 3-5

Incentives: *See* productivity
Income: theory of mercantilism, 73-74; iron law of wages, 74-75; marginal productivity theory, 75-76; dual labor market theory, 76-77; conflict theory, 77; median weekly earnings (table), 78; annual family income (tables), 80, 81; percent of aggregate income received (table), 82; union and non-union workers, 129-30
Industrial revolution: advantages of, 30; in England, 31-42; in U.S., 42-53. *See also:* canals, child labor, railroads, steam engine, Protestant Ethic
Industrial sociology: defined, 2
Industries: employment in (table), 64
Inflation: rates in selected countries (table), 69
Iron: early use of, 10; in industrial revolution, 32-33

Japan: 139-42
Jasso, Guillermina: study of opinions on income distribution, 79
Job enrichment: *See* work reforms

Kahn, Robert H.: on satisfaction and productivity, 95
Kahn, Robert L.: study of workers who would choose same type of work again (table), 104
Kanter, Rosabeth M.: on women workers in corporations, 48
Kochan, Thomas A.: 36, 128
Kranzberg, Melvin: 8n23, 13n42, 16n50, 25n66

Labor force: definition of, 54; rates of participation (tables), 55, 56
Labor law: 119-21; National Labor Relations Board, 121-23; collective bargaining, 125-31. *See also:* labor unions
Labor unions: in England, 40-41; in U.S., 51, 123-25. *See also:* labor law
Lawler, Edward E.: 147n35
Lenin: on applying scientific management in the U.S.S.R., 49n46
Lenski, Gerhard: on speech development among hunter-gatherers, 4; on proprietary theory of the state, 11, 6n17; on prestige, 85
Limited liability: defined, 46
Lincoln Electric: 142
Linton, Ralph: on Sumeria, 8-9; on Egypt, 11-12
Lipset, Seymour M.: 108n3
Luther, Martin: *See* Protestant Ethic

Manorial system: origins of, 17-18, 19-21. *See also:* guilds, putting-out
Marx, Karl: theory of revolution, 40; theory of wages, 74; on location of revolutions, 135
Middle Ages: 17-27. *See also:* manorial system, guilds, putting-out
Miller, Delbert C.: 64, 65, 83n38, 107n1
Miller, Gale: on empowerment among employees, 143
Mills, Ted: on co-determination in U.S., 131
Mobility: *See* occupational mobility, geographic mobility
Montagna, Paul: 73n27, 77n31

Mowday, Richard T.: 96n77, 107n1

Nakane, Chie: 140n12
National Labor Relations Board: *See* labor law

Occupational mobility: in 19th century England, 35; intragenerational mobility defined, 107; (table), 109; intergenerational mobility defined, 110; explanatory variables, 111-13; (tables), 114, 115; women's mobility (table), 116
Occupations: distribution of the labor force (table), 59; and education, 60; and race and sex (table), 61
Organizations: by employee size class (table), 73
O'Toole, James: 104
Ouchi, William: 143

Parke, E. Lauck: 144
Parkin, Frank: on privilege, 92
Perrow, Charles: 95n76
Polanyi, Karl: on market transformation, 2
Porter, Lyman W.: 96n77, 107n1
Prestige: origins of, 85-86; defined, 86; consequences of, 86-89; and occupations (table), 90-91
Price, James L.: 96n77, 107n1
Productivity: annual rates of change (table),84; and work satisfaction, 93-96; and material incentives, 96, 140-41, 147-48
Proprietary theory of the state: 11
Protestant Ethic: 35-36
Putting-out system: 25-27, 38-39, 133

Quality circles: *See* work reforms

Railroads: in England, 34-35; in U.S., 44
Ritzer, George: 83
Rome: 14-17
Ronan, W.W.: study of satisfaction and productivity, 95
Rossi, Peter H.: study of opinions on income distribution, 79; study of prestige of occupations, 89n62, (table), 90-91

Seligman, Ben: 44n33
Service industries: defined, 29n1; (table), 64
Sheppard, Harold L.: study of work satisfaction and task attributes (table), 100
Siegel, Paul M.: study of prestige of occupations, 89n62, (table), 90-91
Smelser, Neal J.: 38n18
Smith, Adam: on pin making, 39; on national wealth, 74
Smith, Hedrick: 135n5
Steam engine: invention of, 33
Steers, Richard M.: 98n77, 107n1
Sturmthal, Adolph: 124n34
Sumeria: 7-9

Tannenbaum, Arnold: 144n24
Tausky, Curt: on work outcomes, 70-72; on prestige, 86
Taylor, Frederick: on scientific management, 49, 94
Thurow, Lester: on conflict theory, 77; on incentives, 142
Tilgher, Adriano: 35n10
Treiman, Donald: on origins of prestige, 85, 87n49, 92
Turnover: 96; defined, 107; discussion of, 107-108; 143

Unemployment: 53-65; rates of
(tables), 65, 66; in eight countries (table), 67
U.S.S.R.: 135-36

Van Houten, Donald R.: 73n31
Vogel, Ezra: on education in Japan
and the U.S., 139; 140n15,
148n37
Vroom, Victor H.: on satisfaction
and productivity, 95

Walker, Jon E.: study of work
satisfaction and job facets
(table), 101
Ware, Norman: 50n49
Watt, James: *See* steam engine
Weber, Max: 11n37, 36n11
Whyte, William F.: 86n46
Wittfogel, Karl: on the origin of the
political state, 7n22
Women workers: by age of children

(table), 56; and husbands' incomes, 57; occupations of
(table), 61; and occupational
mobility (table), 116
Work outcomes: defined, 70-71.
See income, prestige, work satisfaction, occupational mobility
Work reforms: job enrichment, 40,
143-44; participation, 144-45;
quality circles, 145-46; flexitime, 146-47; results of, 147
Work satisfaction: measurement
of, 97; distribution of (tables),
98, 99; and task attributes
(tables), 100, 101; and workers
who would choose same type of
work again (table), 104
Wright, James D.: on age and work
satisfaction, 97n81; education
and work attitudes, 103n85

Xerox corporation: 138

THE BOOK MANUFACTURE

Work and Society composition was by Printech, Inc. of Schaumburg, Il. Printing and binding was by Edwards Bros. of Ann Arbor, Mich. Internal design was by F.E. Peacock Publishers art department. Mead Design designed the cover. The type is Times Roman.